Terri Walker

Mc Grimm

Shades of
Darkness

Best Wishes

M. E. Brine

D1378083

Shades of Darkness

A black soldier's journey through Vietnam, blindness, and back

By George E. Brummell

Silver Spring, MD
2006

ISBN: 0-9788917-0-8
Library of Congress Control Number: 2006907686

Published in the United States by George E. Brummell
c/o Pie Publishing, 2914 Fairland Rd., Silver Spring, MD 20904.
(301) 890-1564 ~ E-mail: info@GeorgeBrummell.com

Inquire about discounts for bulk orders.

Visit www.GeorgeBrummell.com for current information about
author appearances, news, and links to resources for disabled
veterans and for the visually impaired.

Cover design by Foster Winans

Cover photo of George Brummell was taken about 1962 during his
Korean assignment.

Printed in the United States of America

Dedicated to my grandmother, Susie Simms,
for shaping the child I was
into the man I became.

Table of Contents

Acknowledgments

Thanks to the Littlejohns for welcoming me into their family when I needed it most.

Thanks to the late Carstell O. Stewart Jr., a fellow Vietnam vet and professor, for encouraging me to go back to school, leading me to the University of Akron, assisting me with enrolling, staying until I was comfortable, and then turning me loose. Were it not for him, I doubt I'd have made it this far.

Thanks to Cathy Levingston Knowles and Cathy Weatherholt, fellow students and my writers/readers in undergraduate school, for their hard work and encouragement from this project's earliest stages.

Thanks to my old Ohio friends: Nathaniel Johnson for his constant encouragement and his confidence in me; and Willie Robinson, and Nathan and Yvonne Oliver, for always being there during my grooming process.

Thanks to Dr. Margaret Stephens and Professor Neil Gaby, my teachers at University of Akron, for reviewing my work and offering suggestions.

Thanks to my high school classmates, Rosetta Garfield and Virgie Mae Johnson, for inputting edited corrections; to Lovelyn Powell, Joanne McLaughlin, and the late Clarisse Hayes, who were staff assistants at the Blinded Veterans Association; and to Kenneth Toth, a volunteer who helped me with the manuscript.

Thanks to my cycling partner when I returned to Vietnam, Robert (Bob) Steck, for all his support, suggestions, motivation, encouragement, and friendship.

Thanks to Wayne Smith, a cycling teammate on my return trip to Vietnam, for his interest in and suggestions for the manuscript.

Thanks to my beloved wife, Maria S. Brummell, for her constant support and nurturing, and for tolerating the many hours I sat in front of the computer pecking away.

Thanks to my "king," Arthur Gerold, a Navy vet from World War II who I met at a VA facility in Connecticut, for believing my manuscript was worthy of publishing and hand-carrying it through a snow storm to help me reach my goal.

Thanks to Julie Boken, Arthur's friend, for reviewing my writings and confirming Arthur's suspicions.

Author's Note

How does a blind person write a whole book? What about a blind person with his left hand compromised by a battle injury?

I started writing "Shades of Darkness" in 1977 after being inspired by a book, "If You Could See What I Hear," by Tommy Sullivan, who had attended Harvard University as a blind student and described with humor and honesty how he overcame his limitations. The book was a success and was later made into a film. I believed I could write a book that would also be inspiring, but from the perspective of a black man's journey from modest roots, to combat in Vietnam, sudden blindness, and beyond.

I started getting up in the early mornings, with a tape recorder, sitting at my basement bar and trying to remember as much as I could. The process of transferring from tape to paper was a huge obstacle and I dropped the project for a while, until I enrolled at the University of Akron.

There I found a writer willing to assist me with class work, as well as transcribing bits of my manuscript. I persuaded my English instructors to grade my personal writings as class projects.

When I became computer literate in the mid-1980s, I managed to get what I had on paper scanned into digital form. But it was a mess. When I finally got the text cleaned up, my writing project picked up speed. Nearly every night after returning home from work, I sat typing with my one hand, telling my story to the hard drive. Many nights I only got down a sentence or two, but it was progress nonetheless.

Thanks to the technology that allows a computer to "speak" words, I could haltingly write and edit my thoughts. For a short time I had a couple of volunteers who stopped by and took dictation. The years flew by, but I kept up my routine.

I finally completed the manuscript five years ago, but it just sat on my computer, awaiting the right moment to be born. That came in December 2005 when I went to the VA Blind Rehabilitation Center in New Haven, Connecticut, for computer enhancement training. There I met a veteran of World War II, Arthur Gerold, who was learning to cope with macular degeneration.

After telling him my story, he was convinced I should get it out of the computer and into the hands of someone who could help me polish it for publication. He volunteered to carry a printed copy of the manuscript in a snow storm by train to an author friend in New York City. That started a process that ends with the book you hold in your hands.

The stories I've told here are all true, although I have changed the names of most of the people whose lives intersected with mine, out of respect for their privacy.

I hope you get as much pleasure and inspiration out of reading them as I did in the writing.

—George E. Brummell
Silver Spring, MD 2006

Introduction

The last image I ever saw—the instant before my eyes were seared by a landmine explosion in the jungles of Vietnam—is always with me. Many times during the past forty years, I have thought of myself as unlucky. But a soldier I met recently left me wondering. The meeting happened on a visit with a friend and fellow Vietnam veteran to Walter Reed Army Hospital in Washington, D.C., where some of America's wounded warriors from Iraq and Afghanistan were being treated.

We met an Army captain who lost an arm and suffered severe head trauma, a couple of soldiers who had lost both legs, and a sergeant in the Green Berets who'd lost an arm and a leg. As we were walking down the hall to leave, we were stopped by one of the staff psychiatrists. Noting I was blinded, he said blinded soldiers at Walter Reed—at this writing some two hundred American soldiers had their sight impaired in combat since September 2001—often have an especially difficult time adjusting. He asked if we would visit one of his recently blinded patients, a young sergeant a couple of rooms away.

"Absolutely," I said. "Lead the way."

We entered the room and introduced ourselves. The young sergeant, from his bed, mumbled a weak and dispirited "Hello." We thanked him for his service to the country, and I cracked a few lame jokes that seemed unable to penetrate his gloom.

Then I tried to encourage him by mentioning a few of the things I've accomplished since my own loss of sight—getting a degree, heading up the Mid-Atlantic Blinded Veterans of America Association, and bicycling twelve hundred miles through Vietnam, from Hanoi to Saigon, on the back of a tandem bike.

This young sergeant reminded me so much of myself. I, too, had sat in darkness at an Army hospital wondering if my life was over or, if not, how I could ever hope and laugh and love again. I wanted desperately to leave this young man with a spark of optimism that he could have a full life in spite of his injury.

As I prattled on, I seemed to be scoring points. His voice strengthened, I could hear he had tilted his face up rather than speaking at the floor. He began asking questions, and I could hear that his wife had left her chair and come to his side. Then she, too, began peppering me with questions. My sighted buddy later confirmed that the two of them responded like sunflowers turning to face the warmth of the sun.

As a blinded father, I was curious to know if they had any children. "Yes," he said proudly. "Two kids, with a third on the way."

Then his wife interjected, softly, "No, sweetheart. Our daughter, our third child, was born two and a-half years ago." There was an awkward silence and then I changed the subject.

When it came time to go, I wished the couple good luck after telling the sergeant how to reach out to the Blinded Veterans Association for help when he got home.

We were puzzled by the soldier's mistake until one of the doctors explained. She said more than sixty percent of the injured soldiers also suffered brain trauma, a result of the upward blasts produced by the primary insurgent weapon—improvised explosive devices (IEDs). The blasts caused their heads to bounce around inside their helmets like they'd been caught inside a deadly pinball machine.

"These injuries are invisible," she explained, "but often more severe than the visible ones. No one knows if mental functioning will ever be fully restored for these soldiers. It's heartbreaking to see."

It hit me hard that while the blind young sergeant and I shared something, injured four decades apart, his additional mental injury made me feel lucky in ways I'd never considered. We'd both experienced a world of hurt, a common expression among young grunts in 'Nam, but there was a world of difference between our experiences.

shades of
Darkness

Prologue

Cong had been harassing the company with sniper fire, so we foot soldiers had to "unass" ourselves from the top of the snorting bulldozer or risk getting picked off. I'd already lost too many men to our elusive enemy, the North Vietnamese or Viet Cong or Charlie or, as we grunts called them, simply Cong. Traver, the squad leader, ordered Alpha and Bravo teams to each side. On high alert, fingers on trigger guards, we crept down the dusty road with the clank and roar of the dozer's engine in our ears and exhaust in our snouts.

Everyone in front had taken cover, firing forward. Traver trotted crouching ahead to report to Captain North and Sergeant Jade. I held up my hand, to halt the bulldozer and men, and left to join Traver and the Captain. The dozer's engine dieseled to a stop as I passed. The big blade sank slowly toward the soil with a hydraulic wheeze.

Captain North stepped fast in my direction. "Go ahead, Brummell. Take the men back to your platoon and prepare to move out."

"Let's get moving!" I yelled. I looked right, just as the dozer blade touched the soil. A deafening explosion. The air pulsed. I whirled upward, floating in a bubble of quiet. Minutes seemed to pass. The grey darkness flashed red.

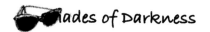

Confused, helpless, doubled over, I reached the apex of my flight and began to fall. The air pulsed again—a second concussion. The shock wave slammed me to the ground.

Silence. Darkness. Stillness. Then screams. Shouting. The pop-pop of rifle fire. Heat and smoke that smelled of grilling meat. Crumpled, paralyzed, I struggled to catch my breath. FUCK! I've been hit! Fuckin' Cong finally got me, man! How bad was I? Dying? Already dead?

Grandma's face popped into my head and I could hear her scolding me. "Lord sakes, child! What kinda unholy mess you got you'sef in now? C'mere boy, and let's get you cleaned up."

Chapter 1

I was an extra mouth to feed in a family that already had too many. My mother, Elsie Gladys Brummell, gave birth four days after Christmas, 1944. I was her fourth.

My mother named me after George Bryan Brummell, better known as Beau Brummell, a London dandy, gambler, and playboy around the turn of the nineteenth century. Credited with inventing the modern man's suit and tie, Brummell claimed he spent five hours a day dressing, and polished his boots with champagne. My mother had been required in high school to read about him, and it left quite an impression.

My father, Walter, earned just twenty-five cents an hour, hardly enough to make ends meet. When I was barely two, with jobs plentiful because all the able-bodied men were off fighting World War II, Mom went to work driving a rig for a local trucking company. One Saturday she took me with her to pick up her paycheck. While she waited for the cashier, I wandered over to the snack bar and clumsily pulled two apple pies from a rack that was waiting to be loaded. The owner of the trucking company caught me red-handed and nick-named me "Pie." It stuck.

My parents divorced soon after. Dad moved to

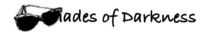

nearby Finchville, a village on the border between Maryland and Delaware, and went to work in a primitive sawmill. He and a mule named Mike wore themselves out skidding giant trees out of the woods to an old gas-powered saw that reduced them to two-by-fours. The county made Dad pay most of his paltry earnings to my mother for child support.

Mom lost her trucking job the same year she and my father broke up. Trying to raise four kids took its toll and she was declared an unfit mother. Besides driving a semi-truck, she'd done other mannish things—wearing pants, cussing, driving fast, and most of all, shooting craps with the fellas down at the bar. She stayed busy and had little time for us kids. One day the county people came and shipped us off to new homes.

Donald was the oldest and I was the youngest. He and I ended up together with our maternal grandmother, Miss Susie Simms. Our only sister, Ida, landed in a foster home. Walter Jr. was taken in by an elderly woman in rural Virginia. It would be years before I would see either of them again.

Grandma Susie was widowed, illiterate, and poor in a wholesome sort of way. She welcomed us with dignity into the tidy little four-room house she'd bought with the money a developer paid to evict her from her old neighborhood. Her place was nestled among a handful of other cottages and shanties along Brooklyn Avenue, a dusty unpaved stretch of road in Federalsburg, Maryland. The neighborhood sat on one of the few high spots in town, on the Marshyhope Creek in the southern-most part of Caroline County, the heart of the DelMarVa Peninsula between the Chesapeake Bay and

George Brumm

the Atlantic Ocean. It was flat, productive farm country about an hour or so across the bay from Baltimore.

Grandma had been just fourteen when she married twenty-seven-year-old Manship Simms. He was, Grandma told us, a short, dark, strong-looking man: "Not handsome, mind you, but a good man."

Manship Simms and Grandma's folks had all died before I was born. She never talked about her father, but she often spoke of her mother, Mary Hopkins, who was part American Indian, except no one ever knew which tribe. "She was slender, with a reddish, fair complexion and, Lord be, she had the longest hair! Came below her shoulders," Grandma told Donald and I.

Great Grandma Mary never learned to read or write either. She supported herself by picking vegetables and cooking for the migrant field hands. Grandma's life was pretty much the same. She never cooked for migrants but she did work alongside them, picking vegetables in the sun-baked fields and peeling tomatoes in the steam-filled cannery.

Before I was old enough for school, each afternoon I could be found standing on a little rise near Grandma's house, waiting for my buddy Nelson and my brother Donald to come home and tell me about their day. They came from where Brooklyn Avenue dead-ended, into a winding trail that led to a narrow foot bridge, known as the Brooklyn Bridge. It led to the back of a Methodist Church for coloreds, as we were known. Less than a quarter mile away from the church was the for-coloreds-only, four-room elementary school, painted dark green.

Nelson was three years older. He lived in the four-room bungalow across the road and came from a family of seven children. He and his sister Effie were the closest to my age, and we quickly developed a great friendship.

By the time Nelson started junior high, and I was in fourth grade, the Brooklyn Bridge was gone, stripped by pilferers to fuel their stoves. The bridge's demise meant school children had to take the alternate route to school, the long way 'round. We walked to the other end of Brooklyn, onto Academy Avenue, past Chambers Park and Maryland Plastics.

Halfway to school was the local theater where we often loitered to admire the lush photos and giant, gaudy promotional posters. I fantasized about being a movie star but rarely got to see any of the movies.

Our route took us past two white congregational churches, Mary's Ice Cream Parlor, Mount Zion Methodist Colored Church, then up a short hill to the school. The four small rooms were separated from each other by accordion doors. A large heater dominated each room. I was hypnotized by the stove's cherry red glow in winter, and watched with pride when the teacher gave my big brother the privilege of stuffing its belly with coal. Donald seemed very grown-up, with a chore as important as keeping the school warm.

The playground was small, with a swing set and a seesaw. Much more interesting to us kids was the stream behind the school. It meandered through a thin, well-lit forest, tucked away in soft green splendor in the summer. Sometimes at recess we dared to jump across the water and explore the forbidden far side. The older students who had failed a few grades would gather switches and chase us back across the stream, claiming the foreign territory for themselves. We younger ones learned to run fast, to stay out of the reach of their stinging blows.

Every day before we left school, we'd all line up to use the bathroom so we wouldn't have to go on the way home. Then we walked in a quiet, polite single file, back through the white neighborhood, into the center of town. If any of the young kids got curious and strayed toward one of the store windows, the older kids would yell at them because blacks couldn't go into those places. Even if we had the money, we couldn't sit in the Rexall to have a cherry Coke or a banana split at the Tasty Freeze. But there were always black men loafing on a rail on the corner by the town's only stop light, waiting for day work.

In town, our little line of black ants dispersed in two directions, some of us going home to Brooklyn near the cemetery, the others crossing the tracks near the city dump.

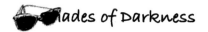

Chapter 2

The school bus had to travel nearly twenty miles for me to get to the only colored high school in the county. It picked us up at the end of Brooklyn, stopping at Federalsburg Elementary to drop off the younger kids who rode in from the rural areas. After the little kids got off, we junior and senior high students claimed empty seats. I preferred to sit in the rear, out of the driver's hearing where we could talk our adolescent nonsense. The bus made a dozen stops before finally pulling in beside four other buses coming from small towns around the county seat of Denton.

One Christmas I got a rusty, fenderless bicycle. In spite of its age, and even in the snow, I wheeled it proudly around Brooklyn Avenue. One summer day I asked Grandma if I could go for a ride. She said "no" as usual, but I went anyway. It was a hot, breathless day. In Chambers Park, I stopped to watch the fish jumping in the crystal-clear stream. I rode past the local store and coasted down Bakery Hill, where the smell of freshly fried doughnuts filled the air like a cloud of heavenly perfume. I passed fields of cucumbers, tomatoes, and corn. Even the cow manure smelled good.

I continued peddling and crossed the state line into Delaware. It was only five miles from home, but I felt like I was on a grand adventure to faraway lands. I stopped now and then, distracted by a frog that I helped cross the road, and to explore a storm drain for tadpoles.

On my way back home I swung around town, past the grade school and toward School House Hill. The closer I got to the hill, the more speed I mustered for the long, steep descent. Three quarters of the way down I decided I was going too fast. But when I back-pedaled to engage the brake, nothing happened. I tried dragging my feet on the asphalt. My worn shoe soles with their cardboard linings were useless. The wind blasted my face as I hurtled out of control toward the bottom, toward a cross street and a house on the other side of the intersection.

Two fast-moving trucks flew through the intersection. I spun the handle bars left then whipped them sharply to the right to avoid them. I flew, bumping, through a front yard, a flower patch, and finally crashed into the back yard of Mrs. Collins, the principal of Federalsburg Elementary. The wreck scraped me up a little but I was devastated to find my beloved bicycle demolished—spokes broken, front rim bent, frame twisted. I dragged the debris home.

When Grandma saw me pulling it across the back yard she shouted, "What you done now? Boy, you cain't keep a blessed thing! Ever'thin' you put your hands on you tear up. You think money grows on trees?"

I retreated to my bedroom in despair. She continued scolding through the closed door, finally commanding, "Come here, boy!"

I threw down an old Superman comic book I was

pretending to read and opened the door.

"You know, Son, you're gettin' to be a big strong boy." She had her hands planted on her hips, a sure sign of trouble to come.

"Your Uncle Noble got a big field of cucumbers, and I been helping him with hoein'. You could be a big help to me. I want you to go with me in the morning, and I'll show you how it's done."

If hoeing was anything like picking cucumbers and tomatoes, I wanted no part of it. But I knew better than to squawk. "You turn in early tonight, boy, and get yourself a good night's rest."

———————

Grandma woke me before dawn. "Make a little ice water for the jug. It'll get hot and we'll need sumpin' cold to drink. After that, you go to the smokehouse and grab a coupla hoes. Well don't just stand there gawkin', child! Uncle Noble's comin' in fifteen minutes and he ain't never been late yet."

Uncle Noble pulled his 1951 Hudson into the back-yard at precisely quarter to six and tapped the horn.

Grandma grabbed her old gray rag and tied it around her head. Uncle Noble's sons, Russell and Virgil, were in the car with him.

"Are y'all ready to get some hoein' done?" Noble asked as he spun the steering wheel and accelerated out of the yard. He zipped through town, bumped over the railroad tracks and swung into the parking lot at the poultry plant. We got our hoes from the trunk and headed toward the field. It was only a few acres, but the rows and rows of cucumbers seemed to stretch to the horizon. It made me tired just looking at all those cukes.

Uncle Noble was a World War II Navy vet and he still kept himself neatly dressed, in a blue shirt and tan khakis. He had a warm, broad smile as he assigned each of us our rows. He usually tried to cheer me up with a lame joke, but that day his demeanor was stern.

"Pie, since this is your first time, you take this row alongside your Grandma. I 'spect you to hoe all the grass and weeds out. If them weeds is too close to the cukes, you got to pull 'em by hand. I need a good crop this year, so you do me a good job.

"Now, I got to pick up another load of field hands. You all get started, and I'll be back soon as I can."

Uncle Noble stepped away and Grandma yanked me by the arm.

"Come on, Boy. Let's git goin'! Noble ain't payin' you to stand around lookin'."

I was amazed at the energy with which she attacked her work, paying no mind to the sucking mud puddles left by last night's rain. The hours crept by, and I grew tired and cranky. My hands sprouted blisters and my back ached like it was going to break.

"Grandma, can I take a rest?"

"Take a rest!?" She looked over at me with eyes narrowed, brow furrowed—outraged. "No!"

"But Grandma, my back is killin' me!"

"Son, you don't got a back yet. You too young. What you got's gristle, and gristle don't tire. Keep up with me, now. You been laggin' all mornin'."

The sun climbed toward noon and seemed to be concentrating its hottest rays right at me. I sneaked as many breaks as I could by dropping to my knees and pretending to pull weeds that were too close for hoeing. When Uncle Noble yelled time for lunch, I felt like I'd been delivered from the grasp of the devil that Grandma prayed so hard against at church every Sunday.

We gathered for lunch in the shade of Uncle Noble's car. Grandma had packed fried bologna sandwiches with salad dressing.

"George, you step on over to the store and fetch us some cold Pepsis."

I was shaky with hunger and my throat was dusty. When I got back to the car, Grandma was resting in the passenger seat with both doors open. I attacked my sandwich with gusto, even though the salad dressing had turned the bread soggy.

Soon as we were done eating, Grandma sprang to her feet. "Ready, boy? Let's git started!" I stood slowly, my muscles as stiff as old, parched leather, and dragged myself back to the field in a dark mood.

By the time the sun hovered over the western horizon, we had only hoed two rows each, hardly a dent. We gathered up our tools and water containers and headed back to the car. Fatigue gave way to relief, but just as I was about to step into the car, Uncle Noble shouted.

"Wait a minute, you guys! I *know* you ain't gettin' into my nice clean car lookin' like *that*."

I looked down. My shoes and pants were caked with mud from working in the puddles, and my arms were covered with sweaty dust.

"Wipe that mud off your shoes, dust your pants off, and put some paper on the seat 'fore you get in."

Russell and I completely covered the rear seat with an old newspaper and we were on our way. Uncle Noble drove fast through town and as he turned onto Brooklyn, a car behind us honked. He craned to look in his rear view mirror. "That's Elsie." It was my mother, who I saw infrequently. I got up on my knees to look out the back window. I flashed her a big smile and waved. She waved and followed us up the hill and into Grandma's driveway. Before Grandma could open the front door, I was out the back. I ran to my mother's car. "Hi!" I shouted.

"How you doin', Pie?"

"Okay. I've been hoein' cukes."

"You're gettin' to be a big help to your Grandma."

"I know," I said, trying to sound like I really wanted to be.

Then she reached into her bra, pulled out a dollar bill, balled it up in her palm, and slipped it into my right hand. In a low, conspiratorial voice she said, "Stick this in your pocket."

I shoved it into my front right pocket before Grandma could spot it. It was a thrill to share a secret with my mother.

"Thank you," I whispered.

"Where you goin'?" Grandma asked my mother as she walked toward the smoke house with the hoes in hand.

"I'm goin' back to Big Frank's Beer Garden and have a couple. Then I'm goin' home to cook."

"Can I ride back with you?" I begged.

"Now what would Grandma think of that?" She paused. "I'm comin' back over this way tomorrow afternoon, after I get paid. I'll have another dollar or two for you then. Come back to the Beer Garden when you see me ride by. I'll blow my horn."

I skipped into the house, feeling flush and loved.

By the time Grandma got inside, I had pumped two tubs of water and had them heating on the gas range. Grandma was impressed I'd done the chores without being told. She reached into her bra, and pulled out her little change purse.

"Here's a dollar, George. For helpin' me t'day."

Wow! I was getting rich!

When the water was heated to Grandma's satisfaction, she took the foot tub into her bedroom to bathe. I grabbed my tub and headed for my room. By the time I finished washing up, Grandma was in the kitchen preparing one of my favorite meals, hot dogs and pork-n-beans. After three frankfurters, two helpings of beans, and my routine chores, I staggered to bed, as weary as I'd ever felt.

But I tossed and turned, scheming to sneak off to Big Frank's the next day. I imagined the night-life crowd meeting up at the Beer Garden after getting their pay. They drank liquor from half-pint bottles, shot craps, and played cards: Pitty Pat, Tonk, and sometimes Poker.

I knew my mother would be there because I often heard tales of her crap-shooting and other gambling expertise. Everyone said she was one hell of a shooter. I wanted to see for myself. I drifted off to sleep, trying to come up with an excuse Grandma would buy.

Chapter 3

I woke to the smell of frying scrapple from the old sow we'd slaughtered a few months back. I reached over to the window and pulled the cord to raise the blind. A soft breeze flowed through the torn, rusty screen. The sun made a pathway across the floor, reflecting off the cracked dresser mirror onto some old overcoats hanging on nails in the back of the door.

I lay there luxuriating in my creaky spring bed, stretching, yawning, and watching dust motes dance in the big ray of sunshine.

"George! Breakfast ready!" Grandma hollered. "Time to get up. Today's Saturday and we ain't goin' to the field, but I got some shoppin' to do and I want you along."

Most times I went shopping with Grandma it was to tell her the prices of things, and do the math. I enjoyed adding the prices in my head as Grandma put the items in her basket. She had a strict budget, never more than twenty-five dollars. My job was to add it all up right so she'd stay in her budget and wouldn't be embarrassed at the check-out counter by having to put stuff back.

My foot hit the floor and a sharp pain stabbed me in the lower back. If what I had was gristle, then my gristle was stiff and sore. Grunting with pain, I pulled my pants on slowly, like an old man, grabbed my chamber pot, and went to Grandma's room to collect hers. I picked it up carefully and carried both of them through the back door, trying to avoid looking down at the floating feces in murky water. My miserable job was to consolidate the two containers.

I was embarrassed for anyone to see me carrying a chamber pot, so first I checked for nosy neighbors or passing cars. Then I dashed the fifty yards to the white-washed outhouse. I went in, put down the pots, and shut the door behind me. Holding my breath, I dumped the contents of the bucket through the seat hole, and made a quick exit. At the water pump, I rinsed the pots, dropped both by the pine tree, thoroughly washed my hands, and went in for breakfast.

I tried hard to think of an excuse to visit my mother at the Beer Garden, but came up empty.

"Finish that scrapple, so we can go shopping."

"Yes ma'am."

"The taxi be here any minute to take us off to the Acme." Grandma dropped her dish in a pan of hot water.

Shopping went fast. At the check-out counter, I nervously waited for the cashier to total the groceries.

"That's twenty-four dollars and thirty-nine cents, please."

That was close! As we loaded the groceries into the taxi, I made my move.

"Grandma, Shelton asked me a few days ago if I could come over to his house and polish a couple pairs of his shoes."

Before Grandma could think of a reason to say no, I added, "He said he would give me fifty cents, or pay my way to the movies."

Chances were better that Grandma would say yes if money was involved. Shelton was my first cousin—Uncle Noble's son—and about ten years older. But he was short and skinny. He'd been born with a heart condition and sported a long surgical scar across his chest. He was a slow learner as well, old enough in sixth grade to quit school and go to work washing cars at a local service station. Even though I was much younger, we got along. He often paid my way to the movies and passed me down his old shoes and pants.

Grandma studied my face for a moment. "Alright, boy. But first I want you to help me put these things away."

As soon as the groceries were organized, I ran toward Shelton's house with no intention of stopping—he worked all day on Saturdays. I continued running to a wood line marked by a single wire and a sign: "State Game Reserve." Down the little hill I ran, following the wire, past tall scattered pines and maples, to the back of the Beer Garden's cinder block outhouse. Through a crack in the outhouse door frame I saw a woman squatting on top of the toilet seat, her apple-red dress up around her light brown rear.

The Saturday afternoon crowd was drifting in. Several people, mostly men, hung around outside drinking beers and swigging from half-pint bottles of whiskey. Underneath a pine tree near the back of the Beer Garden, several craps shooters were getting a game started. Beside a tree, Lucky Leon and Big Barney, two local mavericks, had cleared the dead grass from a level spot and were shooting for nickels. As people passed, each gambler asked, "Wanna make some of this money?"

I sauntered up, trying to appear as cool as possible. "Has my mother been back here?"

The gamblers continued shooting. Big Barney crapped out, and Leon grabbed the nickels. Then he snatched the dice off the ground, locked them into his palm, shook vigorously, sat back on his heels, and shouted, "Shoot all of it! Shoot the entire thirty cents!"

Leon broke his concentration for a moment and looked up at me. "Barney, there's Elsie's boy."

"I ain't seen your mother," Big Barney said. "But she should be here in a few minutes."

Leon shook the dice a few seconds more and rolled them, palm up, off his fingertips. The spots totaled eleven, so Leon picked up thirty cents from the pile.

"Shoot thirty," he said, smiling.

I was captivated by the white cubes tumbling across the black dirt. I dropped to my knees to see better.

"Hey, Pie!" It was my mother, getting out of her car. She came right over and sank to her knees beside me.

"Jump on that thirty cents, Elsie," said Big Barney.

"I'll catch you next time 'round." She reached into the front of her dress and pulled out a wad of greenbacks. She carefully separated it into three stacks. She set one on the ground and the other two disappeared back into her bra.

"Let's make this an interesting game, and shoot for a dollar."

"That's talkin'!" Lucky Leon placed his dollar on the ground in front of him. Scooper and Buck, two other regulars, came from the Beer Garden's side door, stepping quickly. Both dropped to their knees in front of me.

"Atta girl, Elsie," Scooper bellowed.

My mother snatched the dice, shook and turned them loose.

"She stumbled on an eight!" Buck shouted.

"You don't make eight for two dollars," Big Barney challenged.

"Bet I will!" my mother boasted.

"I bet you a dollar over here, Elsie!" Scooper dropped four quarters.

"Okay, that's a bet, too, cause I'm gonna make it!"

This time my mother shook the dice a little longer. Finally, she let them go.

"You have to do better than a four," Barney said, eyes never leaving the dice.

Mom repeated the ritual several times and finally shot seven, a loser. Everyone who had bets grabbed for their share of the loot. Each time the dice made their way back to Mom, she lost. The stack she had on the ground disappeared quickly. She started on the second, even though she told me she had set the money aside for household expenses. Almost as quickly as the first, the second parcel diminished too.

Mom had a bewildered look the next time the dice came around. She passed. She sat on the ground, crossed her legs, handed me a dollar and said, "Here's

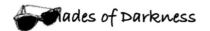

the dollar I promised you, son. Put it in your pocket for now. When the dice comes 'round again, I'm gonna let you shoot. Maybe you'll have better luck."

I was thrilled. "You think I should?"

"Why not? I'll tell you what to do."

The dice slowly moved in our direction and finally it was my turn.

"Okay, let's see what my son's gonna do!" Mom pulled out two dollars from her bra and asked. "Who wants to fade him?"

"I'll fade him. He's just like you Elsie! He ain't gonna hit nothin'," Leon jeered.

Others bet the dice were going to lose also, but Mom had confidence. She accepted all of their challenges until her last pile of money disappeared. I picked up the dice, feeling the pressure, and rattled them in my little fist several times, waiting until all bets were down. Then I released the ivory cubes. Everyone quieted. I prayed: Let me be a winner. She's got a lot of money riding on me. The dice totaled nine.

"I bet fi' dollars he don't make nine!" Leon again.

Now my mother was nervous. She reached into titty city, as she called the inside of her bra, and pulled out a folded ten dollar bill. Mom accepted the five dollar bet and some other smaller bets. I delivered a six, five, three, snake eyes, an eight, and finally...nine!

"Oh, I knew you could do it!" Mom squeezed the back of my neck. She snatched all of the money with the exception of a ten dollar bill and said, "Shoot ten! This boy's hot! Come on suckers! Let's shoot!"

Each time I grabbed the dice I shook them a little harder and prayed a little longer. I thought about

Grandma. If she knew I was shooting dice and praying to win, she'd kill me.

"Wait! Before you shoot, I wanna get my money straight. I'm not gonna lose this," Mom said placing two stacks back in her bra.

My good luck continued. I won three more times before finally losing the dice.

"Okay, son, guess we shot enough dice for today. Here's five dollars. You better get back home now before Grandma starts yelling for you."

She patted my head. "You meet me here next Saturday, we'll try our luck again, okay?"

"You bet!" I laughed, and dashed back to Grandma's, stopping now and then to look at that five-dollar bill.

I shot dice with my mother several weekends in a row, until cucumber-picking time began. Picking was worse than hoeing, but it was comforting to know that Grandma did not pick every day along with me. On days she didn't make it to the fields, Uncle Noble watched me like a spider with a trapped fly, and reported back to Grandma my every move. If Noble was not in the field, his wife, Aunt Eleanor or his sons and daughters continued the vigil.

Uncle Noble's sons and daughters were the ticket holders. Every time someone filled a basket of cucumbers, one of the holders gave a picker a twenty-cent credit. The picker then carried his filled basket to a turn

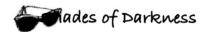

row where a truck traveled along, loading baskets.

Uncle Noble drafted me to stack baskets on the truck. I often got to drive, which was a lot more fun than picking. One of the permitted breaks during those blistering days in the sun was when the lunch truck drove up, always greeted with relief. Its driver peddled ham and cheese sandwiches, buns, candy, and the best homemade chocolate cupcakes. A glass of Kool Aid sold for a nickel, a bottle of soda went for a dime, and since tickets were redeemable for refreshments, I spent my tickets almost as fast as I earned them—when Grandma wasn't around.

She eventually figured out why I had so few tickets at the end of the day, so for the balance of cucumber season, she set a quota. I had to bring home at least fifteen tickets a day, requiring me to work hard and spend little. Cucumber season ended, only to be replaced by tomato season. Wouldn't you know it? Uncle Noble's money making ventures included the tomato business.

Tomato picking was as frustrating as picking cukes, but since tomato plants are taller, there was less bending. When tomatoes were wet, I hated the way the dew soaked my overalls. The hot sun baked my pants dry, leaving a dusty green residue.

It was exasperating to reach for a red-ripe tomato and discover it was rotten on the bottom. I hated plunging my fingers into that mushy, spoiled fruit but I got rid of the foul smell with the juice of a fresh, ripe tomato.

By the end of the long hot summer, I had earned almost a hundred dollars. I handed all the money over to Grandma, who then doled out my share—twenty dollars to go school shopping. That year I learned a fundamental economics lesson—twenty bucks didn't go far.

Chapter 4

The following school year began with news that my brother was joining the Army. Donald's departure for Fort Jackson, South Carolina, left me with extra chores. In addition to my usual tasks—pumping water, and taking out the chamber pots—I now also had to cut the wood and feed the hogs. But I could handle everything. I was in the eighth grade and Grandma said I was her little man.

Was Nelson getting to be a man, too? I was surprised to see him and his sister Effie one day at the bus stop, each puffing on a Pall Mall.

"I didn't know you guys smoked," I said, approaching them.

"We been smokin' a long time," Effie declared.

"How long?"

"Oh, 'bout two years," she answered, puffing with exaggerated sophistication. "Wanna try one?" Effie pulled a cigarette from an almost new pack.

"No, I don't want the habit."

"Why not? You chicken?" Her big brown eyes gently mocked me. She held out the cigarette.

Nelson looked on, puffing furiously, wearing that striped brown sport jacket I admired.

Effie waved the cigarette in my face. "It's a

good feeling. You can get a buzz if you inhale," she promised.

"Inhale?"

"Yeah. Like this," Effie said, lavishly demonstrating her technique, inhaling slow, deep breaths.

"Okay, I think I can do that." I reached for the cigarette. "Lemme try."

Effie lit my cigarette with hers, then handed it to me. I put it to my mouth and, following Effie's example, pulled a stream of smoke deep into my lungs. My lungs exploded in a fit of coughing and choking. It was bad, but smoking bothered me less than the thought of Grandma finding out I was doing it. She flatly opposed smoking anything: "If God 'tended for folks to smoke, we'd of been born with chimneys."

As for Nelson and Effie, their mother also abhorred smoking. But their father, who always had a cigarette dangling from his lips, bought Pall Malls by the carton.

Nelson finished his cigarette, stamped it on the ground, then twisted his foot from side to side, just the way the grown ups did. He reached into his brown pants pocket and produced a shiny steel lighter. He flipped the top open and closed it several times. It clicked shut like a trap.

"Man, where did you get that tough lookin' lighter? Lemme see it." He tossed it to me, and I inspected it carefully.

"B-bought it." Nelson had an occasional stammering attack.

Effie continued tutoring me and within minutes I got the hang of inhaling smoke. I didn't like it, but puffed anyway.

After a few drags, I started to feel wooly-headed. "I'm dizzy as hell. Is it supposed to make me drunk?"

"No man!" yelled Nelson.

"Here comes the bus!" Effie warned. They quickly hid the evidence.

School that day was boring and I spent most of it with a bad taste in my mouth. I was glad when it was finally over. Still fascinated with the lighter, I sat with Nelson instead of in my usual seat at the back of the bus.

Malisa Cummings, who also lived on Brooklyn, sat in front of us. She was in the tenth grade, kind of pretty, but hardly ever talked to me.

Feeling reckless, I turned and said in a sarcastic tone, "How are you, Miss Cummings?"

"Hi, Pie," Malisa answered dismissively, then continued chatting with her seat mate, Tammie Gable, a short, plump honey-brown cutey who lived on the outskirts of Federalsburg.

I leaned over to Nelson and whispered, "Where's that lighter you had this morning?"

"W-wait, Pie, 'til we get rolling."

As soon as we got outside the city limits, Nelson handed me his lighter. It was the most elegant thing I'd ever seen, a Zippo, all shiny and scratchless, shaped like a match box, with rounded edges. With the least amount of pressure, the top snapped open with a satisfying click. I rotated the Zippo in my palm and snapped it open and closed for a mile or two. When pressure was applied to the little black wheel, the blackened wick burst into a dancing blue-red flame.

"G-gimme my lighter. You're g-gonna use up all the fluid."

I knew better than to defy him. Nelson was short-tempered and hated to explain things more than once. He snatched the lighter, flipped back the top and tested it several times to make sure it still worked.

A sudden gust of laughter from Malisa and Tammie made me turn around in my seat. Tammie was clutching her pudgy belly while Malisa was clasping her hands and appeared to lose control of her upper torso, which was bobbing up and down.

Malisa's long, green nylon scarf concealed her short, sparse hair. The other children gossiped that she was cursed, insisting that a bird once flew from the heavens and plucked her head near bald. As Malisa jerked back, Nelson lit his lighter again. Somehow, the flame caught the end of Malisa's nylon scarf and it caught fire. I looked on in frozen terror as the flame rushed toward Malisa's fragile hair. Nelson looked terrified, too. He jumped up and starting batting at the flames.

Oblivious to the danger, Malisa snapped, "Pie! What in the world? "

"I didn't do nothin'!"

Tammie stared at Malisa's smoking scarf until Malisa finally noticed it too and shrieked. I jumped up and opened the window to let out the smell of scorched fabric while Nelson patted Malisa's scarf between his palms, preventing the flame from reaching her hair, just in the nick of time. The bus driver turned a few times with his head raised as if he smelled something, but then acted as if nothing had happened. Thank God for short hair. If Malisa had had long hair, it could have been a disaster.

"What're you doin', Pie? You tryin' to kill me? You coulda burned up my hair!" She patted her head and scowled at me.

I laughed, and then the laugh grew harder at the thought of Malisa with an even balder head.

"You're crazy. This ain't nothin' to laugh about!" She wagged her finger at me. "You gonna buy me a new scarf. I just got this scarf and you gonna buy me another one. Look at this! It's ruint!" She squeezed the destroyed scarf into a ball between her palms. "You nearly had to buy me a wig! You're forever getting' into trouble!"

"Hey, I didn't set you on fire. It was..."

"You did! You did! The lighter's right there in your lap."

I looked down. Sure enough, there it was. I looked at Nelson. He leaned back in his seat and looked out the window.

Malisa stared at him until he turned back and their eyes met. Nelson looked at me, his face unreadable.

"I d-didn't do n-nothin'." He shrugged and put on his best nonchalant expression.

"You see, you did do it, Pie!" Malisa was convinced, and I was too afraid of Nelson's temper to rat him out.

I arrived home with a bad feeling in my gut. So I quickly changed into overalls and started my chores without waiting for Grandma to tell me. I pumped and carried in enough water for the following day. I also cut the wood, fed the hogs, and took in both chamber pots, all the time looking over my shoulder for trouble.

As I was coming back out of the house, a black and white '57 Ford with a Continental spare tire kit on the rear eased up to the front of Grandma's house. I recognized the man behind the wheel—Malisa's father!

My heart leaped to my throat. I was in for it. I knew Mr. Cummings was not paying us a friendly visit. I scooted around into the back yard, waiting to see what would happen. I decided I needed reinforcements. Where was my brown and white terrier, Bootsy? She always barked when a stranger came to the house.

"Come here, Bootsy!" I called. "Come here!"

Finally she came sprinting from the woods across the field, barking happily. I squatted and she jumped up on me with both paws hitting my chest, wearing a wide dog grin. She always smiled, with her tongue lolling out the left side of her long snout. I stroked her head a few times, picked up a small stick, and threw it into the field. Bootsy raced after it, her white tail wagging like a windshield wiper. Before she returned, I heard footsteps inside the house approaching the back door. I knew those footsteps: they were Grandma's special footsteps that meant trouble was coming. I was doomed.

"George! Come on in here, boy."

Mr. Cummings stood in the living room, his narrow dark eyes glaring at me. As soon as I entered, Cummings stepped toward me, shaking a short, fat index finger in my face.

"I don't appreciate that sh... " He paused, and cast Grandma a frustrated look. She was well known in the community as a respectable church woman. Anyone who knew Grandma would never use foul language in

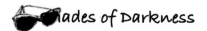

her presence.

Cummings put his hands on his hips. I could see he wanted to wail on me in the worst way. "You think you're bad, huh? Now if you're so bad..." Cummings turned, pointed to the back of his big round head, and raised his voice. "Why don't you just set MY head on fire!"

Cummings spun back around, and stepped closer to me.

"You need a good whippin'!" He held his arms out like he was ready for a fight, bent slightly like backward chicken wings. He pulled in his paunchy stomach, puffed out his chest, and shook his stubby finger closer to my face. "You're gonna get it, you little..."

Grandma looked at me with enormous, flashing eyes. "Tell the truth, boy! Did you set that poor child's hair on fire?"

"No, Grandma. I didn't do it! Honest!"

"Well, who did do it then?" Cummings demanded.

I looked down and muttered, "I don't know."

"You did it!" Cummings shouted.

Malisa's father went to work convincing Grandma I was lying. It worked. Grandma promised him, shaking her head as she looked at me, "I'll take care of him, Kelly. Don't you worry, son. I'll take real good care of him."

After the sound of Cummings' throaty V-8 faded down the hill, Grandma went to the refrigerator, pulled out a frozen beef bone and began humming "Precious Lord" while preparing a pot of soup. I knew from experience that Grandma was biding her time. I also knew I'd never convince her it was Nelson, and I finally knew that even if I did, I'd get a beating from Nelson.

That night I dawdled while getting ready for bed. I ironed my favorite blue pants and red shirt, then packed a lunch of two homemade biscuits, each with a hard-fried egg tucked in the middle. I climbed into bed, relieved that I had gotten through the rest of the day in one piece.

Just as I was drifting off to sleep, I heard Grandma's voice, as stern as it ever got.

"Boy, get out here! You know you're gonna get it!"

I threw back the covers and stumbled, half asleep and in my boxer shorts, toward the doorway, where her enormous silhouette loomed.

"Pull them drawers down, boy! Turn 'round! You know you shouldn't of done it!"

I steeled myself for the stinging lash of the old fan belt from the 1948 Buick she owned but never drove. I tensed and tried to block my mind against the blows. The doubled-over fan belt wrapped around my skinny butt, digging into my black flesh. I clenched my muscles tight, hard and long, exhausting myself, but I held out until the severity of the blows lessened.

Grandma was pooped. Nevertheless, just before the last blow she said, "This one's for good measure! Don't let it happen again! You coulda killed her!"

When Grandma turned me loose, I ran, my skin on fire with pain, jumped into bed and curled up in a tight ball. The beating was a sad way to wake up, but it was over and now I could go back to sleep.

Although I hadn't been responsible for Malisa's near scorching, I did manage to get myself in trouble. Bobby Good and I fought violently one afternoon on the bus because I told him his mother didn't wear underwear, and when she did, they were dirty. Then a classmate ratted on me when a section of the school was closed because of the unbearable smell created when I soaked a bathroom radiator with urine. A few weeks later, I was caught with my head hung out the same bathroom window smoking, trying to make smoke rings.

By the end of my freshman year, I thought I had gotten all the dumb pranks out of my system.

Then I bought a set of white dice, similar to the pair I first shot with my mother, but a little smaller. My square "pearls" and I were a team for the entire summer, and by fall I was a competent crap shooter. All the big-time gamblers in town knew me. They called me "Hot Shot."

Sometimes I gambled out of town with the high rollers, in big-stakes games, as high as one hundred dollars. Usually the excitement took place in the back room of the barber shop or in an after hours house. When school started, my cubes went to class with me.

Almost every day I gambled, in the rear of the bus or in the school bathroom. During a losing spree I thought of a way to increase my winnings.

The next day in agriculture shop I waited until the teacher left the room and drilled three tiny holes in the dice. On the first die, I took aim at the side with the single dot, which I carefully drilled a bit deeper. On the second die, I drilled two holes on the six-dot side—one at the bottom of the left column, the other at the top of the right column. Then I filled each hole with mercury I stole from the chemistry lab. Finally I plugged the holes with wood filler and painted them black so they disappeared.

After that, I won consistently. The weight of the mercury usually caused the dice to fall on a winning seven, on a six and one. I won so much my gambling buddies were hesitant to shoot with me, so most of the time we gambled by flipping coins. But I had a trick for that, too. Whenever possible, I used a dime. I learned how to shake the tiny coin in my right hand so that when I slapped it into my left palm it was on the edge and I knew which was heads and which was tails. After the other boys revealed their coins, I expertly let my dime drop on the winning side. Often I cleaned out the group, but I never let them go without money for lunch, as long as they paid me back, with interest.

Chapter 5

My gambling success made me a celebrity. My pockets bulged with bills most of the time, and I grew less and less interested in schoolwork. Toward the end of the year, Mr. Elsey, my math teacher, called me to the blackboard.

"Here, George," he said handing me a piece of yellow chalk. "Solve this equation."

I tried desperately to work out the problem, but I had not been paying attention.

"That's what I figured," Elsey said, pointing his finger close to my face. "You've been running your mouth with Gwendolyn like a dummy, and she's as ignorant as you!"

Mr. Elsey embarrassed me, so I took a step toward my seat. He snatched my head around with his yellow chalky hands. "Where are you going? I'm not finished with you, boy!"

The class fell apart with laughter, but I couldn't see what was so funny.

"You look like a painted black Apache!" yelled a classmate, pointing at the chalk on my face. Insulted, I grabbed a piece of chalk and smeared several white lines across Elsey's dark delicate expression. He glared at me for an instant and then grabbed on to my shoulders and violently shook me. I retaliated by grabbing his shoulders, swinging my right leg behind his bony knees and pushing him backward onto the floor. He recovered and lunged back at me like a tackling lineman. We tangled and rolled frantically on the classroom floor, while students screamed and scrambled out of our way.

"Get 'em, George. Break that fucker's neck! Get that sucker good for me!" yelled my friend Bobby, trying to camouflage his voice. Instead of pulling us apart, Bobby slipped in back of Elsey, pulling the little fellow to the floor.

Finally the principal and two of the biggest teachers in the school came rushing in and dragged me off to the office. I sat with my arms defiantly folded, awaiting my inevitable destiny with justice. Finally two state troopers and someone from the Welfare Department arrived. Grandma showed up an hour later. After they had a brief meeting, the two troopers gently handcuffed and hauled me off to the county jail, since there was no juvenile detention center.

The sheriff locked me alone in a small cell about the size of a large closet, with a stinking, dirty, yellowish-gray toilet, no lid, and a filthy sink. The tiny room was cold and uncomfortable. I was miserable and yearned for home. The bunk, chained against the wall, was just a slab of wood and there was just one thin, rank-smelling blanket. The cell had two small openings, in the door and a barred window over the bunk, where I looked out all day. There were adult prisoners in the other cells I could see through the cell door.

When I'd been in for a couple of days I spotted two

classmates walking on the sidewalk but didn't dare yell to them. I was too embarrassed. If I crammed my head in one corner of the window, I could see down a wooded hill where I sometimes saw wild ducks paddling the small river. They were going somewhere. I, however, was going nowhere.

The other opening was in the thick steel door where I received food, and from time to time I saw other prisoners walking down a hallway that led to the visiting room, where I met with Miss Reed, my social worker. She was short with long pretty brown hair, and big blue eyes. She scolded me as she handed me some books through the little window in the iron door.

"At least you can read until you get out of here." She looked around for a moment, then she said in a quiet voice, "I've been talking to the judge and the sheriff. The judge, after reviewing your records, thinks you may have something on the ball. He's willing to give you another chance."

Miss Reed explained that the sheriff was taking a prisoner to Maryland State Penitentiary in a few days. "He'll take you too, to let you see what prison life is all about. If you're not careful, prison will be your new address. Read this book, *Huckleberry Finn*, and good luck." Then she waved me off.

The week crept slowly by. The food was terrible, always cold, and never enough. Hardly a day passed without runny eggs, under-cooked scrapple or an over-cooked hot dog.

Monday morning, the sheriff's keys rattled like wind chimes outside the big door.

"Are you ready to go to prison, George Brummell?" Mr. Andrews, tall, blond, and lanky, barked at me. "We're not going to leave you there. We're just going to show you Maryland State Penitentiary."

I was just eager to get some fresh air. As we walked out of the building, I wondered, "Do you have to hand-cuff me?"

"Not if you promise to behave and not try to escape. Get in the back seat," he ordered.

The sheriff's wife was sitting on the passenger side, so I gently pushed her seat forward and stepped in behind her. James, a jail mate, was sitting behind the driver's seat with his hands cuffed behind his back. He was a white man, about fifty years old, tall, with thick gray hair. I don't remember where he was from or what he was in for, but he had treated me okay, rolling cigarettes for me until my case worker gave me enough money to buy a pack, at an inflated price, from another prisoner.

"Are they taking you to prison?" I whispered.

"Yeah. I gotta do a six-month bit," he answered in a deep southern drawl. "Sorry I can't roll you a smoke."

"I got some cigarettes," I said. "I'll light one and hold it for you, if you want." James wiggled his lanky body around and faced me. I lit him a Pall Mall as the sheriff started the Chevy and pulled slowly away.

The trip was too quiet most of the time. The sheriff and his wife passed a few remarks to each other about their four-year-old grandson. James fell asleep before we crossed the Chesapeake Bay headed toward Baltimore, so I settled back and enjoyed the scenery.

Finally Sheriff Andrews pointed and announced we had arrived at the prison. Shit! I thought. It was a massive, dismal, isolated building, just like one of those ugly castles in a Dracula or Frankenstein movie.

While the sheriff checked James in, a prison official took me on a tour of the facility. It was like the county jail but many times bigger. Similar cold quarters, foul language and odors.

The sheriff joined us. "Would you want to be in a place like this?" he asked softly, but in a grave voice.

I answered without hesitation: "No, sir! This place gives me the creeps."

"Let's get started back, then. I believe you've seen enough."

I fell asleep almost as soon as I got into the car. It seemed like only a second had passed when I was being shaken awake. "Wake up, boy. Lemme get you back in your cell."

A prisoner again. "Dang it, Sheriff," I said. "Do you have to put me back in that crummy little pen? Can't you find something for me to do?"

"'Fraid not, boy. But you should be gettin' out soon enough."

Seven days and five chapters of *The Adventures of Huckleberry Finn* later, Miss Reed came to tell me the judge had decided I'd done enough time. She took me straight to Grandma's. Grandma met us at the back door, head tied, smiling, wearing her silver-green apron. She always sat by the living-room window, so she saw us long before we got there.

"Welcome back home, son. I hope you learnt a lesson."

"Oh he has," Miss Reed said, smiling. "Remember what I was telling you on the ride from Denton,

George? Your previous behavior simply cannot persist. You take care and I'll see you soon."

I was relieved to see her drive away. I went straight to my bedroom, put my things away, lay across the bed, and soon drifted to sleep. I awoke refreshed a couple hours later. Letting the shade roll up, I found a half sun setting behind the little forest of tall pine trees behind the house. I opened the bedroom door, and glanced at the kitchen clock on the wall above Grandma's spotless old Tappan gas range. It was not quite five-thirty in the afternoon.

"Grandma, I'll be back in a few minutes. I'm going to see Nelson. If you want me, that's where I'll be." I grabbed my jacket, threw on my baseball cap and dashed out the back door.

Nelson was at the wood pile swinging an axe, slicing logs into pieces for their cook stove.

"Hey, Nelson!"

"P-prisoner! When did you get back? Come on. G-gimme a hand with this wood, hoss."

Nelson called everybody hoss, even his sisters. I reached down and grabbed an armful of what smelled like pine and cherry wood and followed him into the house. The table was set but without the usual pan of Mrs. Mary's hot homemade biscuits. She had not gotten home from work yet. Mrs. Mary made the best biscuits on Brooklyn Avenue. She often asked if I liked to stay to supper, but the only thing I ever accepted was a hot buttered biscuit or two.

"Hey, hoss. M-man, you're a convict. W-what's your number?" Nelson asked. "W-what's prison like?"

"I'll tell you after we take in more wood."

39

We went back to the wood pile, gathered more armloads and took them inside. In a little while we had taken in all the wood Nelson cut. Soon we were outside again, across the road sitting on Grandma's whitewashed, wooden fence. I talked about the jail until the sun went down, and Mrs. Mary arrived from her long day of domestic duties for a rich white family.

A white woman driving a new Chevy coupe pulled into the driveway. Mrs. Mary slowly got out and looked across the road to where we were sitting. She managed a tired smile. "Hi, Pie! You're growing into quite a young man."

I blushed and watched her trudge into the house and slam the side door shut.

Then an even newer black Ford turned the corner, cruised down the avenue and pulled to a stop in front of us. It was Chris Canter.

"Hey, Pie! When did you get home?" she asked, peering out a half-lowered window.

"This afternoon."

Chris was married with two children. She had an unremarkable face with a remarkable body supported by two big, smooth, wheat-colored legs. We chatted about my prison experience for a few moments until a car pulled up behind hers and the driver tooted his horn impatiently.

"Stay out of trouble," she shouted as she pulled away. "I'll try!" I yelled back.

"Nelson, how'd she know I was in jail?" I asked

"You kn-know how word gets around."

We sat on the rail fence for an hour or so, greeting people as they drove and walked by, talking about school and jail. Finally, I got up to go.

"I guess your dinner's ready," Nelson said, dusting the white wash from the back of my pants.

"I know you're probably ready for those hot biscuits."

"Yeah."

"I'll see you tomorrow at the end of the road."

"Okay, hoss."

At school my friends welcomed me back with teasing. They called me "Con," "Prison Bird," and "Loser," but I took their insults with a smile. I was determined to stay out of trouble.

Chapter 6

My celebrity soon faded. For the rest of the year I managed only a few minor mishaps and even passed to the tenth grade.

That summer I lied about my age. I wrote to the Social Security Administration requesting a Social Security card before my sixteenth birthday. Within a month, the card came. I was elated! It was the next best thing to getting a driver's license.

On my way home from the post office, I stopped at the filling station where my cousin Shelton worked. He was busy washing a black hearse. I flashed my new card.

"I'm going to be making some real money soon," I boasted. "I don't have to work those fields no more." I waved the card in his face.

"That's good," Shelton replied, without breaking his rhythm with his chamois. "Here's a nickel. Get yourself a Coke. I'm gonna go play some cards at Chris's house tonight. We're gonna play Pitty Pat. You want to go?" Pitty Pat is a rummy game where the objective is to make three pairs starting from a five-card hand.

"Sure, man, I'll go, if you let me have fifty cents."

"Here you go. Meet me at my house at seven."

On the way to the card game, Shelton told me

Chris's husband Ronny, her brother Mike, her uncle James, and he, frequently played Pitty Pat for nickels and dimes. Sometimes they shot craps.

"Really?" I fingered the loaded dice in my pocket. We walked past the Beer Garden. Next to the tavern and under the yellowing tall pine, Lucky Leon and a guy named Scooper prepared to shoot dice, on an old army blanket they'd spread on the ground.

I considered ditching Shelton and joining the crap-shaking duo, maybe get them to use my doctored dice. But I instantly reconsidered. If those two discovered I had tampered with the cubes, they'd probably hang me. When we got to Chris's unpainted, clapboard cottage, she yelled before we knocked, "C'mon in! We been waitin' on you! I've shuffled these cards for twenty minutes! They should be good an' hot by now. Ya ready to get started?"

Walking toward the kitchen table, Shelton reached into his pocket, pulled out a dollar, kicked the chair back and sat. "Give me change for a dollar," he ordered.

"How much are we gonna play for?" I asked.

"Let's start with a nickel."

"Deal me in a hand!" a voice yelled from the back room. It was Mike, Chris' tall, lanky brother, a thick coat of Clearasil smeared over patches of acne.

Ten hands flashed by quickly. Mike won repeatedly. The pot increased to a dime and, shortly, I was broke. Chris lent me a quarter, but still I couldn't catch a break. I lost every hand.

By midnight, everyone was weary and the game ended. As we walked home, Shelton counted his winnings—a dollar twenty. "I'm gonna let you have another quarter, Pie. But I'm gonna keep it for you 'til tomorrow night."

For several weeks, Shelton and I got into the habit of walking to Chris's house for an evening of Pitty Pat, with similar results. One Saturday, we went to the movies instead. On the long walk home, we devised a signal code to let each other know what cards we held and try to gain an edge.

The plan was simple. If either one had an ace, we were to scratch one side of our nose. A deuce, both sides of the nose. A three, scratch one ear. A four, scratch an ear and one side of the face. If there was a king, we were to say something that included a word ending in I-N-G, and emphasize the "ing," as in "play-ING" or "try-ING." If either one got to deal, if we had the chance we were to deal each of us an extra card. We were to tuck the extra card under our legs, and when we had the chance we would use it. Sometimes we would pretend to drop a card on the floor to make the switch.

The night we were to put our plan into action, Chris sat between Shelton and me. She seemed to have every card I needed. I was losing again. Chris put coins in the pot for me, to keep me in the game.

Then my luck changed and our plan was beginning to work. I won a few dollars and, it seemed, I won Chris, too—she rubbed her leg against mine all night.

It was clear I wasn't going to get rich playing Pitty Pat, and Grandma was badgering me to get a job. Alex and Nelson had been working for slave wages at Donaldson's Vegetable Canning Factory, putting in sixty to seventy hours a week. Alex was a shift leader and drove some of the other workers to the plant.

I flagged Alex down one day when he drove up in his truck to drop off Nelson at the end of the shift. "They hirin' at Donaldson's?"

Alex gave me the once-over. "They hired some migrants yesterday, so you might be able to get a job. Wanna give it a shot?"

I nodded.

"Be in front of your house tomorrow morning at four-thirty."

Nelson and I were waiting the next morning when Alex arrived. We clambered into the back of the enclosed pick-up truck bed, along with at least five others with familiar faces. I dropped my bag of three peanut butter sandwiches on the floor beneath the bench and sat.

Like the tomato and sweet potato factories Grandma had worked in, Donaldson's cannery was decrepit. The building listed like a sinking ship, looking like it might fall over any minute.

I went to the office and filled out an application. While I was waiting for Sam, the boss, I threw rocks at birds on the roof of a nearby building. Then, impatient, I left to explore the factory.

"Where you goin', Pie?" June Bug yelled as he drove up in a forklift.

"Just walkin' around, waitin' for Sam."

"I saw him a few minutes ago, walking back there," he said pointing behind him. "Wanna ride? Hop on!"

He shifted the forklift into gear. It spun forward and nearly lost the palette. But June Bug was as skillful as he was reckless. He tilted the forks back and up in one motion, correcting the balance of his cargo, then threaded the lift through a small opening and expertly placed the palette of boxes high up. June Bug then stopped where Dave, another rider in Alex's truck, was running a boxing machine.

"Did you get the job, Pie?" Dave asked, as he bent his sweaty, swollen body, placing an empty box onto the boxer. He jerked the lever toward him and the box instantly filled with twenty hot 303-size cans of tomatoes. Dave closed the flaps and stacked the box onto a palette.

"Man, they got my black ass humpin' today!" he complained. "Orvill got drunk last night and didn't show, so I'm all by myself. Orvill 'posed to be stackin' these damn things."

"Think the boss'd mind if I give you a hand?"

"Don't think so. Come on. They're hot and heavy. You see how I got 'em stacked? Every row of boxes go in the opposite direction."

An hour passed quickly. I was so involved in what I was doing, I didn't notice the older, dusty-looking white fellow standing behind me.

"Who are you?" he asked.

"I'm a friend of Dave's. I came over to look for a job."

"Okay! You got one! Name's Sam Donaldson. Go to the office and sign up, then meet me in front of the factory."

"Welcome aboard!" shouted Dave.

For the next few weeks, I stacked boxes, operated the boxer, and worked with the labeling crew. A couple of times I drove the lift truck, which I really enjoyed. I guess Mr. Donaldson thought I was having too much fun, because the driving lasted only a short while.

Next I worked on a machine that put the tops on each can. I was shoveling the tomato slush into a drain when Donaldson showed up yelling. "Wait, boy! I paid good money for those tomatoes! Pick them up off the floor and put them back on the line."

"But I've been sloshing through them all day!" I protested. "I figured no one wanted tomatoes I been walking on, especially after goin' in that nasty toilet."

"Damn it!" he fired back. "I know that, boy! And you know that! But the customers don't!" He walked away.

I worked at the factory all that summer, gambling on some weekends. I had been winning a lot, as much as twenty-five dollars a night. Shelton and I had perfected our signaling scheme.

One Saturday afternoon after school started again, I was at Chris's house when she asked her husband if he wanted to go out to a dance hall.

"You know I don't like to go to those places," he groused. "Too much fighting. But if you wanna go, go ahead."

"I wouldn't wanna go by myself," Chris whined.

"Maybe Pie'll go with you," Ronny suggested. "He won all that money last night."

"Pie, you wanna go with me?" Chris asked, dealing the cards.

"I don't mind," I said, trying to sound casual. "What time?"

"Pick you up 'bout seven-thirty. We won't stay too long."

I ran home, pumped water for the night, pressed a pair of pants and a shirt, and took a quick sponge bath.

Then, I sat down to a slice of fried scrapple, two hot dogs, and some left-over fried potatoes.

"Where you goin'?" Grandma asked.

"The Blue Savoy, with Chris."

Grandma made a face. "You been fooling around a lot with that older woman. She 'most ten years older than you. I hope you don't get in no trouble. You two ain't doing somethin', is you?"

"What makes you think that, Grandma?" Before she could answer, a car horn tooted outside.

"That's Chris, boy!" Grandma scolded. "Look at you. You can't even finish eatin'!"

I grabbed the greasy scrapple, tucked it between two slices of bread, put the plate on the pump bench, and ran toward the door. Grandma had recently added two rooms to the house, a third bedroom and a room for the pump.

"Wash that dish when you come back here!" Grandma hollered. "And I want you to go tomorrow after church and get some day-old bread!"

I hopped into Chris's car, stuffing the sandwich in my mouth and watching her shift the gears. Every time she raised her leg to step on the clutch, the hem of her green plaid skirt slid up above her smooth, round knee. A couple of good glances at Chris's glossy thighs and we were there.

A local band stumbled through top twenty tunes for the nearly empty house. We decided to check out The Flame, another club over the Delaware line. The parking lot was full and the highway next to the old building was lined a half mile with cars. We circled the converted one-room schoolhouse. In one corner of the parking lot, two cars faced each other with their head-lights on. In the middle, crap shooters with dollar bills balled in their fists were shouting and carrying on.

A bootlegger named Big Barney was bent over into the trunk of his car, exposing the cranny of his fanny. His business depended on discrimination: colored establishments were denied liquor licenses. He sorted through cases of whiskey and handed a half-pint bottle of Calvert to a fidgety customer.

A few cars away, a city slicker was hustling hot hats. Farther around the building, a well-dressed man shoved a woman who was protesting but laughing as she got into a car. They left, spinning wheels, kicking up dust, beer cans, and gravel. Chris quickly pulled into the space.

"Pie, if you wanna go into this place, go ahead," she said, in her soft, husky Eastern Shore drawl. "But I'm not going in. Too many people."

"Okay, I'm goin' in, to see what's happening."

"Bring me a soda."

"I'll be back in a few." I circled the joint, hoping to find someone I knew with a bottle of Thunderbird wine, but no luck. I climbed the six wooden steps and pushed my way through dozens of people standing outside the door.

"Hey, man! You! Let me have a quarter so I can get in," demanded a grimy old woman. I ignored her, and paid the dollar admission. I squeezed sideways down a narrow hallway into the crowded room. I saw a few people I knew, but no one I had ever hung out with. After two bump and grind dances with girls I recog-nized from Delaware, I returned to Chris's car. She was sitting in the middle of the front seat trying to tune a distant station on the radio. I slid onto the driver's side.

"Let's go for a little ride," I suggested, turning on the ignition before she could answer. "I know how to drive."

The car's eight cylinders burst into a rumbling idle. I let up on the clutch and the car lurched out of the lot.

"Be careful, Pie. If Ronny knew you were driving his car, he'd kill me."

She sat as straight as a pole, peering ahead, but after a few minutes, she sat back, relaxed, and slid closer to me. Instead of taking the direct route home, I detoured on all the lonely back roads through miles of forests.

"I got to be gettin' home," Chris finally said. "It's one o'clock."

"Okay, when we get to the cemetery, I'll stop and let you take over the wheel."

Soon after we changed seats, Chris stopped in front of my house and switched off the ignition and turned to me.

"I had a real good time. Maybe we can go out again, soon, huh?" She put her hand on my leg and caressed it.

"I had a good time, too," I admitted. "How 'bout a little kiss before I go in?" My heart pounded.

"Okay," she said smiling, sliding toward me.

I kissed her lightly on the cheek, but Chris turned her head until her wet lips met mine. She pressed harder. Headlights approached from around the corner, so I drew back and quickly leaped out the car.

"I'll give you a call tomorrow!" I yelled, running into the house. That night my sleep was restless. Although I had already lost my virginity, I had never been with anyone like Chris. Over twenty years old!

The next day, in school, my thoughts were filled with fantasies. Minutes before the final bell, Mrs. Puscito caught me nodding. "George, what was the last statement I made?"

"I don't know, Mrs. Pusci...," intentionally dropping the last syllable.

The room filled with sniggering.

She was furious. "Smart aleck! Get out of my classroom and don't come back until you bring permission from the principal's office."

"I need a vacation anyway," I said defiantly. When I got to the principal's office, Mr. Washington sprang from behind his desk, strutting like an angry rooster. "You again? What now?"

I told him my side of the story, but he wasn't biting.

"Come with me!" I followed him out of his office and down the long hallway to a connecting corridor.

"Hurry up!" he barked.

He stopped in front of the janitor's storage room, reached into his pocket, fumbled through some keys, and unlocked the door.

"Get in here!"

He followed me into the dim, dusty room, pulled off his jacket, and hung it on the stair rail leading to the back of the auditorium stage. He made a fist and started pounding it, hard, on my chest.

"You think you're tough shit!" he began. "For two cents I'd give you the worst ass kicking you ever had!"

I reached into my pocket and found two pennies. "Here you go, Mr. Washington. I'm ready when you are."

Sweating like a sprinkler, he stepped back. "Get out of here, asshole! You wait for the school bus outside!"

When I got home, Grandma was across the road talking to a neighbor, so I headed straight for the telephone to call Chris. I told her about my three-day suspension. She lectured me about the mistake I made and the importance of education.

"Let's go riding tonight, Chris," I interrupted.

"I can't. Anyway, we're 'spectin' company. Wait 'til tomorrow and come meet me at the Goldbergs' where I work. Come at one o'clock. There won't be nobody there but me."

I was excited to see Chris and to visit a white family's house. The next day I showed up at the Goldbergs', at the snowy-white back door, and let myself in to the large, brick ranch house.

"Come on in!" Chris called out. "Have a seat. You can fold while I finish the ironing."

An ironing board stood in the middle of a small, tidy utility room. A basket of clothes occupied the only chair, so I hopped up onto the countertop. Chris pulled a sheet from the clothes basket and draped it across the ironing board.

"You bored from bein' off school?" She slid the iron smoothly across the blue lace-edged fabric. When she finished, she stretched the sheet and handed me one end.

I heard a key slip into the back door, and before I hopped off the counter a well-dressed, slender, silver-haired man walked in. His head snapped in my direction. My feet took forever to hit the floor. The man focused his deep-set gray eyes on mine with a disgusted look.

Chris dove right in. "Mr. Goldberg, this is my cousin, George. When I finish the ironin', I'm goin' to get him to he'p me move some furniture, so I can vacuum behind."

"Hello," the man said in a flat voice. He opened the refrigerator, put some ice cubes in a glass and went into the next room. A few minutes later, he reappeared with his briefcase. "If the store calls, tell them I'll be back there shortly." He slammed the door behind him.

When I heard the engine of his car crank up, I moved toward Chris's shapely behind. I put my arms around her small waist and kissed her softly on the neck. She was wearing a low-cut white blouse and a tight-fitting black skirt. The skirt clung to Chris's buns like she'd been poured into it. Her hair was loosely curled. Her shiny skin smelled like soap. Slowly I followed her curves, up her sides to her chest, and lightly rotated my index fingers and thumbs around her nipples.

Chris sighed and set the iron upright. She pushed her rear into me, then turned to wrap her arms around my neck. Just as quickly, she broke away.

"I'm gonna put these things away," she said, picking up a stack of folded sheets and a handful of panties from the counter. "Come on. I'll show you 'round. Bring Mr. Goldberg's underwear."

I grabbed a handful of monogrammed tee shirts

and boxer shorts and followed her through the spa-
cious kitchen and into a living room more glamorous
than I imagined, decorated with antiques—all wood,
silver, and brass. A fancy hi-fi set was recessed into a
wall, with rows and rows of buttons.

"Do you know how to turn this thing on?"

"I don't even fool with it," Chris said. "If somethin'
busted, I'd get the blame."

I thought how good the Hoppy Adams Show
would sound, blasting through those big speakers.

The master bedroom was out of a magazine. The
ceiling had four large gilt mirrors right over the bed
and the walls and lace-edged drapes were a light lav-
ender. Chris laid her laundry stack on a white antique
dresser. She separated the women's underwear, leaned
over, pulled out the bottom drawer and tucked the
delicate lingerie inside.

I sat on the corner of the bed, intensely focused
on her neatly designed buttocks. I kicked my shoes
onto the plush sand-colored carpet and sprawled back
onto the bed. When she finished her tasks, Chris sat on
the edge of the bed, rubbed her leg against mine, and
sighed.

"I'm really beat."

Then she turned onto her stomach, resting her
chin between her hands. "I think I've been bending too
much. My back is sore. Why don't you rub it a little bit
for me?"

"Where's it hurt?" I straddled her just below her
rear.

"Right above my bra."

I began rotating my thumbs between her shoulder

blades.

"Wait a minute, Pie." She lifted herself up and started unbuttoning her top.

"I'll get it." I marveled at her soft, brown back.

"Could you unsnap my bra for me?"

I unsnapped the black bra, slipped the straps over her shoulders, and let it slide down her arms.

"Where did you say it hurt?"

"All over."

I rubbed her shoulders, gradually working my way to the small of her back. Chris turned over and faced me, nipples hard and red. I massaged and stroked her small breasts for awhile, and soon I was absorbed by the warmth of her love making.

Hours later, I walked back through Chambers Park beside the lake under the cool shadows of swaying pines. On the weed-filled bank, an old man in bib overalls stood smoking a corncob pipe, holding a bamboo fishing pole. He got one. He yanked his pole, but it was just a sunny. I stopped to watch until he caught another small one, then continued toward home. I stepped with purpose, feeling manly and optimistic.

Maybe I was a man. A grown woman appreciated me. An uncontrollable smile crept across my face. I couldn't wait to tell Nelson. After all, how many fifteen-year-old boys had had sex with a twenty-three-year-old woman? THAT was something!

After that, Chris and I usually made love in her car in the woods near Brooklyn. Only once did we do it in her house, while her two children were at her mother's. Her husband had gone to Boston to visit his sister. We spent hours in bed, loving and talking.

"I do love you, Pie," Chris confessed. "I'd like to leave Ron. But I got the kids to think of, and you're so young. I just don't know what to do."

The rays of approaching headlights lit up the curtains, flickered, then grew brighter. Chris leaped out of bed. "That car's comin' here! Get up!"

I threw back the spread and slid out of bed. I stumbled into my pants as the sound of the engine grew louder. Scooping up my socks, I slipped into my shoes, grabbed my shirt, and crawled out the half-opened window, dropping the short distance to the ground. The light came on in the kitchen just as I hit the soil.

"I'm home!" Ron's voice echoed through the open window.

Keeping low, I hobbled to the back corner of the yard. The outside light was on and I feared running where I might be seen. I darted for the tree line. Halfway there, a dog began barking. Then a chain reaction of barks erupted. A light flashed on in Chris's bedroom. A shadow appeared behind the blinds so I hit the dirt, like soldiers did in the movies. One side of the shade lifted and Ronny peeked through the narrow opening.

As soon as the shade fell back into place, I sprinted into the dark woods to a place where a large downed tree made a bridge across the river. I carefully crossed it, ran through back yards, and slipped into Grandma's house and to bed.

The next morning Chris called as soon as Ronny left for work.

"Can't let that happen again. Just can't."

"Does Ronny suspect?"

"Don't think so. But we can't keep this up."

In spite of the danger, our bond grew. Once during that first year, she even picked me up after school. When the fellows saw me get in the Goldbergs' new Ford I became a celebrity again, driving that big red car through the parking lot with the radio blasting as my schoolmates trudged onto the dusty old buses, scowling at me.

That was the last time I rode home with Chris. The principal found out and suspended me for five days, for skipping the bus. He contacted Welfare and somebody from the agency wrote Chris accusing her of contributing to the delinquency of a minor. If she didn't quit, she'd lose her kids.

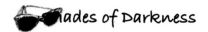

Chapter 7

Neither Welfare's threat nor my suspension could cool our attraction. As it grew, my school work suffered. I cracked jokes, threw spitballs, and slept in class. In agriculture, the teacher, Mr. Smith, got so fed up that, after he took attendance, he sent me to the tool room to clean and arrange tools, or just sit around.

I talked a girl I knew from church into meeting me in the tool room. I'd lock the door and when Jerrie and I weren't making out, she helped me clean tools. She was the good-girl type, wouldn't go all the way. I liked her anyway.

One day after Jerrie left, I was putting together an A-frame turkey coop that the senior class had been working on and played a trick on a boy by locking him in the cage. That got me another five day "vacation," and again Welfare was alerted. On the second day, Miss Reed's stubby Volkswagen sputtered into our driveway. I met her on the front porch and she sat in the green metal rocker.

"You've complicated matters, George. I hear you're still seeing that woman and now you're suspended again." She sighed heavily. "My supervisor and I have decided to place you in a foster home."

My heart fluttered with anxiety.

"Do you know Julius and Iola Littlejohn?"

I nodded. "They live out in the woods on Houston Branch Road."

"Then you know they take foster children. They're much younger than your grandmother, so we think you'll be better suited living with them. At least until you're eighteen. You should get your belongings together. I'll come day after tomorrow to take you over there."

Grandma had been at the unemployment office, and returned with her shopping. While she unpacked, I broke the news to her.

"Lord help me, what am I gonna do?" she wailed. "I prayed they wouldn't do this, but you're just too hard headed. Lord have mercy! I told you, boy. A hard head makes a soft behind." Grandma slammed a head of cabbage on the kitchen table. "But you just wouldn't listen."

"I'm sorry, Grandma." I hugged her and kissed her on the cheek as tears flooded my eyes.

"Get away from me, boy," she fussed, grinning.

I dabbed at my face with my sleeve. "It's close by. I'll be over every day I can."

Miss Reed returned as promised and I loaded my two shopping bags of clothes into her tiny car. Grandma, her eyes red, handed me my first baseman's mitt and my old pair of black tennis shoes.

"I hate seein' you go, son. Don't forget about me. You come and see me."

I wanted to cry too, but that day the tears wouldn't come. Grandma stuck her head through the rolled-down window. I kissed her again on her satin soft cheek. Then Miss Reed drove the five-minute ride to the Littlejohn's.

We turned left at the end of Brooklyn, up the hill and past the colored cemetery. Then we turned onto a dirt road that had water-filled potholes just about deep enough to swallow the car.

Mrs. Littlejohn was waiting on her porch. She looked tall for a woman, and her skin was coal dark against a long white dress and a pair of black and white high-top tennis shoes. Her fogged-up glasses had slid down her nose and her wild, woolly hair almost brushed the bottom of the low awning.

"How ya doin', honey?" she said, wrapping her right arm around my neck as soon as I got out of the car. "I've been hearin' lots about you, son. Go on in."

Mrs. Littlejohn held open the storm door and we entered a small, dimly lit room. Two large freezer chests dominated the left side wall. On the right was an old clothes press, tucked in a corner with boxes of old garments piled on it. The floor boards creaked under the battered linoleum.

"Your room is 'round to your left," said Mrs. Littlejohn. "Bathroom is back over there, straight ahead. Did y'all have a bathroom at your house?"

"No ma'am."

A large picture of Elijah Muhammad and a "No Smoking" sign caught my attention as I entered the living room.

"Follow me." She stepped gracefully through an accordion door which separated two bedrooms.

"This side is Clair's and Martha's. Clair is seven,

and Martha's three."

She continued through another door. "This room is for Manny and Louis. Manny's fourteen, and Louis is eleven. Your room will be back here on the end. Why don't you put your things away and meet us in the living room."

The bedroom was smaller than my room at Grandma's. Even with only a single bed, wall locker, and a small table, it was crowded. But it felt homey and I quickly settled in.

Soon after I arrived, I started working for Mr. Littlejohn's custodial service. He was a big, meticulous man with a sparkling gold tooth. He was a Black Muslim, a devout follower of Malcolm X. He ate no pork and, on Sunday mornings, he and a few other brothers attended a small temple they organized on the outskirts of town.

"What black people need is to be more independent," he told me. "We need to create more jobs for ourselves. That's why I quit one of the largest industries around and started my own business."

I seldom visited the Muslim Temple. Grandma had insisted I keep going with her to the Baptist church.

Working for Mr. Littlejohn's janitorial service had its rewards. The job gave me a chance to explore the bank, the post office, and other white-owned institutions around Federalsburg. He paid me the minimum wage, same as his other employees, but unlike at Grandma's, I got to keep it all.

Six months passed quickly. I stayed busy but not too busy to see Chris. On a Saturday afternoon in early January, while I washed the bank's glass door, I saw a reflection of Chris's car in the blue-tinted glass. She pulled to the traffic light and leaned out the window.

"Are you gonna be home later?"

I nodded.

"I'll call you. It's important."

I started to walk over to the corner, but the light changed and she pulled away.

"I'll be home about four!" I shouted after her.

When the black wall phone in the Littlejohn's kitchen jangled at four fifteen, I was waiting and snatched it up on the first ring.

"Hello, Pie." She sounded sad. "I don't know how to tell you this. I just came from the doctor and...I'm a couple months pregnant."

"Pregnant! You?"

"Yeah me, pregnant. I'm gonna have a baby, and you're gonna be a father."

"Me! A father?" A wave of heat raced up my neck. "But...but... Why me?"

"You did it, Pie," she said impatiently. "I don't know how to tell Ronny. I'm scared. Him and me haven't been messing around too much, and when we did, we used protection."

For days I was in a stunned fog. Chris told Ronny and he threatened to kill me, so I tried to make myself scarce. I was filled with endless anxieties, hopes of fleeing Federalsburg, and daydreams of a better life. On one of those days, on a routine trip to the post office, I spotted an Army recruiter in the post office lobby, handing out brochures.

As I took one, the recruiter stuck his chest out and said, "Uncle Sam wants you."

George Brumm

The Army. Of course! I went straight home to the Littlejohns and called Chris.

"After I'm seventeen I'm joining the Army."

"What about school?"

"I don't care about school. Besides, the soldier at the post office said I could continue my education in the military."

As for the baby, the idea of fatherhood was terrifying. I was just sixteen. Even more than Ron's death threat, that made the Army an irresistible alternative.

The school year finally ended and I was promoted to the twelfth grade. That summer Mr. and Mrs. Littlejohn gave me more independence. Mr. Littlejohn often let me clean the bank and do other jobs alone. Mrs. Littlejohn even trusted me now and then to run errands with her station wagon, without a driving permit. The confidence they showed in me was important. I didn't want to break their faith, so I did the right thing. The summer breezed by, and I was back in school before I knew it.

Within the first couple of weeks, trouble started all over again. I talked back to my home room teacher and was sent to the principal's office for insubordination.

"This time, George, I'm going to send you to work with the janitor," Mr. Washington said. "You return to class tomorrow. I'm not going to suspend you but if anything else happens, you'll be out of here,"

Even though Mr. Washington didn't suspend me, I worried that he would tell my foster parents, who I did not want to disappoint. They were good to me, like a real mother and father. I didn't want to be placed in another home before I was old enough to join the

Army. A day or two passed and I knew I was in the clear because neither of the Littlejohn's mentioned Mr. Washington calling.

The next week Chris asked me to spend the weekend with her at a girlfriend's house. I was elated, but it would take some planning. I asked Mrs. Littlejohn if I could stay at Grandma's Friday night. She agreed. On Friday I stopped by Grandma's after school. I waited until dark to call Mrs. Littlejohn. She seemed satisfied because she heard Grandma's voice in the background. As soon as I hung up the phone I told Grandma I was returning to the Littlejohn's. I left, running to the end of Brooklyn Avenue where Chris was waiting in her car.

She reached over and unlocked the door. I hopped in. She smiled and started the car, stretching her left leg so her toe could reach the clutch.

"I'll be having the baby soon," she said, shifting gears and wriggling a little. "She's moving now! Feel my stomach! I just know it's a girl!"

I placed my hand on her hard belly. Almost in time with the music from the radio, throbs bumped against my palm.

"Persistent bugger, ain't she?"

"Yeah, she is. I just know it's a girl. Hope she sleeps tonight so I can rest."

That next week Chris called me from a downtown phone booth, her voice filled with excitement, to tell me she had picked up a used crib. "Would you like to see it?" I couldn't get enough of her, so I agreed. She showed me the crib and we drove for awhile, then parked on a deserted road until past midnight.

The next morning I was having my breakfast of evaporated milk and Corn Flakes when the phone rang. It was Chris, sounding groggy.

"I had the baby, a six-pound seven-ounce girl."

"Already! I just saw you a couple hours ago."

"Soon's I got home I had some real bad pains. Ronny drove me to the hospital, complaining the whole twenty miles that it wasn't his. You'd think he'd have stayed, but he just dropped me off and went back home."

"Does she look like me?"

"Well, it's a little early to tell yet. She's not even a day old."

Chris called me from the hospital each morning of her three days stay, timing it for when she was nursing, so that I could hear the little girl exercise her lungs. I couldn't wait to see them, but seven weeks went by.

We finally arranged to meet at the end of the road that led to the Littlejohn's. I got there first. It was freezing cold, so I stamped my feet to stay warm. She was late. A car finally approached, flashing headlights from bright to dim. Before the car stopped rolling, I hopped in. The old Oldsmobile felt like a toaster inside. Chris leaned, planted her lips against mine and then spun around, looking into the back seat, where the baby was bundled in a blanket.

"Why don't you bring Theresa Ann up front, Pie?"

I squirmed. "I...I don't like to handle babies that small. I've waited this long. Might as well wait 'til later."

She shrugged and started the car.

We stopped near the city dump, on a road that was seldom used at night. A full moon lit the way as Chris backed into a small opening of trees. She settled the car and reached back for Theresa.

"You wanna hold her?"

"No, you better keep her. She sure is little."

Chris slid toward the center, put her feet up on the hump, and opened the blanket. Theresa's large wide-set eyes glowed inquisitively, almost motionless, hardly blinking.

"She's kind of quiet. Is she alright?"

"Yeah. Theresa's just being a good girl."

I cooed and brushed a kiss on her tiny chin. Theresa wriggled and began a whimper that grew into a continuous cry. "She must be alright," I said. "She's doing just what babies do."

I gently worked my hands under her body and picked her up from the pink blanket. "By the way," I said, trying to sound as casual as possible. "Welfare gave me permission to join the Army. I'm gonna take the test the middle of January. If I pass, I guess I'll be on my way."

Chris tucked a pacifier in Theresa's mouth. I knew she liked having me around. But my mind was made up, even though it did feel kind of good to cuddle, kiss, and play with Theresa's tiny hands and feet—until she started to cry again. Then I handed her back to Chris.

She gave the baby a bottle. "Oh, Pie. "Don't you want to watch your baby grow up?" She wasn't quite begging, but she was earnest. Finally, she sighed. "I'm wasting my time, I guess."

The three of us sat in the darkened car in silence,

watching the rats scurry between the piles of trash.

The weeks passed and as January rolled around, I tried to talk my buddy and classmate, Ruben, into joining too. At first he was skeptical, but I was determined.

"We can go in at the same time and be stationed at the same place."

"That does sound good," he admitted. "I'm tired of school, too." We made a pact.

On test day, I was wide awake at five o'clock. Just before I left, I knocked on the Littlejohn's bedroom door to let them know I was leaving.

"Good luck, Pie!" Mr. Littlejohn called out.

I walked at a fast pace to the Safeway parking lot where the recruiter was going to pick us up. I kept my fingers crossed all the way, hoping Ruben hadn't been bullshitting. Around the corner by the theater, I spotted Ruben in a telephone booth.

"Ruben!"

He hung up the phone and walked, smiling, toward me. "Well, here I am. You can see I wasn't jiving. You and me are gonna set the Army on fire! Before you know it, we'll both be generals!"

We waited inside the laundromat, huddled by the heater, watching the parking lot and sharing a package of peanut butter crackers. At exactly six o'clock, the recruiter's car circled the parking lot and stopped.

"Who's that brother in the car with him, Ruben?" Walking closer, we recognized Bill Thomas, the older brother of one of our female classmates. He lived in Preston, five miles from Federalsburg. He and I played on the same high school baseball team.

"Where you guys going?" Bill yelled.

"That's a hell of a dumb question," I said, climbing into the green sedan. "We're going the same place you're going, the Army!"

Bill, Ruben and I talked nonstop the nearly two-hour trip to Baltimore. When we got there, our recruitment officer turned us over to a soldier, a sergeant first class, and we found ourselves in a big classroom filled with young men my age. We weren't the only ones trying to escape our lives.

The testing took all morning, then we were lined up and we marched raggedly to a mess hall. It was a long line but the food was worth it. I filled my tray with a bit of almost everything and ate 'til I felt stuffed. Ruben and Bill went back for a second helping of steak, potatoes, and apple pie.

There were some more tests in the afternoon, then we had to wait a long hour for the results. Finally, our recruitment officer came out of the office carrying three folders. Ruben, Bill, and I all stood up at once.

"Okay, fellows, this is it. George! William! Congratulations. You two passed. But Ruben, you didn't quite make it. You can take the test again later."

"Shit!" he muttered. I was disappointed, but mostly glad for Bill and myself.

"When would you two like to leave?"

We answered in unison. "Soon as possible!"

"Well, you could leave tomorrow, or the day after."

I looked at Bill. "How about tomorrow?"

"Sounds alright to me."

Bill and I teased Ruben on the way back. He was smiling, so I knew a part of him was relieved. The recruiter dropped me off at the Littlejohn's, with orders to report to his office the next morning at six o'clock. As soon as I walked into the kitchen, I told Mrs. Littlejohn the news. She said she was happy for me, but she looked sad. Later, I called Chris to see if she could meet me before I left. Chris broke down crying. "Ronny and I promised to go see my mother. She's been sick."

I hung up feeling bad for Chris and sad for myself. It would have been nice to see the baby and her one last time. Who could say what the future held? I shook off the mood and went to my room to pack, such as it was—all I owned still fit in the two shopping bags I arrived with.

I hardly slept that night, terrified I'd oversleep and miss my date with destiny. I walked to Grandma's in the bitter cold and pre-dawn darkness and she and Aunt Mildred, her daughter, drove me to Easton, to the recruiting office. Bill met us there.

I had a tearful but dignified goodbye with Grandma. I took a few extra moments to study her face before she turned to leave. She had stuck by me through thick and thin, and taught me plenty, even though I had adopted the Littlejohns as mother and father. She was an old lady. Who could say what the future held for either of us? I wanted to remember her well.

Chapter 8

Full of purpose and enthusiasm, Bill and I boarded a military train full of escapees like ourselves on Groundhog Day, 1962. The train couldn't go fast enough for us, chugging leisurely through the countryside, stopping in just about every small town. It took all day and then, finally, the portly colored porter strode through the five cars of recruits, calling out: "Fort Jackson, South Carolina! Next stop!" The train wheels shrieked and the car jerked to a clamorous halt.

Before we could even gather up our belongings, the door at the end of the car flew open and a tall stone-faced sergeant came bursting into the car. "Alright you fuckin' recruits," he bellowed. "You're in the Army now. Off and on! Off your ass, and on your feet! Line up in one straight line! Okay, come on, come on! GET ON IT!"

Thus began my Army career. Bill and I lucked out—we drew the same barracks in Basic Training, and were assigned to the same outfit—A Company, Eighteenth Training Group, Fifth Regiment. We seldom saw each other during Basic, but we survived and after graduation went home on our two-week leave and showed off our spiffy new uniforms around town and at the high school.

I saw Chris and Theresa a few times, but Feder-alsburg and all that it represented was already behind me. After a few days of attention and affection, I was ready to get on with things.

When we got back to Fort Jackson, I spent eight weeks in Advanced Infantry Training, which sounded interesting but seemed more like a repeat of Basic. The two months flew by, and we were marching in the graduation parade. Most of the men got their orders that day and were sent to military posts throughout the United States and overseas. Some were delayed, including Bill and me.

We waited in suspense for two weeks and then our names were called: Korea! I felt so lucky. I had never been on an airplane, never been anywhere except Maryland and Fort Jackson.

They flew us to San Francisco and then bused us over the Oakland Bay Bridge to the Army terminal where we spent two days filling out forms and getting shots. Next stop was the harbor and the USNS *Barrack*, the biggest thing I had ever seen, with a huge ramp angled down to the pier. A sergeant in a Class A—full dress—uniform read off the names alphabetically, without bothering to look up.

"Private Brummell, George." I slung my stuffed duffel bag across my shoulder and followed the others up onto the main deck. A young-looking buck sergeant leaned against a stairwell rail leading down to another level. He glanced at my name tag. "Follow the arrows to C Berth," he said.

Shouldering my duffel, I followed the green arrows down several flights of narrow metal steps and into C

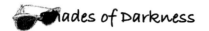

Compartment.

"Stack your duffel bags on top of the cargo hatch and claim a bunk," ordered yet another sergeant.

I loitered as long as I dared at the bottom of the step, waiting for Bill. He never showed, so I went and chose a bunk. When the big metal room was full of soldiers, our first sergeant came in and took another head count, then assigned details. I was an acting Military Police. The first sergeant handed me a blue arm band with "MP" printed in big yellow letters.

"Your job is to guard top deck, where the dependents' quarters are. Keep the little kids off the outer rails. We don't want to lose anybody. Your shift will be assigned later."

I slipped the band onto my left arm. It felt good and snug. For the first time in my life, I had authority. After a lifetime of being ordered around by Grandma, teachers, and the factory boss, I had my first real responsibility—in charge of the safety of others.

The Officer of the Day stationed me just below the sun deck, circling the dependents' quarters and shooing the kids away from the guard rail. A plump, freckle-faced blond, Private Brandon, relieved me for lunch. Each lunch line had about five hundred GIs creeping down three flights of stairwells and around the main deck. Since I was being relieved from duty, I was allowed to jump the line.

"Who does he think he is!" an irritated voice yelled. A chorus of GIs joined in—"Come on, you guys! Wait in the back of the line like we do!" But they quieted down when the commander of relief escorted me to the front.

Near the end of the serving line I was surprised to see Bill Thomas. He was handing out a tasty-looking strawberry shortcake, but he had on a sour face.

"Hey, Pie, what're you doing with that MP band? You wanna trade duties?"

"Hell, no. I had enough KP in Basic. I've got it made. I'm on the deck where the dependents and beautiful female bodies are. I'm in Berth C, Bill. Stop by!" We were both glad to have found each other again.

The *Barrack* steamed westward, crossing horizon after horizon. Each day I grew more comfortable about being at sea. On the fifth day Diamond Head rose in the distance, and then a pineapple-shaped water tower. The temperature spiked to one hundred degrees as we docked at Pearl Harbor to refuel. Hula dancers greeted us at the gangplank with multi-colored leis. But within a few hours, the *Barrack* was resealed and we resumed our journey.

Late that afternoon, a low pressure front moved in and the sky filled with black clouds. The ocean boiled with pounding waves and the big ship dipped, rolled back and forth, and heaved from side to side. My sea legs wobbled, and walking became increasingly difficult.

"Attention, all passengers!" the loudspeaker boomed. "Clear the decks. We are trying to avoid the eye of a typhoon. Military personnel, with the exception of cabin MPs, report to your quarters."

Leaning against the howling, salty wind, I stumbled around my watch, making sure all dependents were below decks. Then I found shelter in a corner between stacks of lifeboats. I grabbed a vertical rail and braced to ride out the storm until the commander of relief came to transfer me to an inside hallway where I was to block the entrance to the outer deck.

The storm raged for days. Many GIs got seasick, even some seasoned sailors. Hallways were lined with sea sick bags and most were used, as well as the floor. Riding the storm in the bunks was an adventure. At times the motion was just right for a peaceful sleep. Other times the ship leaped and dipped like a roller coaster out of control. What was supposed to be a two-week voyage lasted three.

We finally arrived at Inchon, South Korea. The ship buzzed with anticipation. We GIs were glad to be getting off the heaving bucket and eager to start our tour. We quickly gathered our gear only to find ourselves standing for hours around our bunks awaiting instructions. I was impatient, excited to be seven thousand miles from home!

At last we were allowed to tramp down the gangplank. My name was called. "Second Battle Group, Eighth Cavalry." An officer pointed to a waiting convoy of military trucks.

Land, and elbow room! Huge mountains reached up and through puffy white clouds. Korean soldiers sat behind some of the steering wheels in the convoy of trucks. The air was redolent with a cocktail of sewage, cooking spices, dried fish, and other intense smells. I hopped on a truck and found a seat, looking for Bill. I wondered if Chris had written me yet. I hoped to find a stack of mail waiting for me at my new company.

Finally the convoy lurched into gear. We rumbled through hamlets and past huts beneath mountains barren of vegetation. Cluttered fishing villages dotted the coastline. We passed rice fields, some divided into tiny plots, and others the size of small lakes. After two dusty hours of bouncing over unpaved roads, we arrived at Headquarters Company, Second Battle Group, Eighth Cavalry of the First Cavalry Division.

A sergeant major assembled everyone on the parade field. With exaggerated hand gestures, he told us, "Our job here in Korea is to keep Communist soldiers of the North from infiltrating to the South! Your job will be patrolling the Demilitarized Zone, manning observation posts, and 'staking out' overnight in three-man groups. We're in a real hot spot here."

It sounded dangerous but I was ready. I was assigned to C Company, Second Battle group. Bill had been assigned to nearby Headquarters Company, so we would still be able to hang out together.

Bill marched off down the road with about twenty others while I remounted the truck and our convoy rolled on, down winding roads, up steep hills, across small bridges, through darkened deep valleys, and finally into a long lane. At the end there was an entrance marked by a big jagged white rock with a sign painted on it in fancy black letters, "'Charlie' Company, Home of the Roadrunners," and a drawing of a red Roadrunner speeding away from an Army green hut. It hit me that I was on my own now in a foreign country, with no ties to home.

I was assigned to the Second Platoon as a rifleman. My buddy Brandon was still with me, as a radio telephone operator. We were about the lowest ranking men in the company, but we had the eight months of training that entitled us to automatic promotion to Pri-

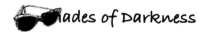

vate First Class, Pfc.

We new arrivals had to stay on the compound for the first two weeks. My bunk neighbors included Donnie Dant, a specialist fourth class, from Beaver Falls, Pennsylvania, and another Pfc., Andy Miller from Akron, Ohio. Miller took the bunk to my left and was appointed Bravo Fire Team Leader of my squad. Dant was assigned to the second squad as Alpha Team Leader and claimed the bunk to my right.

Miller was black, a draftee, and dapper. He had a sophisticated air and almost graceful body movements. Dant was also black, taller and thinner than Miller or I. He was on his second hitch in the Army in the "Frozen Chosen," as Korea was known due to its harsh mountain winters.

Dant had requested assignment to an infantry company from the Honor Guard because promotions came quicker there, even for blacks. The trick was surviving. Old timers said, "There are more blacks in infantry outfits because the Army don't mind losin' a few of us." In fact, there were a lot of us blacks in Charley Company.

Dant had big, amazingly clear light-brown eyes and kept his hair short, shaping a crisp line across his forehead with a razor. His brass always glittered and his shoes always gleamed. I admired him from the start. Even his underwear looked tailored.

While we waited to have our first chance to explore the local town, Dant regaled us with stories about the fun he had with the girls in the villages. That was a major reason he came back.

Finally, orientation was complete and we got our

first pass. Dant said for two dollars a man could have a "short time" with any girl working the streets. Dant, Miller, Brandon, and I got ourselves all spiffed up to explore the nearby village of Shang Par Re. We scrubbed our belt buckles with Brasso until they shone like the sun, and our insignias sparkled like kaleidoscopes.

"I am the shoe-shiniest nigger in the world!" Dant said as he laced his shoes. I shined mine like I never had before, applying multiple coats of Kiwi to my "low quarters." I couldn't put my shoes down until they were as clean as Dant's.

Finally, Dant straightened his "gig line," aligning his fly and belt buckle with his shirt flap. "Okay, you guys," he said. "If you're goin', let's go."

"You ready in there?" Brandon yelled, poking his freckled white head in the back door.

"We're coming," replied Miller, grabbing his garrison cap, known as a "cunt" cap for its shape.

In the orderly room, a large box hung from the ceiling filled with small packages of condoms. During orientation, officers warned us about the many varieties of venereal diseases we could expect to encounter. The sergeant who signed us out chuckled at our eagerness. "First night to the village, eh? You better take some rubbers."

"Yeah. I think I'll take five because I'm going to screw myself to death," Dant bragged.

A mile walk and we could see the village of Shang Par Re across the slow-moving Imjin River. Children played on the far bank. Women moved about retrieving clothes from the water and scrubbing them on rocks. In the distance, against a clear blue sky and tall mountains, men plowed behind oxen in muck up to their knees, preparing the rice paddies for the harvest.

We presented our identification cards and passes to the sentry at the bridge—Liberty Bridge, we called it—and entered Shang Par Re, a town with three bars, a few produce stands, restaurants, whiskey shops, and photography shops everywhere. Cluttered windows displayed photos of GIs with their arms around beautiful Korean women. The smell of spicy food was heaven and American servicemen were gorging themselves on large plates of rice with diced pork, covered with a layer of fried eggs and a ketchup-like sauce.

As we walked through the village, old-looking women known as mammasans approached, asking, "Catch short time? Two dollars can do." We declined, looking for an inviting bar.

"If you're going to use those five condoms, you'd better get started," Miller said. "Fuckin' twelve o'clock comes awful fast. We gotta be back by curfew."

I needed a drink to loosen me up so we bought a fifth of White Horse for a dollar and passed it around. Then we threw the empty in a ditch and headed on our adventure.

As we walked I heard a stream of Korean with my name in it: "Yeo bo se yo, Brummell. An nyeong ha shim ne ka?" It was Corporal Kim, a Katusa who I'd made friends with. Katusas were Korean soldiers assigned to our units for training. The other GIs called them "gooks," "slopes," and "yellow jacks," but I didn't, because I wanted to learn some Korean I could use with the Korean dolls in the village. He taught me a few words and phrases. "Sigae" meant "watch." "Myou sim ni ka" meant "what time is it?" "Tambae" was "cigarette."

Corporal Kim had plans to catch a short time and invited me along. We walked down the road and into an alley past several huts they called hooches, up another road at the back of the village, and through yet another narrow alley. Finally, we stepped down into an open-air parlor. Kim asked for a makuli, a native alcoholic drink made of rice. Then he began talking in Korean with a mammasan.

The standard price for sex for a GI was two dollars, but Kim could get the same lay for one. He asked her to charge me his price, since we were good friends. With some reluctance, the mammasan agreed. She disappeared for a moment and returned with three attractive young working women, called "choson."

"Which choson GI like?" I looked them over and picked the smaller one in the middle. Her working name was Cindy. She had a big cheerful smile, and seemed pleased I'd chosen her. She was slender and her hair was slightly longer than the others. Cindy's eyes were rounder than I expected on a Korean.

Mammasan stepped forward and held out her hand for the dollar. I pulled out one MPC—military payment certificate. MPCs were the only currency we were supposed to have in a combat zone. And we weren't supposed to spend them in town. But everybody did, and the Koreans used them to trade for black-market dollars.

Mammasan tucked the MPC in her baggy brown pants pocket. "Come, we go now." I set down my drink and followed her and Cindy out the door to the rear of the hut.

Mammasan pointed to a tiny hut that sat apart from the others in the crowded neighborhood. "You go hooch."

A neat fence made of sand bags surrounded what was a mud shack with a roof shingled with flattened tin cans. Cindy slid open the rice-paper door and stepped inside. I took off my shoes and followed, stepping up to a hard earthen floor. The room was surprisingly cozy. Close to the ceiling were two windows covered with the same rice paper. Both were open, letting in a warm breeze. On two opposite walls, below the windows, hung brightly-colored paintings of mountains, rice paddies, and oxen.

"Sit," Cindy commanded, pointing to the a mat on the floor. She sat down beside me, flashing an enormous smile but making no move to shed her clothes. This was my first time paying for sex and I was nervous, even though I often thought that when I took a girl to the movie or bought her drinks, it was about the same thing. I didn't know what to expect or do, so I waited for Cindy to make the first move.

"What name?"

"Private Brummell."

She tried to pronounce it a few times, but it wouldn't come out right. I tried to teach her how, but then realized I had paid for a short time, not to give English lessons. "Close enough," I said.

Finally, she stood up, walked across the room, and hooked the door latch. Still smiling, she came halfway back, stopped, and began peeling off her long, black silk dress. She folded the dress neatly and placed it on a wooden box to one side of the room. In her black cotton panties, she slowly walked toward me. The sight of Cindy's curvy yellow skin sent chills up my spine.

Nice little body. I fumbled for the top button on my shirt.

"You catch short time before?" Cindy asked, her voice slow and sweet. "How long been Korea?"

I watched transfixed as she peeled off her bra. "I no catch a short time in Korea. I been Korea only few weeks." I continued unbuttoning my shirt.

Cindy placed her warm palm on my chest. She pushed me back until I was lying flat. Then she got close to my ear and said, in almost a whisper, "I do it."

I felt as nervous as a virgin, sweating. I pulled out my handkerchief, which I had sprinkled with Old Spice, and dabbed at my forehead and neck. When Cindy finished unbuttoning my shirt, she removed it and fumbled at my belt buckle. She was too slow. I practically tore off my belt, stood, let my pants drop, and sat back on the mat. She pulled off her panties. Her breasts were small and firm, like little yellow volcanoes, with hard, pink nipples. I began examining every centimeter of her smooth skin with my sweaty palms.

Cindy soon responded, slowly at first, then more vigorously. She said it was her first time with a colored GI. White soldiers often told the Korean girls that we colored men had tails like monkeys. Cindy laughed. "Maybe tail in front."

A few minutes passed before we were entangled, burning with heat, locked tightly but passionately, massaging, stroking, and exploring. We loved long and slow, long after the short time had passed. Finally, her mammasan banged on the door.

"Hey, GI! You stay, you give money. Two dollar!"

Cindy asked if I would stay longer. Without answering I got up and handed Mammasan another MPC through the door. We finished our love making, and I closed my eyes for a moment.

"Wakey GI! Your bus come!" Cindy was shaking me. I looked at her alarm clock. It was eleven-thirty! Holy shit! I jumped up, slipped into my pants, ran to the door, and grabbed my shoes. I threw my shirt across my shoulders and darted out with a hasty goodbye.

"See you! Come back, please!" Cindy yelled as I ran down the road. I yelled back, "Sure!" and sprinted for the bridge. Miller, Brandon, and Dant were already on board the idling bus. "You musta use all them condoms," Brandon slurred, so drunk he seemed to be talking in his sleep.

"As a matter of fact, I forgot I had them."

Everyone on the bus looked beat, even the driver. Miller and Dant leaned against each other, snoring.

Chapter 9

Morning arrived like vengeance. We were rousted before dawn and my fifteen-person squad, many nursing savage hangovers, marched three miles over steep treeless hills and valleys, along shallow creek beds, past mine fields, and back up to a high plateau. A deep rugged valley, a stream, and the Imjin River wound into the distance toward a range of mountains. Korea! What a beautiful land at a beautiful moment, the morning serene, just as the sun was rising.

Our mission was to build a machine gun bunker that could be operational in minutes, and allowed a protected escape route in case we had to beat a retreat. We spent the day clearing brush, and roughing out an eight-foot-square pit. We made it back to the barracks just in time for mail call at three o'clock.

It was my lucky day—I had three letters from Chris. Two had been mailed to my old address and held up at headquarters. I was relieved to hear that she and Theresa were doing all right, but she had a way of making things emotionally complicated.

Pie, I love you a lot and miss you even more. Ronny sure have been giving me a ruff time about

Theresa. He continues to remind me that the baby is not his. I'm not really sure now myself who the father is, but I know she is mine.

I wrote fewer letters than I received. There were so many things I couldn't tell Grandma, or Chris, and I never felt motivated enough to write to my brother or my old friends.

Chris, I miss you as well and think of you all the time. I'm sorry Ronny is giving you such a ruff time. I wish I was there with you even though I don't know what I could do since you are married. I would marry you but I know it is not an option. I look forward to seeing you when I get home but for now hang in there.

For several mornings we marched out to the mountains and hacked away at our machine gun emplacement. Once the hole was complete, we lined it with sandbags, covered it with four-by-four beams, added more sandbags, and camouflaged the whole thing with scoured vegetation.

When we stopped for lunch, we downed C-rations of canned meats and desserts. I lit a cigarette and sat gazing out on the barren windswept hills. It was hard, as a soldier, to look out on the landscape without imagining the fierce battles that raged there during the Korean War. Everyone had heard accounts of GIs who'd been on the receiving end of waves of fanatic Chinese soldiers blowing bugles and swarming down on their positions in the middle of the night.

Evidence of the violence lay scattered among the ratty vegetation—expended shells and rusted metal parts of weapons and other equipment. A river of blood had soaked that soil. But, I thought with relief, that was a long time ago, ten years at least. The border was tense, but nobody expected a real war to break out anytime soon.

When I'd joined up, I had to name a beneficiary for the ten-thousand-dollar insurance policy in case I was killed—Grandma, of course. Other than a casual joke, I figured on a quiet tour of duty and didn't think much about finding myself in a real shooting match. That changed in October, 1962, when President Kennedy ordered the blockade of Cuba during the Soviet missile crisis. With nuclear war looming, anything was possible. But not, it appeared, in Korea.

At the end of a long week of hard labor, our sergeant gave us some good news, greeted by hoots and hollers. "Okay, you guys! It's Friday! We're goin' in early! Get an early start for the ville!"

We made record time jogging back to the Company to pick up our three-day passes. This time we were headed for Yong Gee Co, farther than Shang Par Re. We rolled past our "romper rooms," waving at familiar girls standing along the main drag.

Yong Gee Co was a lot like Shang Par Re, only bigger—more idle people, more prostitution, more poverty. Men squatted along the street, playing cards and board games, talking and gawking. The girls were mostly young, pretty, and available. They looked for tricks in the bars, on walkways, and in the open air markets. I wondered how many were mothers of the

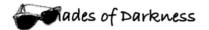

desperate-looking children in the streets, begging for anything. "Tambae yi sum ni ka?" Do you have a cigarette? "Ton yi sum ni ka?" Do you have money? Some children were nude as they ran along side of the bus.

Before I got to Korea, I thought poverty was bad in the States. I'd certainly seen enough poor people—blacks and whites—living in the Eastern Shores' migrant worker camps and shacked up down its remote country lanes. Korea showed me in stark terms how good we had it in America. We GIs tried to always carry whatever we could spare—candy, food, spare change—but we always suspected that the poor kids were put there by their parents, to make money.

The bus finally arrived at a regional military recreation center, which we promptly abandoned to head into the village.

"Catch short time GI? Two dollars can do," an old woman offered.

"O.K. mammasan, two dollars. I'll take you!"

"No, no, no!" She waved her arms wildly as I grinned. "No can do! Me too old! Mammasan no do! Have number one virgin girl can do. Come, me show."

Miller had no patience for banter. "Quit bullshitting Mammasan, man! Let's go! I see some pretty interesting bodies up ahead."

So we commenced what we called our "browse of promiscuous intent." The streets were as crowded as the Chicago Loop at Christmas with pimps and prostitutes—even children were pimping for the girls—promising "good short time." Out of the crowd, I spotted a girl I liked.

"Two dollars no can do!" she spat back. "I fuckin'

number one choson (prostitute)."

Miller was astounded. "You're not going to give that whore three whole bucks, are you?"

"Hell no! No can do," I told her and stepped away. "That chick must've been crazy," I muttered to myself. "I must look like a real sucker."

Our destination was the "Alley"—that part of each honky-tonk town set aside for us coloreds. I'd heard about these from other colored GIs who'd been in Korea awhile. There were a few whites who frequented the Alleys, but only the hip ones. Rumor had it the girls only laid Negroes. I didn't believe it. I figured they'd lay with anyone for the right price.

The Alley was muddy, too narrow for a car. Hooches with flimsy cloth or paper doors lined the walkway. The air was fetid with the smells of primitive life—wood and tobacco smoke, fish, spices, and the ubiquitous smell of sewage. Open air market vendors hawked suspicious looking meats, strange fruits and vegetables, and souvenirs.

In the Alley we found a bustling joint called the Tropicana Club. Behind it was Joe Mammasan's, another popular spot. At the end of the walk, inconspicuously, sat the Paradise Club, where we began. Miller, Dant, and I scanned the dimly lit room and found three vacant stools at the bar.

"Two beers, and a shot of White Horse for my friend Dant," Miller told the barmaid. She quickly gave us our drinks. Then she went to the record player at the other end of the bar and flipped through the platters.

Miller hollered a request. "You got 'You Don't Miss Your Water 'Til Your Well Runs Dry?' I don't know who

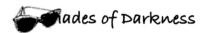

it's by."

"Memphis Horns," I said.

"Yes, we have," the barmaid called out, smiling. "I play for you."

Five girls and a couple of GIs sat chatting in a far corner. A crack of lightning lit the window. Within minutes the skies opened, the downpour driving the street girls and GIs into the club.

"Miller, there's a couple fine lookers near the corner dancing together," I said. "Why don't we split 'em? You take the tiny one in red. I'll take the one in green."

I stepped between the two and started dancing the shimmy. Miller slid in, Twist-ing away beside me. We gave the girls a good work out, and they didn't want to stop. Record after record, we made all the latest moves—the D.C. Hand-Dance (a Washington version of jitterbug or swing), something we called a Wrap Around, the Cha-Cha—or we just stood in place grinding.

Finally we took a break. A bossa nova tune was playing, with Sonny Rollins on his big saxophone.

Miller peered out the window. "Looks like the rain ain't stoppin'."

Dant had already left with a tall dark girl who looked like she might have been part colored. There were a lot of mixed-race young people, left over from the Korean War.

"Whatcha gonna do?" Miller asked, sipping his beer and glancing at the two girls we'd been dancing with. "There's a cute young piece outside. She's been standing out there in the rain looking in for quite some time." He put his folded white handkerchief into his back pocket.

I peered out the window. "I wonder what her problem is. She's wet to the bone. I'm gonna see if anything's wrong."

I found her standing by the door, drenched, with her black stringy hair hanging below her waist. She looked at me and then lowered her round face, with its slightly pointed chin. Tears fell from her eyes and mixed with the rain on her chest. Turning her back toward me, she moved closer to the window.

"What name?" I asked.

"Me GI name Connie," she said softly. "I speak little GI talk."

From inside the club, a record scratched and popped. Then Jerry Butler belted out "He Don't Love You."

"Do you dance?"

"Little," she answered.

"Come, let's Cha-Cha."

"No can do. You come hooch-ee." She pointed to the right. "Not far."

I nodded, told Miller, and followed Connie to her room. Dropping my shoes at the door, I stepped in and flopped onto her sleeping mat.

"You stay. I fix fire." Sliding the door open, she ran outside to put more wood into the fireplace, outside under the hooch, that heated the floor. Connie's mat was cozy and warm.

She returned and changed out of her wet clothes behind a portable screen, and put them with my wet socks under her sleeping mat on the toasty floor. Connie got a pillow and tucked it under my head. I stretched out and relaxed, staring at the ceiling. The hooch was clean and dry. Its few furnishings were neatly arranged.

"Why you no go inside club?" I asked.

"No likee club."

She said she was sixteen, from a village near Seoul. She had a younger sister and a sickly mother. Her father had died a few months earlier. Her family needed money so she came to Yon Gee Co to work as a prostitute. Then, bursting into tears, she said, "Tonight number one time catch-ee GI."

She said a first sergeant had given her three dollars earlier. But when they went to the hooch and she pulled off her clothes, he didn't want sex, only to look at her body. She was frightened and turned out the lights. The GI got angry, so she ran and told her mammasan, who refunded his money but threatened to kick Connie out.

I had heard similar stories back in Shang Par Re. This one I believed. She seemed so innocent I almost cried. I reached for my wallet and fished out a Military Payment Certificate—the gaudy currency the Army printed up to pay us soldiers in combat zones—and handed it to her. The bill was equal to five American dollars. "Here, I know I'm a sucker, but I believe you."

Connie's face glowed and her eyes lit up like high beams. "You number one GI," Connie said almost in a whisper, fluffing my pillow. Then she stood, smiling. "Stay!" she commanded, and dashed out the door.

Minutes later she returned with a plate of rice. I wasn't hungry but ate anyway. Connie slid closer, putting her arm around my waist. "You can makee love to me," she said with a kittenish grin, tugging me closer.

"Maybe some other time." I had another girl in mind, one of the girls I hoped Miller was still entertaining. Connie had the money to satisfy her mammasan. I downed most of the rice and got up to leave. "Thanks for the meal. See you soon."

"You come back?"

"Yes, soon," I said, sliding the door shut .

Back at the bar, Miller had beat me to the girl I wanted, leaving me a message with the girl in red. We danced awhile, then left for her hooch.

The following week, the week of my eighteenth birthday, just after Christmas, we were assigned stake-out duties. Sgt. Terry, Brandon, and I bivouacked out in the boondocks on a trail between two mine fields. Our job was to block infiltrators from entering South Korea. A thousand meters from the Demilitarized Zone—the DMZ—we found a clump of bushes, cleared an area, and laid out our equipment: basic loads of ammo, sleeping bags and air mattresses, grenades, Claymore mines, a shotgun, a Browning automatic rifle, and an anti-intrusion device the size of a pocket dictionary, which contained hundreds of feet of catgut wire.

Then there was the clothing. I wore a steel pot (helmet) and liner, t-shirt, long underwear top, sweatshirt, wool shirt, fatigue shirt, tailored insulated vest, field jacket and liner, parka liner, and parka. Also boxer underwear, long drawers, fatigue pants, pant liners and shell, and insulated boots. I felt like a stuffed, black and green teddy bear.

"Brummell, string that catgut," Sarge commanded. I pulled the wire forward and stretched it all around our position. If anything touched the wire, a soft red light would glow and a low-frequency alarm would sound. The mine fields provided excellent protection for our flanks. Nothing could get through. We were impenetrable.

After we organized the equipment and had our watch assignments, we climbed into our double sleeping bags wearing almost all our clothes. The temperature had fallen below zero degrees Fahrenheit.

Inside the bags it slowly became cozy enough to quit shivering. I glanced at my illuminated watch. It was one o'clock, another hour before my watch. My air mattress squeaked as I shifted restlessly. I stared up at the dark star-lit dome, unable to sleep.

Sergeant Terry stirred, then whispered, "Somebody's out there." I rolled over and grabbed my rifle, straining to hear. The anti-intrusion device was humming and the indicator glowed red. A bush, about a hundred or so meters away, trembled as if someone were crawling low to the ground.

"Halt!" the sergeant shouted.

Silence. Just the wind sighing in the grass.

"Blast that bunch of bushes over there!" the sergeant growled. I aimed my rifle and, for the first time in my life, squeezed the trigger intending to do harm to another human. I felt no fear since there was nothing to suggest we were being attacked. Our job was to prevent infiltrators and whoever was on the receiving end of the violence knew he wasn't supposed to be there.

In a few seconds my twenty-round clip had spit its lethal load into the quivering bush. The night lit up for frozen moments as grenades that Terry threw exploded, and Brandon cut loose with his M-1 rifle. Terry raised his arm to cease firing and the explosive sounds faded echoing. The bush was still. My heart pounded. We surely had killed somebody.

A faint voice broke the radio static, "Pancake One, this is Pancake Two, over."

"Pancake Two, this is Pancake One, go ahead," acknowledged Terry.

"What's going on over there? Did you get one? What's all the firing about?"

"Detection device went off and we saw movement. There's nothing now. Must've got'em."

"Stay in your position. I want two men awake at all time. Keep your eyes open. Joe Chink's tricky. I'll be there at daybreak, with reinforcements."

None of us slept the rest of the night. We hardly blinked, our eyes fixed on the motionless bush, our firing hands resting on our weapons. At first light, I grabbed my black-insulated boots and slid them on. Ice lined the inner soles. A cold sharp pain cut through my aching legs.

"Get the lead out," Terry ordered. "We got to inspect the area. The trucks'll be around to pick us up soon."

Brandon and I struggled into our frigid field gear. No sooner had we wiped the sleep from our eyes than Terry barked the first order of the day.

"Get on line!" he yelled. "Move forward! Weapons in assault position!"

The three of us, stretched over an arm's length apart, stepped off. Brandon took the left flank and I moved to the right of Terry.

About a hundred meters ahead, Brandon shouted, "We got'em, alright. Dead as hell!"

I rushed to get a look at our kill. At first I thought the wild firing had cut the man to pieces, scattering his hair and flesh. But then I realized it was a wild boar!

"Fuckin' hog!" Terry said, shaking his head in disgust. "I thought we killed a Joe Chink. Okay, let's get back to the position and pack up."

A three-quarter ton pickup sped up the road and closed in on our position. Ice in the potholes shattered like glass as it rolled to a stop. Almost before the engine cut off, another larger truck pulled in behind it. The Officer of the Day (OD) stepped out in a hurry, and commanded everyone to get out of both vehicles. A squad of men quickly got into formation.

"Get ready to assault!" a young second lieutenant yelled.

"Oh, shit!" Sergeant Terry said, running toward the OD.

Brandon and I continued packing our equipment, laughing as Terry got his ass chewed.

"A fucking PIG! You shot a fucking PIG!" The lieutenant shouted loud enough for all of North Korea to hear. "You had us come all the way out here, combat ready, for a fucking harmless PIG!"

The OD finished blasting Terry while we loaded our gear into the trucks, sniggering, and headed back to the company.

That afternoon, I hopped the bus back to Yong Gee Co. Connie spotted me as I walked through the grubby streets on my way to the Alley. We lingered in front of a movie house and decided to go in to see *Ben*

Hur. I had seen it three times already, but I thought it would be funny to hear Charlton Heston speaking his lines in Korean.

Afterward, we went to the Recreation Center for hamburgers. Connie was unimpressed. She said she couldn't swallow the meat and insisted I take her to her favorite rice joint across the village. By the time we finished eating, it was time to catch the return bus to A Company.

I went back to her hooch the next night and we made love for the first time, long and slow, until it was time to catch that eleven o'clock bus. From then on, we were a couple. Connie would stop whatever she was doing when I came to the village, just to be with me. There was no charge. Our relationship grew into a caring, trusting conspiracy.

Both of us enjoyed climbing mountains, so we tramped up some of the rugged high trails she knew. When the weather warmed up, we took cooked snails, and bottles of the popular Korean rice beer. We climbed to a spot where we could enjoy the breeze and make love in the warm, quiet splendor of the outdoors.

Most of the time, we just sat in the hooch and I told her stories about home. Sometimes I had to be creative in my explanations. I became adept at using my hands to describe people and events, and sometimes the confusion was entertaining. I once used the traditional two-handed curving motion to comment on the full figure of one of Connie's girlfriends. Connie dashed off and returned with a bottle of Coke.

I assumed Connie was servicing other soldiers, but figured, what the hell—she had to make a living. Prostitution seemed like a practical way to combat poverty. At least some of the women were employed and some, I suspected, even enjoyed the work. I couldn't see the harm in a man and woman agreeing to sex for money.

Our next assignment meant spending two weeks in the field. Tanks and armored personnel carriers (APCs) from our support units roared into the assembly area early in the morning. Kim, Miller, three others, and I were assigned to APC 31. We crammed in and tracked out. Instead of crossing Liberty Bridge, our vehicle splashed into the cold Imjin River. I was nervous. The APC was an iron casket with tracks. I expected it to sink, but it stayed afloat and we began the crossing.

"Hope those water pumps keep working!" Miller shouted. "I hear the river gets to twenty feet or more! If the water pumps fail, we'll sink like a stone."

We chugged and wallowed slowly and safely to the other side and up the bank. Then we roared down the main road, out of the village, and into the country-side. For days we roamed the northern mountainous territory of South Korea.

Every day I looked for Connie—she'd said she would find me in the field and bring Suzi, Miller's girlfriend. Knowing where the GIs were training was expected of the villagers. Security leaks were so common the Koreans knew as much about our training exercises as we did, and often more.

The fourth day of the exercise we spent charging up a steep mountain, attacking an imaginary enemy that—faced with our ferocious, superior forces—I was sure would have scattered down the other side like cockroaches.

Part way up, Miller flopped to the ground, gasping for breath. "Brummell! I'm stopping! Too damn tired! Can't make it!"

I was already at the top of a mountain known as Nightmare Ridge. Miller and the rest were at least twenty-five yards behind. When I got over the rocky summit, I pulled the legs down on my rifle and assumed the prone position, as I would in a real combat situation, to provide security for my slower comrades.

The company commander, Captain Knight arrived at the ridge, gasping for air. "I see you did it again, Private. First one up,"

"Yes, sir!" I replied smiling.

"I hope we don't have to climb any more of these big fuckers today," Miller said, stumbling onto the ridge.

"This is it," the Captain said. "We're defending this mountain for the rest of the night."

When he left, Miller turned to me, teeth chattering. "Do you think tonight's the night C-Connie and Suzi will show? It sure would be nice having a warm b-body in the bag with me."

"No way are they climbing up here," I said, shedding my heavy pack. "You must be out of your head."

He chuckled. "I guess you'll just have to sleep with me."

I snorted in mock disgust. "Get the fuck out of here, man! You know I don't play that shit!"

We started digging our foxholes, but the earth was hard as rock. A jackhammer would have bounced off it. But the squad leaders were unrelenting.

"Dig in! Prepare for the counterattack!"

Exhausted, we tried but could barely scratch the surface. So we played war, pretended to be hiding like kids playing cowboys and Indians, except I'd never heard of colored cowboys. I knew colored soldiers fought in combat during the Korean conflict. At home there had been talk in the old days about a local man who'd been killed in one of the big battles.

At dusk the temperature at the top of Nightmare Ridge dropped twenty degrees or more. Never had I felt such bitter, dry cold. There was neither snow nor ice—just a depressing, motionless freeze, as if everything but us was dead. Even the wind-blasted trees looked defeated, growing sideways with their limbs drooping to the ground. The heavy gusts made a howling noise like a candy Halloween whistle. I began shivering. "Th-This is b-bull shit!"

I looked down the steep mountain and realized that if we had launched an assault from down there against an enemy up here, we would have had our asses fried and served on a silver platter. None of us would have made it to the top. The pitch was so steep, they could have knocked us all off by throwing rocks.

Miller stamped his feet and hugged himself. "I sure would like to be back home right about now."

"This f-fuckin' Korea and this Army go together," I agreed. "You can take 'em both and shove 'em straight up your ass!"

Chapter 10

Brandon came tramping up to our position, out of the dark through a patch of briars. "Brummell! Miller! You ain't gonna believe this. They're here!"

Miller chuckled. "Those broads came way the hell out here? On a night like this?"

"They're over by my position," he whispered, struggling to untangle himself from a prickly bush.

There was no question how I was spending that night. I went to the truck, pulled off my sleeping bag, and hiked the short distance to where Connie and Suzi were sitting huddled, near a clump of bushes, eating pound cake from a C-ration can that Brandon had given them.

"Brummell, you think I no come, but I come," Connie said, smiling, eyes bright with mischief in the glare of my flashlight.

I led her by the hand to my so-called foxhole, nervous as hell that Sarge, or anyone else, might discover the girls were in our defensive position. Connie's teeth were chattering, so I told her to get inside the bag.

Miller and Suzi left for the other side of one of the graves that dotted the landscape, for a bit of privacy. I laid out my down-filled sleeper and Connie dove right

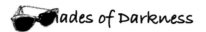

in.

"No! No!" I said. "Too warm. Take clothes off, take shoes off, too." I wanted to be sure none of our clothing got sweaty in the frigid air.

Once Connie was settled, I spread my poncho on top to keep the frost off the bags. Then I squeezed in with her. After a toasty and passionate night, I hustled Connie from the bag just before sunrise. I went to wake Suzi and Miller but they were already up. The girls got dressed, we kissed them goodbye, and they slipped and slid down the frost-covered slope. We could still see them fifteen hundred feet below, waiting alongside the road for the bus home.

The borders of the DMZ were marked by two-inch engineering tape, white so we could see it easily. The area was clear of tall vegetation to increase visibility to the front and our flanks. The tape also identified mine-fields. When we patrolled the DMZ, we followed the tape.

Our fifteen-man squad marched miles and miles, up and down the border between North and South Korea, through rugged, harsh terrain in all kinds of weather. We were instructed, if we encountered any North Korean soldiers, to observe and report what we saw. My job was to pay attention to their gear and when we returned, explain in detail what types of weapons and ammunition they were carrying. The only obser-vation I made was that their winter uniforms appeared bulkier than ours.

The few times we did run across a patrol, the exchange was often friendly. Sometimes they shook our hands, or offered us candy and other tokens of friendship, such as a picture postcard or a book of matches. We'd been warned to refuse souvenirs, but some of the daring American dudes took them anyway, without incident. There was never any attempt at conversation.

Miller, Brandon, and I finished our DMZ duty with just over a month left in our Korean tour. That Friday afternoon Miller and I raced to the bus stop with three-day passes in our pockets. We each carried only a toiletry kit which we camouflaged in a paper bag so the Military Police wouldn't suspect us of staying in the village overnight. Three-day passes were only to be spent in Seoul, where there was an Army-run hotel. But most of the guys in my outfit sneaked off to the local village instead, risking being caught in an MP raid.

Miller and I parted company in the Alley. Miller strutted straight to Suzi's and I went to Connie's. She wasn't there, but the door was unlocked so I stripped and settled on the mat for a snooze.

The next thing I heard was Connie shouting. She was sitting up on the mat beside me.

"Wakey, Brummell! Wakey hurry! MP's look-ee hooches!"

I was too close to leaving Korea to get busted now and have my trip home delayed. I grabbed my pants from Connie and slipped them on like they were greased. I picked up my shirt and went to the door. I peeked around the corner into the Alley. Shit! The MPs were a few hooches down, working their way toward me.

"I'll come back later," I whispered.

I sidled out the door, hugging the hut wall. A few sidesteps and I made the corner, slipping between two hooches and around back into the shadows.

"HEY! GI!" an American voice shouted. "Where the hell you think you're going? Halt!"

I darted between hooches, pulling on my shirt. I leaped across a dike, stumbled through a rice paddy, hopped a ditch, and splashed through some puddles. I peeked over my shoulder. I'd lost the MPs, but something smelled awful bad. I slowed my pace and checked again for MPs. My left foot sank into something soft. I plunged to my ankles, to my knees, and my chest...in a honey well—a hole in the ground filled with human waste.

The ultra-frugal Koreans saved everything, even their shit. I'd seen them, buckets of the stuff hanging from shoulder poles, on their way from the outdoor toilets to a hole in a corner of a rice paddy, where they dumped it. During the planting season, they used it to fertilize their crops.

Disgusted, retching, I reached up and dug my fingers into the ground, pulling myself out. I was covered with funk. When I had worked my way out, I reached into my pants pockets. Thump! A big turd popped out and hit the ground.

I couldn't get that shirt off my back fast enough. I shook it out and hiked, wide legged and sloshing, back toward Connie's. A few ditches from her hooch I paused to look for the MPs. The coast looked clear so I stripped, stuffed my pants into my shirt, tied my sleeves together, and dashed nude to Connie's door. She let me in, giggling uncontrollably when she saw my condition, toilet paper and newsprint clinging to my skin.

"No funny," I said, stone-faced. Connie wrinkled her nose but couldn't stop laughing.

"Where pants?" she finally asked.

"Outside door."

She got a bucket of water and methodically sponged the mess off my tired body. But it was a long time before I got the stink out of my head.

The next morning, I sent Connie out to find Miller and tell him what had happened. He caught the next bus back to the Company to fetch me a change of clothing.

Within a few days, I had put the shit episode behind me. I had gotten my orders for a thirty-day leave, to be followed by a new assignment in Fort Hood, Texas. Connie and I had a good cry and I promised I would return. I intended to make a career of the Army.

We carefully packed up our things and early one morning a truck carried eleven of us from A Company and sped back to Battalion Headquarters, where we joined a convoy taking other rotating GIs to be processed out of country. I didn't see my buddy Bill Thomas. I was looking forward to going home with him, but his name wasn't on the roster. I wondered, what had happened to him?

The convoy headed south and a couple miles down the road there was Bill, policing alongside the dusty road with a group of others.

"Thomas!" I yelled as the truck rolled by. "What happened?"

He shouted back, "See you soon! Two weeks!"

"What happened?" I hollered, but the truck was already out of range.

I settled back on the bench seat and mentally pho-
tographed my company area, nestled beneath the big
mountains. There was activity all around the Quonset
huts. I felt heavy-hearted, almost teary. As difficult as
the duty had been, I was sad to leave the scenery and
some of the friends I'd made, both the Koreans and my
fellow American troops. Korea had been where I had
fully become a man.

By nine o'clock in the morning we had driven the
fifty miles and arrived at the Company that would
handle processing us out of country. Our bunks for the
overnight stay were assigned. The sergeant in charge
ordered us, "Dump everything out. Every goddamn
thing. If you have any boxes, open 'em. We'll see if any
of you are smuggling any goodies back Stateside."

I had spent three days meticulously packing. Now
I had to scramble it all up. An inspection team—a dozen
men, all starched and spit shined—clattered into the
barracks. Most of them were old sergeants, and tough.
They checked everything—toothpaste, shoe polish,
even long underwear.

"Look what we got here!" a big Mexican staff sergeant crowed in mock falsetto. "Something to remember
her by, huh?" He held up a small blue panty, stretching
it so everyone could see. They looked like they were
old and dirty, but the sergeant didn't seem to care. The
entire barrack roared with laughter.

At the other end of the big room a sergeant found
opium in a body powder can.

"I didn't know it was there!" the young buck sergeant pleaded. "I got a family!"

"Right!" the sergeant said sarcastically.

The inspection went on for two hours before we were released. As I was repacking, I had a visit from Pfc. Elmore Cannon, a black soldier I'd met in a bar. He was from Baltimore, in the finance battalion, and wore thick glasses.

"You goin' home with us?"

Cannon laughed. "Don't I wish! I just came to see you guys off. You free after you finish packing?"

"Yep," I nodded, handing him my overcoat to roll.

"Let's go to the enlisted men's club," Cannon said, stuffing my overcoat in the bag. "I thought maybe you might wanna get stoned before you take that trip back to freedom." With Cannon's help, the bag was packed in minutes, and as tight as it was before.

I locked my duffle and we left for the club. Cannon handed me a twisted filtered cigarette.

"Try this."

It was opium mixed with tobacco. Lots of guys smoked it. "No, I don't do that, remember?" Some of the guys said it made them sick and could become a habit. Cannon had tried to get me stoned numerous times, but I always declined.

"Brummell!" Miller trotted up from behind a platoon hut. He was out of breath, but smiling.

"One of the guys said Connie's here, outside the fence, over near the water tower."

I was shocked.

"Did Suzi come too?" I asked.

His smile faded. "Nah. Just her."

I started running in the direction of the tower. "I'll see you guys later."

As I approached the fence, I saw Connie right away. She was shouting. "Brummell! Hey, Brummell. I come!" She had tears in her eyes. I pressed my nose up against the ten-foot fence. I poked my fingers through the wire, pursed my lips and put them through one of the rusty square holes. Connie locked her fingers over mine and pressed closer, greeting me with a long, warm kiss.

I drew back and told Connie for the first time that I loved her.

"Me love you too, a lot," she said weeping. "No go. You no go Stateside, please! You catch-ee pass. We make love one more time."

"No can do. No can leave." I tried to make her understand.

Connie slumped. More tears ran down her cheeks and onto the exposed mounds of her lovely, full breasts.

"Brummell, I go to mountain," she said, drawing a line across her wrist. "I cut hand away."

She had talked that way before. Going to mountain and cutting hand away meant suicide.

"Connie, no do!" I pleaded. "I come back Korea sometime."

I racked my brain for a way to get on the other side of that fence.

"Stay here," I told her. "I come back soon."

I ran as fast as I could to the enlisted men's club. I found Cannon sitting at a table with a crowd, so I went to the bar and signaled for him to come over. "Two drinks, Scotch on the rocks for my friend and a shot of I.W. Harper and Coke for me," I told the bartender. I handed Cannon his drink and pulled him closer.

"Listen, I need to borrow your uniform, pass, and ID card. I want to be with Connie one more time. Oh, I forgot, your glasses too. Otherwise the ID's no good if I don't have the glasses."

Cannon took a thoughtful sip. "Why my uniform?"

"Because mine is rolled and wrinkled," I answered. "You know I need to have on a class A uniform to go on pass. It'll be a piece of cake. There's a white dude on the gate. You know white people think all us darkies look alike. He won't be able to tell the difference."

"Okay," Cannon said. "I don't see any problem with it. I just need to stay in the hut. I don't see well without my second set of eyes. I've got glaucoma."

We downed our drinks and left for the sleeping quarters. I fitted easily into Cannon's uniform. He gave me his ID card and pass. I checked his birth date so I could repeat it if asked. "Don't forget the glasses," I reminded him. "They'll make it a lot easier for me to get past the guard."

Cannon slowly pulled his frames off, hating to part with them. "I'll just hang around the bunk 'til you get back. Don't be gone too long," he said quietly.

"Okay. Thanks. I owe you!" I blurted, and rushed out the door.

Just before I reached the gate, I slipped the glasses on. The lenses were so thick everything was a blur, so I lowered the frames and peeked over the top. Remembering Cannon's ramrod-strait posture, I threw back my shoulders.

The sentry took the pass and ID card. I bent and fooled with my shoe laces.

"Nice day," I said, keeping my head down.

"Yeah, it is. Here," said the guard, handing the pass back.

It gave my heart a big lift to see Connie's face lit up when she saw me. We embraced and cried so hard my muscles ached. Neither of us had much to say, communicating with touches and looks. She squeezed my hand tight, as if she was holding onto life itself.

I didn't want to venture far from the holding area, so we circled close to the small compound. On the opposite side of the front gate near the back entrance, we climbed to the top of a hill. On its back slope, we found an isolated mound of dirt—a neatly trimmed grave, shaped like an igloo. We sat with our backs against the mound, embracing and making promises. I promised to re-enlist within six months, so I could return to Korea. Connie promised to wait in Yon Gee Co until I returned.

We made love, passionate but quick, then just lay there clinging. Three hours flew by and I had to get back to the compound.

I made a joke about waking the dead, and got her to smile a little. But when we got near the gate, she burst into tears again. I told her I would meet her back at the fence.

I ran to the hut to change. Cannon lay on my bunk, sound asleep. I woke him up, we swapped uniforms again, and I hurried back to Connie. We sat and reminisced for hours. We took a break so she could go and get some rice with pork.

Then she fed me through the fence. The last minutes ticked away, filled with powerful and tangled

emotions. The sun set and it was time to part. Sick with sorrow, I watched her stumble, sobbing, out of sight.

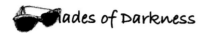

Chapter 11

As I traveled east across the Pacific and the States, my grief at losing Connie gave way to anticipation of my thirty-day leave at home, and about seeing Chris again. I conjured her smiling face and warm embrace. I wanted to think of the future, of Chris, and my new assignment.

My brother Donald picked me up at the bus depot in Easton, Maryland. As we neared the corner by Uncle Noble's house, he tapped his horn and pointed out the windshield. "There's Chris's car. I know you'll be seeing her while you're home."

I had written her about when I'd be in town. As the car passed, she smiled at us from the passenger seat. Ron, her husband, stared straight ahead, oblivious.

I found Grandma bent over in her flower garden, transplanting her pink roses from the front of the house to the side of the white-washed outhouse. She was wearing the same red head-rag she had on when I left, and a long, loose-fitting cotton dress covered with a pattern of green flowers. I wanted to surprise her, but she looked up, dropped the hoe and ran toward me in old-lady slow motion, her chubby arms wide.

"Welcome home, son," she said, kissing me and huffing. "How come you didn't tell me you was comin' home, boy? I woulda fried up some chicken and made some biscuits."

"I wanted to sneak up on you." I gave her large waist a firm squeeze.

"You sure enough did, you scamp. You go in and unpack. How long you gonna be home?" Before I could answer, she continued, "You go on, now. I'll be there in a minute and cook you somethin'. I bet you starvin' for some home cookin'!"

I rushed into my room and searched the bag for my stash of pot that I'd picked up on layover in San Francisco. As Grandma came in, I was on my way out. "I'll be back in time for dinner. I'm going over to Nelson's." Nelson, I was sure, had never smoked grass. I was curious to see how it would affect his speech.

I found Nelson outside, playing catch with Terrence, an old classmate of mine. When he saw me, Nelson balked in the middle of his left-handed pitch, ran and hugged me.

"What's happenin', P-Pie?"

"I got some pot. You guys wanna get high?" They nodded with foolish grins.

"I've seen people smoke it on TV," said Terrence. "I'd like to see what they get out of it."

We walked to an old pig pen in the woods behind Grandma's. Then I remembered something.

"Papers! We need papers to roll it in."

"They g-got some at the store," Nelson said. "G-go get some, Terrence."

When he returned, I rolled my first joint. It was sloppy, more like a tiny banana than a cigarette. I passed it to Terrence. "You went to get the papers, so you get to go first."

"My pleasure, soul brothers. Gimme the matches."

We shared the joint, and it didn't take long before I felt amazingly relaxed. Then the laughing started. We laughed until it became exhausting and then until it became painful. Nelson doubled over the rail of the pigpen.

"W-we g-got to stop laughin'," he stammered. "M-my stomach's hurtin'."

"Nelson, if you're not careful you're gonna have your nose in hog shit."

Like a chain reaction, our laughter redoubled. Finally, hungry as hell, our sides aching, we split up after agreeing to meet later at the colored cemetery. Then we would ride to the hill just above the landfill, our old hang-out.

I returned to Grandma's to sit down to a feast of fried chicken, mashed potatoes, fresh corn on the cob, and homemade biscuits, all of which—stoked by my first case of the munchies—I greedily devoured. Grandma just watched, glowing with delight.

Chris called during dinner and swung by to pick me up, without Theresa. Chris sped the car to our lover's lane with me holding her hand, letting go only so she could work the gear shift. Even in the dim light of the dash, I could see her black skirt and beneath it her light brown bare legs. The green and red glow reflected off her smooth, sleek thighs. I was full of desire. When the '55 Ford picked up speed, the wind coming through the open window lifted her skirt, revealing black pant-ies. We stayed in the car for hours, trying to catch up on love.

It was two weeks after I got home that Bill Thomas finally showed up. I dressed in my Class A uniform and got a ride from Chris to his parents' house, where Bill was preparing his uniform. I was dying to know what had been going on in Korea since I left. Had he seen Connie? "Never did," he said, pulling on his khaki shirt while slipping his left arm through the blue infantry rope. "You want to straighten this brass for me, Pfc. Brummell?"

I aligned his gleaming US and rifle brass on its blue background. He tucked in his shirt. "Now let's get out of here." We took off in the family car, a yellow sedan, and Bill promptly got us into a fender-bender. We shook it off and, as I had neither car nor license, I wound up spending most of my leave riding around with him.

I wanted to see more of Chris but the opportunities were limited. Bill and I visited friends, churches, and good old Lockerman High, still segregated, wearing our uniforms with puffed-out chests. But with Chris unable to liven things up, I soon got bored and left several days before my leave ended.

Bill drove me to the bus station. It was almost as difficult leaving him as it was saying goodbye to Grandma. In three weeks he was scheduled to report to Fort Carson, Colorado. By then I would have settled at Fort Hood, Texas.

I boarded the Greyhound lonely but excited about my new assignment. During the ride to the airport, I took an inventory of where I stood. I hated leaving Chris but what was the use of staying if I couldn't see her? I thought of Nelson, Terrence, and some of my other schoolmates, most of them jobless, or picking vegetables, or working in a cannery or the chicken processing plant. I didn't want to pick any more, nor regress to using an outhouse and foot tub. I was glad I'd chosen the military and happy to be off seeing the world.

I hoped to avoid an infantry assignment but ended up a rifleman in A Company, which had high standards and was always supposed to be combat ready. We spent a lot of time out in the dusty field solving military problems. The outfit was supposed to be mechanized but we usually walked while the armored personnel carriers and other vehicles sat in the motor pool.

One evening, while we were lying around on our bunks, one of my bunkmates said he'd heard a rumor we were headed to Germany. The rumor made sense. There had been too many new guys arriving. It felt like something major was up.

A few days later we learned that we were training for a major NATO exercise, Operation "Big Lift." In October 1963, with the Cold War with the Soviets the main event on the international stage, the US was sending fifteen thousand troops to Germany for war games. The purpose was to show the Soviets how prepared we were to meet any aggression against the NATO alliance.

Overnight, we were transformed from field soldiers to garrison troops, preparing vehicles and undergoing rigorous inspections until the day came for us to leave. In full combat gear, shouldering bulky duffles, we were loaded on the backs of trucks, motored to an

Air Force base near Waco, and marched onto a C-130 transport plane.

Over Newfoundland, the convoy of planes circled an Air Force base. Looking out the small windows I could see large whitecaps rippling the water's dark green surface. An ocean liner appeared to bob helplessly, yet managed to maintain its eastward course. The world tilted as our plane descended through the cloudy dark ceiling and aligned with the runway.

Strong, cold winds blasted us as we disembarked the plane. A hot meal awaited us in the main mess, where thick, juicy steaks crowded hot sizzling grills. I crammed down two sirloins, a baked potato and corn. Plane refueled, soldiers re-inspected, we were on our way again.

Hours later, under cover of darkness, we eased down in Germany. We were handed boxes of C-rations, boarded waiting trucks, and bumped along in a long convoy. We crossed the Rhine River and passed through small towns until we reached our staging area outside of Kaiserslautern, known among the tens of thousands of US troops there as K-town. We marched a couple of miles to a forest and stopped in front of a camouflaged squad tent.

"This is it," said Sergeant Stockdill, our weary, rumpled platoon sergeant. Our first sergeant—Cash— who had arrived with the advance party, stuck his head out of the flaps. Holding a cup of steaming coffee in one hand and a cigarillo in the other, he said, "Platoon sergeants, come inside the mess tent for your orders!"

I looked around. There were no buildings, just forest. It was cold and felt like rain. "Where the hell we gonna sleep?"

Private Smitz, a guy from Philadelphia who I'd gotten friendly with, said, "You and I are just privates first class; we're not supposed to know nothin', just obey orders. You'd think I had enough of being ordered around, the Jew that I am. We'll be lucky if we sleep at all tonight."

Sgt. Stockdill returned and marched us deeper into the woods, through thick underbrush. Finally he called a halt.

First Sergeant Cash jumped up and down trying to keep warm as he gave out assignments. "Okay, we're going to stay in pup tents while we're here. For now, Brummell, you and Smitz stay here." He pointed to the cold, hard ground. The wind picked up, blowing the dead leaves around. Then he walked away. I envied his tent and coffee and cigarillo.

We got our pup tent up in time for chow call and just before a slow, cold rain began. We grabbed our mess kits and joined the long line at the mess tent. I was starving and it seemed to take forever to creep into the tent out of the cold. I finally got my pork chop dinner and joined a group of men who were eating standing at a tall, rickety bar. I found a spot next to Specialist Fourth Class Green, an enormous Negro with slanted-dark eyes who I knew from Texas. He played Army division-level football. He greeted me with a warm Texas howdy. They called him Big Green.

We chatted about his wife and daughter as he wolfed down his dinner. "Why don't you come over to the supply tent later?" he said. "We're gonna have a card game."

That pricked up my ears. "What's the game?"

"Poker, table stakes. I came over with the advance party and we set up a tent for playing. We even got an oil heater."

"Shooting craps is my thing. Do you know where there's a game?"

"There was one over in Headquarters Platoon of Bravo Company a couple days ago," Green said. "Why don't you just check out the poker game for tonight?"

After dinner I trotted off to watch the card players with my butt as close as I could get to the heater. Poker looked easy enough, but the stakes were high. I decided to wait for a craps game, where I knew my way around.

The next day the CQ—the Charge of Quarters, an enlisted man in charge of company during off duty hours—woke us by banging a large spoon against an iron skillet. "Get up, you fuckin' sleepy heads! Let's get this day goin'!"

I dressed as fast as I could and crawled outside. Even though it was cold, I was glad to get out of that damp, cramped tent. After breakfast, I showered—it was a half mile hike to get to the facilities—and spent the rest of the morning cleaning weapons, sprucing up our bivouac areas, and loitering.

That afternoon we marched to a barricaded highway where hundreds of military vehicles were arranged in precise columns. Sergeant Stockdill laid out our details.

"We're going to work on our squad track the rest of the day, because tomorrow we're taking off in hot pursuit of the enemy. The Third Armored Division is the 'aggressor.' After today, anytime you see a Third AD patch, consider it's the enemy. Squad leaders, take your men and get to work!"

We were assigned to an armored personnel carrier, responsible for its maintenance: changing the oil, cleaning the inside, painting, and mending the tracks. At the end of the day, I was drafted along with two others for guard duty. We each took a box of C-rations and patrolled the staging area for the rest of the night.

In the morning, we loaded our equipment in our assigned vehicles and left. The convoy of trucks, tanks, artillery, and other combat supports, thundered for miles through busy towns and isolated villages. For a few days, we chased the Third Armored Division deep into friendly territory, had a few mock firefights, and returned to base camp.

Our first mail call in Germany produced nothing from Chris but, surprisingly, a letter from Sally Goble. Sally had been two grades behind me at Lockerman and shared homeroom with my favorite cousin. After seeing me in uniform on my visit to the high school, she asked my cousin for my address. Sally's letter was filled with love poems and the back of the envelope was sealed with kisses. Why would such a studious girl write me? She must have been one of those uniform freaks. I wrote back, lying about what a fabulous time I was having in Germany. Three hasty pages, a quick lick, and it was on its way.

"Brummell, c'mere!" Green broke the silence, calling to me in an impatient tone from in front of his supply tent. "The old man told the platoon sergeants he's authorizing gambling in the mess tent tonight." Green snapped his fingers and shifted his weight. "You might be able to get that craps game you were lookin' for."

I helped Green separate bundles of clean laundry and then walked to the mess tent. Two games had already started, craps and poker. Each game quickly filled to capacity and latecomers crowded around to be ready to jump in when the first person dropped out.

A Specialist Fourth Class—Pratt—shook a fist of dice near his right ear, thumb locking the "bones" between index and little finger. He dropped to his knees and released the dice outward, palm up. They left his hand tumbling like square wheels. "Seven!" he ordered. The cubes danced across the tightly stretched Army blanket. The dice halted, one on four and the other on three.

"Not bad, Pratt," I said, kneeling.

"Bet five dollars the dice lose!" someone said.

Pratt next rolled ten. After a few tries, he made another ten, but crapped out two passes later.

The game was getting interesting. More spectators began crowding in for a better look. I took out all the money I had—forty dollars—and placed a couple of bets, doubling my money both times. Within an hour the stakes had risen. The casual gamblers, quickly cleaned out or scared away, drifted off leaving the serious shooters to monopolize the ground. My reserves mushroomed. I was hot, far ahead of the game and could afford to bet heavy.

"Suckers! Don't you recognize skill when you see it?" I taunted. "I'm gonna wipe your asses cleaner than your mama ever did." The dice obediently stopped on a five and a deuce. I was a winner. I grabbed the bundle of cash. "Anybody want to raise the stakes? Let's shoot for a hundred bucks. Come on and get some of this big money I got." I shook the wad of bills in their faces.

GIs moaned and groaned. "Shit!" someone belted out. "I got buzzard luck." Another accused me of cheating. "Let's bump the dice against something."

"I ain't bumping against nothin'," I fired back. "If you want some of this money back, we gotta shoot like we been. If not, call it a night."

The hours passed. The game thinned until there were only four of us left. Pratt shook the dice and peered at my stack of money as I counted. Nearly two thousand dollars! I admired my stack of green, meticulously straightening the corners of each bill. Pratt had about five hundred dollars. The others were down to chicken feed.

Pratt shook the dice nervously. He grimaced, showing his even white teeth. "Okay, then," he said, reaching for his stack. "Let's shoot for a hundred."

Pratt was coal black and kept himself immaculately groomed, always wearing starched fatigues and well-shined boots, even in the field.

"I only have two hundred bucks," said the soldier to my right. "I only have a hundred thirty-five," confessed the soldier to Pratt's left.

"Why don't you two put your money together?" I suggested.

The GI to my right hesitated, then agreed. Within minutes, Pratt and I cleaned them out, sending them grumbling through the dark woods to their tents.

I looked at my last competitor. "Just you and me left, brother Pratt."

"Well then, let's get it on, just you and me. Let's bump," Pratt said, moving the foot locker out of our way.

We had been pad rolling, which is rolling the dice out on a tight surface like a blanket, not bumping them against another surface. I was good at rolling, and I knew how to boost my odds. As I picked up the dice I would manipulate them to the numbers I wanted. Then I would hold them together between my pointer and little finger, pretend to blow in my fist as I spit some saliva that helped the bones stick together.

By controlling the shot, the dice would tumble together, eventually stopping on your point. Others were doing it as well, so it narrowed down to whoever could do it best.

"Come on and bump," he pleaded. "I got seven hundred green ones you can get. IF you're lucky," he taunted.

Finally I agreed, being more greedy than I was tired. I wanted to break him, too.

"The dice gotta hit against the foot locker. That's the rule," he added.

Pratt and I bumped until the early hours of the morning, but my luck had turned against me. My lush pile began to shrink.

"Come on, suck-ah," he chided with a grin. "You should have stopped while you had the chance. I'm not gonna stop now, 'til I take every penny from you."

And he did, every bill I had in the stack, as well as what I had in my pockets. I was stunned. I had let it all get away. Pratt took pity on me.

"Here Brummell, my friend. Take this hundred-dollar bill. It comes from the bottom of my heart. Now get back to your tent and go to sleep while I count my winnings." He began sorting through his fat stack of bills as I walked, dazed, back through the damp, cold woods.

Two rainy days later I got the only pass I was entitled to during the time I was to be in Germany. I joined a truckload of wet, excited and optimistic GIs being delivered outside the K-Town post office in the town square.

"Trucks will be here every hour on the hour until twenty-four hundred," barked Sergeant Stockdill. "After that, and you're not here, you're AWOL."

Big Green, a white soldier named Beach, and I took off in the same direction. Beach was from Mississippi but liked to hang with us Coloreds. Our "white shadow" was a shorty with curly black hair. He was playful but a fierce competitor in the military game.

Green took the lead as we window-shopped for a "guest" house. He knew what to look for because he'd been stationed in Germany two years earlier. His big body bounced quickly down the street and was the first to spot a target. "This has to be one. Those two coming out are drunker'n hell." Beach grabbed the door and we followed him in, heading straight for the bar.

"Vait!" a beautiful red head called out, walking in our direction. "Colored Niggers! You're not allowed in here! Vee don't serve your kind!"

The scarlet-faced woman stopped just short of me, standing with her hands on hips, and legs spread. "There are places for your kind, across the tracks."

Green and I knew better than to argue. We spun

and walked out of the all-white bar. Beach followed, calling out over his shoulder, "I'm not spending my money here. If my friends can't stay, I'm going, too."

The red head pointed up the street, "I don't care, you go ahead, nigger lover! The place you vant is zat vay."

It was always the same—if you're black, you belong on the other side of town. So the exciting evening we had planned was spent in a run down guest house eating schnitzel, drinking beer, and watching two tired, old waitresses. At eleven o'clock we went back to the truck stop, disappointed.

The days were all the same after that, one big field problem after another. For days, the Third Division chased us all over West Germany, up and down mountains, woods, through cities and towns. The last few nights were the worst, bitter cold. One night, after a watch, I snuggled deep into my sleeping bag for more heat, but nothing would keep me warm. My toes were freezing so I kept wiggling them, like we'd been instructed during cold weather indoctrination classes. Nothing helped.

The next morning I woke up swearing from pain. My toes were badly blistered from a mild case of frostbite, so I went on sick call. The prescription was light duty, but it came too late. We left for the States two days after. Squads of us quickly filed off the cargo plane and back into the sizzling Texas sun. Even in November, the sun had not lost its brightness.

I assumed my toes would heal now that we were back in a warm climate, but the pain and blistering persisted. The doctor continued me on light duty for three more weeks. I hopped around the barracks in flip-flops, while the rest of the troops were at motor or weapons pool.

Late one November Friday morning, I was watching Pratt, Beach, and Green getting a game of pinochle started. I pulled up a chair.

Suddenly, voices outside were shouting. A moment later, a voice yelled from the hallway: "The President's been shot! JFK's been shot!"

"What?"

"When?"

"A few minutes ago," a voice said.

"Damn! I'll be damned!"

"Turn on the radio," Pratt said, shaking his head.

The announcer was repeating the same message over and over: "This afternoon, bullets were fired at the presidential motorcade in Dallas, Texas. The President was hit, but his condition is not known."

Others gathered around the squad room's entrance, listening to the broadcast. Some soldiers were sniffling, wiping tears from their eyes. By late afternoon, almost everyone was pulled back from pass, and when the President's death was confirmed, the companies held brief memorial services in a parade field near the barracks.

The next few days were chaotic. We were restricted to company areas and placed on standby alert. We kept busy with riot training, cleaning weapons and inspections. No one knew what the future held now. It was a terrifying new reality that just anyone could take down the leader of the free world.

Not long after, I was promoted to Specialist Fourth

Class. In February, 1964, I celebrated my two years in the Army by re-enlisting for three more. I wanted an assignment at Fort Meade, Maryland, the nearest post to home, but there was no open slot for a light weapons infantryman. My second choice was Fort Devens in Massachusetts, an eight-hour drive from Federalsburg. It was a small installation with only two infantry battalions. With so few "ground pounders" there, I figured I could earn a quick promotion to buck sergeant, the lowest of the sergeant rankings.

B Company, Thirty-Seventh Infantry's barracks were more modern than any of my previous living quarters. Each room housed eight men. Rooms were divided in two parts, separated by a four-foot wall, four men per part.

The next pay day I bought a small stereo record player, and separated the speakers as far as I could, on the shelf above my headboard. That March and April were cold. I spent most nights and weekends listening to records. When I wasn't tapping my feet and singing along with Marvin Gaye, Patti LaBelle, or Dionne Warwick, I played basketball.

A few weeks after Christmas, 1964, my first sergeant came to me with orders. "Brummell, you hit the jackpot. You're headed for Hawaii."

"Finally!" I said. "Sweet duty."

"That's what you think. I was there last year. They're gonna run your ass into the ground, and besides I think they're bringing that outfit up to strength for something. They're sending a lot of guys over there."

I was to report to Oakland Army Terminal for transportation to Hawaii. But I was in a quandary.

While I'd been in Massachusetts I met another girl, Blanche, who I'd fallen hard for and to whom I'd proposed. She'd turned me down, but after she found out I was being reassigned, she changed her mind, so long as I'd propose to her on my knees.

On my thirty-day leave, we had a small traditional wedding in Cambridge at the Massachusetts Avenue Baptist Church. I wore my Class A uniform. She wore a beautiful white wedding gown. A honeymoon was out of the question, so we retreated for several days to the guest house on post, loving and exploring.

Six days after the wedding I left for Hawaii. I lacked the time in rank to be entitled to have Blanche or the car I'd bought transported at government expense. So I gave the car away and left my new wife watching through the airport window, her face shining with tears. I promised to send for her in two months.

Chapter 12

Oakland Army Terminal was the same as it had been when I went through on my way to Korea. In two busy days, I'd been processed and delivered dockside to find the USNS *Barrack* waiting.

"This is my third voyage on this tub," I told a recruit in line behind me. "We're gettin' to be old friends."

On the fifth day of a smooth cruise, Diamond Head hove into view. Hotels, palm trees, and colorful buildings were scattered along the base of the big rock and along the shore of the Pacific. This time, I'd get to stay and explore that tropical paradise.

The *Barrack* docked at Pearl, greeted by the usual hula dancers in grass skirts rolling their hips in time to the strumming of a ukulele. Those of us Hawaii-bound soldiers exchanged farewells with the men continuing on to Japan and Korea. I sat on the dock on my duffle bag, enjoying the fragrant island air, hoping Blanche could join me soon. I missed her so much already.

We were bused to our barracks, which had three floors on which I could see soldiers cleaning weapons. In the orderly room, the first sergeant—tall, thin and tanned—leaned over his desk reviewing the roster.

"Specialist Fourth Class Brummell, eh? You're assigned to the Second Platoon. Sergeant First Class

Jade is the platoon sergeant. He should be up there now."

Jade was left-handed, brown hair, blue eyes, with GI glasses sliding down his nose. He took a few seconds to read the paperwork. After giving me the once-over, he walked me to my bunk.

"Your squad leader is Buck Sergeant Richard Traver, a good man," Jade said, extending his hand for a quick shake. When he let go, he held his fingers extended for a moment, then rubbed the inside of his hand down his pant leg. It was probably unconscious but it pissed me off a little, acting like my hand had shit on it, or maybe he thought the black might rub off on him.

"Welcome aboard," he said. "Just as long as you soldier, we'll get along just fine."

Traver was handsome, with clear blue eyes, fair skin, and wide shoulders. He smiled a lot, told jokes, and radiated enough energy for two people. Jade had said Traver had amazing stamina. His uniform was spotless, starched, and flawlessly creased. His boots shone like black glass.

Jade and Traver left. I was unpacking and organizing my wall and foot lockers when Big Green showed up. I gave him a warm, manly hug. "Can't seem to shake you," I laughed.

The two months I had to wait for Blanche seemed like years. We had no money but I was impatient and insisted she take a cab in from the airport. A big blue Pontiac taxi pulled in front of the quadrangle entrance, and out she stepped with her beautiful high cheekbones, her instant smile, and auburn hair swept up high with a wave cascading over the left side of her forehead. Large gold earrings glinted as she raised her chin and offered me her moist lips.

"Where do you want the bags?" the driver interrupted. "I gotta be gettin' back to Honolulu."

Blanche rifled through her big, black leather shoulder bag. "I wonder where... " She started taking things from the purse and laying them out on the back seat.

"What are you looking for?" I asked her.

Blanche opened all the zippers and snaps then finally gave up, looking at me with big sad eyes. "I must have left my wallet on the counter at LA Airport. I'm sorry. I bet that's what I did. I can't find the money."

"You what?"

"I can't find the money."

"But...but... Blanche! That was the security deposit on an apartment!" I reached into my back pocket for my wallet and grudgingly paid the driver twelve dollars. Now we only had enough money for a few days lodging. Big Green bailed us out. He and Rosetta let Blanche spend a couple of weeks living with them.

The next pay day, we went apartment hunting and found out the cost of living was much higher than on the Mainland. We ended up renting a shabby, one-bedroom apartment, owned by an old Korean woman. I tried to be optimistic. Maybe I'd have a chance to brush up on my Korean.

Six lopsided steps led up to the second floor. Painted

olive drab, the apartment looked suspiciously military. In Korea, villagers were notorious for acquiring military goods and equipment through devious means.

A rough wooden door painted red led into a tiny sitting room-kitchen combo. The sitting room had a homemade love seat, kitchen table, and two chairs made from the same wood as the door. The bedroom was little more than a doll-house with a military metal wall locker, a make-shift night stand, and a rough-lumbered double bed, with a scarred wooden floor.

We shared the place with an army of cockroaches and spent the first weeks killing bugs and making love. In a couple of months, Blanche had applied the woman's touch. She made a soft-yellow curtain for the one window, painted the walls and ceiling white and even covered the ugly brown floor with a piece of discarded carpet.

It was great having her around and she was always eager to help. She often scrubbed my muddy field gear, starched and pressed my fatigues and sometimes spit-shined my boots, although once she tried to dry them in the oven and forgot they were there, charring them.

I managed to finance the purchase of a car and from that moment on, we rarely stayed home. On weekends we circled the island, stopping to climb mountains or to stroll along beautiful beaches. Nights when the tropical winds blew warm, we made love on the white sand of a deserted beach.

Not long after, on a ride around the "Rock," somewhere between Wahewa and Sunset Beach, Blanche announced that she was pregnant. It was just what we wanted, although we were unprepared financially.

I could take a part time job since we had a car, but I remembered I was in Hawaii, a tough place for a black man to find work. I was nervous, in spite of telling myself that Blanche was fine and I would soon be getting additional pay. What did I have to worry about? Others made it on military pay and so could we.

The first trimester of the pregnancy went well, interrupted when our battalion was flown to the Big Island—Hawaii—for a thirty-day field exercise. Our short flight touched down at an air force base in the capital city of Hilo. From there we slowly truck-convoyed twenty-five miles up to thousands of feet above sea level at the base of Kilhuea, the volcano, in the Pohacaloa Training Area.

We slept two squads to a hut, same as in Korea. But unlike Korea's grass and sidewalks, but there was nothing at Pohacaloa but barren jagged lava rock. The larger rocks had been bulldozed aside or trucked away to make a passageway for military vehicles. The only visible living creature was an occasional bird. It occurred to me that the military was pretty good at creating life where there was none, and death where there had been life.

In the mornings, when the clouds evaporated, the snow-capped peaks of Mauna Kea revealed themselves. It was astounding to see snow in Hawaii, and experience the temperature extremes, from hot, dusty days to frosty nights. Several of those nights were spent sleepless on sharp rocks near a cliff, sometimes the only level place to lie down. That mountain on the Big Island was a miserable place to be posted but it made an impression—man could make it anywhere.

Back home, the fruit of my love with Blanche appeared to be growing well. Blanche had that glow everyone talks about on a pregnant woman. We immediately made love, and then settled down to my first home-cooked meal in a month. It was good to be back.

Two months later, on a hot January afternoon, I had good news—I had been selected for Non-Commissioned Officers Academy. On reporting day, I nervously signed in at the academy headquarters. It consisted of only two rooms, both spit-shined. I could see myself in the floor and the door knobs. I had heard the training was difficult, but I had mentally prepared myself. Maybe this would help me make staff sergeant sooner.

A tall polished Negro master sergeant handed my orders back to me. "Wait outside with the others, Sergeant," he ordered.

"Yes sir!" I replied, made an about face and joined a formation of several other NCOs standing at parade rest.

When my name was called I took one smart step back, whirled around to a right face, and double-timed out of formation to a new group. I fell in alongside several senior ranking sergeants. When everyone was accounted for, the group leader, a Captain, started his talk.

"The objective of this training is to enhance leadership qualities. The rank each of you held before entering training is now obsolete. As far as we are concerned, all of you are recruits. Your two week course will be focused on individual appearance, drill formations, and methods of instruction. This program also includes a strenuous physical training course, much like basic."

In the days that followed, I wondered why everyone had said the course was so difficult. Classes, practical applications, and drill seemed to be the Academy's primary focus. The first week was a charm—I loved it. In the middle of the second week, the Methods of Instruction class was interrupted by a short, white major. He called the instructor outside. They talked for about five minutes and a first sergeant joined them. The three talked some more and the expressions on the two listener's faces, the sergeant and captain, became noticeably sober.

When the instructor finally returned, he announced: "The training had been discontinued. You are instructed to return to your company. You are dismissed. If you have any questions, wait and ask them when you get back to your units."

A formation was gathering when I got back to the Company, so I fell in with my platoon.

"At ease!" yelled the company commander, a veteran with pale white skin and graying brown hair. He smiled quickly at the first sergeant, then took a couple steps forward and looked at his platoon leaders slowly, one by one.

"You guys are probably wondering why they sent everybody back to their outfits. I guess you think something's up. Well, you're damn right. Something is.

"We're going to Vietnam. Most of you below the rank of E-5 will be transferred to other companies to bring their units up to strength. The rest of you, mainly NCOs, will remain behind with me for six weeks to train a battalion that's coming from Alaska. We will train them in techniques for jungle warfare.

"We have a job on our hands training troops in only six weeks. I know you'll do your best because we'll be going to combat with these trainees, so train them well. Your platoon sergeant has a roster of the names of those who will be departing. Company! Atten-SHUN!"

The old man then stepped vigorously off toward the orderly room. In the field, he was known for plowing alongside his troops like General Patton. A few of the guys said he was an ex-sergeant. I accepted the rumor because he looked old for a captain.

Sergeant Jade started calling out names: "Private First Class Krusack, you lucked out. You won't be goin' to Vietnam at all. You've been transferred to Delta Company, 1-11 Supply Battalion." A subversive chuckle was heard. Krusack had syphilis. We all knew he was going for treatment.

"That's one way of getting out of going to Vietnam," I told Traver.

At the end of the day, I sprinted after Sergeant Jade as he walked toward the parking lot. "Sergeant, you know my wife is going to have a baby soon. Do you think—"

"Hell, no! I know what you're gonna say before you say it," Jade continued to walk. He was from Chicago and talked like Humphrey Bogart, out of the side of his mouth. "Whatever fuckin' shit they're doin' in Vietnam, it ain't gonna stop because your wife is having a damn baby. Forget it, Brummell. You're takin' your ass to Vietnam just like the rest of us."

When I told Blanche, she burst into tears.

"We're having a baby! I want you here with me!

What's going on in... What's the name of that place!"

"Vietnam."

"Will I stay in Hawaii? How long will you be over there? Will you be gone when the baby is born?"

"Don't worry," I said, but started crying, nearly losing my voice. I put my arm around her. "The Army will be sending you home. All you have to do is have the baby and sit tight 'til I get back."

In the days that followed, Blanche and I talked all the time we were together. We grew closer, cried often, laughed and wished a lot, too. The big wish was that I would not leave and there was no place called Vietnam.

Within two weeks, A Company's enlisted men were gone, all but the noncommissioned officers. Two days later the troops from Alaska poured in and their training began. The first part involved a standard proficiency test, including disassembling and assembling weapons, compass course, chemical warfare, and physical fitness. Usually, I was the one tested but this time I was the administrator, which was more fun.

One day while I was grading soldiers on the M-79 Grenade Launcher firing positions, a familiar looking fellow, three men back, fixed his eyes on me while I was squatting to check a trooper's prone position.

"I'll be doggone!" I said, as the familiar fellow drew closer. It was Frank Lacky, an old schoolmate from Federalsburg, two years my junior. We'd known each other well. He wanted to shoot the bull and so did I, but I had many more soldiers to grade.

Lacky, once a high school scholar and trumpet player, failed to meet my expectations, ironic considering his name. He was clumsy, awkward in firing positions, and slow assembling his weapon.

"Hey, Sarge! Homeboy!" Lacky said, reading the grades on the test sheet. "Don't you think you were a little hard?"

"Quite the opposite, Private. I think I've been generous."

Lacky and I did get together once after the test. We met at the Post Gym, went to the Enlisted Men's Club and stopped at a couple of bars in Wahewa. He criticized my grading technique, but we had a great time reminiscing about home.

The newcomers' battalion took to the fields. We instructed men even younger than my twenty years how to make bridges out of ropes, repel off mountains, and other survival techniques. I thought about being married less than a year, with a pregnant wife, and preparing to go to combat in a strange country. I could be killed.

Vietnam. The sound of it began clinging to me like the smell of kerosene. I wanted to be disassociated with that smell, that far away place. It meant being a half-world apart from Blanche.

A day before Blanche was to return to the Mainland, we toured the island for the last time. We stopped at a small clothing store near Honolulu and bought a pretty beige maternity suit for her homeward journey.

The next day we arrived at Honolulu's airport forty-five minutes before flight time. The terminal was bulging with GIs and their dependents. Lobbies and corridors were a mass of humanity. Most of the faces bore sad expressions. Women and children wept and, on occasion, even the tough-looking guys broke down.

Blanche drew closer to me as we maneuvered through the clusters of people, a sea of Army green. Grappling with her two large suitcases, for the first time I started thinking seriously about what was happening. "Now, let's see. Which direction is your gate?" Blanche held a pink tissue dabbing at the wet spots on her cheeks. I set the luggage down. "Honey, you're gonna make a scene."

My chest felt heavy, my throat was tight, and I wanted to cry. I held the tears back, but only for a moment. By the time Blanche and I reached her designated gate, she was bawling.

"G-George, I've been hearing folks talk about Vietnam. I'm scared. They're killing people over there! You be careful! I want you back in one piece!"

"Don't worry," I said, looking deep into her eyes. She looked at my name tag and touched it.

"A year is a long time," she said, picking a bit of lint off my shirt collar. "We'll be waiting for you, the baby and I."

The boarding announcement for her flight came over the loudspeakers.

"Well, that's me," Blanche said, slinging her bag over her shoulder and folding some magazines under her left arm. With her free hand, she picked up an overnight bag and started stepping slowly toward the shuttle bus. I wrapped my arm around her waist and walked with her.

"I love you," I whispered. Blanche's body trembled and her knees weakened. I tightened my arm around her. She kissed me, quick, but sensuously.

"Watch your step," warned a skycap as we started down the stairs. I stopped at the bottom. "This is as far as I can go. How about one for the year, sweetheart?"

We kissed again, then parted, slowly, touching fingers as long as we could.

"I love you," Blanche said, turning to board the bus.

I ascended the steps, trying to keep her in view. She looked up a few times, searching for me. As the shuttle doors closed, we locked eyes until her face had disappeared from view.

Chapter 13

The United States Naval Ship *General Walker* had the same foul odor as the *Barrack*. Sergeant Jade assigned our platoon to Berth C and told us to hang our field packs and weapons at the end of our bunks, and stack our duffle bags on the lid of the cargo compartment. We were to stay below deck.

Finally, after a few hours in stifling heat and the stench of humanity, we were allowed to go above to the main deck. More than four thousand of us scrambled topside, to fresh air. I maneuvered through the mass of green uniforms, and found a tight spot on the railing between Traver and Big Green.

The enormous ship rocked slightly from side to side with the weight of all those soldiers. Below us on the pier the ground crew made preparations to close the gang plank. Further down the platform an Army band played "Anchors Away" and "Tiny Bubbles." Hawaiian girls danced the hula in their traditional orchid leis and grass skirts. A sea of faces of children and mothers looked up like baby birds hoping for a scrap of food, looking for fathers and husbands.

Traver spotted his wife and yelled, "You take care of yourself! Write everyday! And take care of that car!" Traver was crazy about his Ford with its snazzy yellow-flecked red paint, white leather interior, and gleaming chrome wheels.

"There's Sergeant Bosi's family," Green said, pointing.

Sergeant First Class Bosi was the first platoon sergeant, a native Hawaiian. He had dark, straight black hair, permanent tan, and actually spoke the language. His wife stood on the pier waving a yellow handkerchief, with all seven of their children clustered around her. Bosi, not far away from us, caught sight of his wife. Three stories below, his wife managed to squeeze out a smile. Bosi leaned forward with his elbows on the railing yelling at the children, calling each by name, promising he would see them in a year.

"Take care of your mother! Be good! Be sure to write!"

My heart ached. What I would have given to see Blanche down there on the dock. I moved off the railing and another GI quickly slipped into the tiny space. I maneuvered through the swarm of men in a daze, conjuring Blanche's face. I could almost smell the Joy perfume she wore. I had to fight to keep my tears at bay. I headed below. The berth was nearly empty, just a guard and a couple of guys sleeping off last night's drunk.

I scrambled through the huge stack of duffle bags until I found mine. I pulled out my photo of Blanche. One long look and the tears flowed. I held the frame to my chest, climbed into my bunk and plunged my face into my pillow. I was comforted slightly when an older GI ran down the metal steps, sniffling all the way to his bunk. In another bunk a trooper had staked out a corner and was bashfully boo-hooing. Fifteen minutes went by and my pillow was soaked.

I finally exhausted my grief and dried my face. The strains of the band drifted from the pier. Through a porthole I could see the cranes and buildings sliding away. The crowd was roaring. Recovered, I ran back up to the main deck and found Big Green. He managed a brave smile.

"Looks like this is it," I said, knowing how lame it sounded. "We're on our way to combat."

"Yeah, it looks as if we are in for some excitement," Green said. He looked away, covering his eyes with his hand for a moment.

"Maybe too much excitement," I said, trying to fill the silence. "Come on, let's take a walk to the stern."

A tugboat pulled the ship out into the channel, like a parent dragging a reluctant child by the arm. We watched as the Pearl Harbor water tower, shaped like a huge pineapple, shrunk. We were on our way to a land most of us had never heard of. What were we going to do there?

We had a lot of time off, and I spent a fair amount of it with Specialist Fourth Class Andy Andrews. He had earned the nickname Andy Articulate because he spoke with such precision. He was popular in spite of it, a jokester who was always smiling. He had status as the company commander's personal driver, which meant he knew what was going to happen before we did. He was a white angel with curly blond hair, blue eyes, and pale skin that glowed, yet he seemed to like hanging out with the black troops. He and I often went topside together, for a dose of the fresh salt air. The stern was a great place to hang out, talk, and meditate on the relentless churn produced by the ship's huge propellers.

"Would you care to place a wager on who is going to get it first?" Articulate Andy asked one afternoon.

"Yeah. I'll bet on you."

"And what, pray tell, do you bet?"

"I'll bet you that watch you have on." He wore an impressive timepiece—a large luminous deep sea diving watch with built-in alarms and rotating dials.

It was a macabre game being played all over the ship, a way men could talk about their fears without seeming fearful. Groups of gambling men would form pools, each putting up five or ten bucks on a bet that a particular buddy would catch the first bullet. No one wanted to win those pools, but they all knew somebody would.

We steamed across the calmest seas I'd seen in all my travels, under the bright, tropical sun. During the days, hundreds of men sprawled topside, enjoying the sun and air. At dawn and dusk they crowded the railings to catch the spectacular sunrises and sunsets. At night they smoked and gazed at the moon as it traced its way across the star-filled sky. The atmosphere was calm, but a subversive unease lay just beneath the surface. The miles separating us from our destination dwindled, and so did the chatter—conversations became clipped, and there was less laughter and smiling. An air of mass introversion cloaked the decks.

My thoughts always returned to Blanche and our baby that might have been born and I wouldn't know it. Blanche's delivery date was near. I hoped for a boy. I decided I'd name him Mister, so everyone would have to call him Mister Brummell. Growing up, I'd had to call men mister and women misses, especially if they were white. That people would have to call him Mr. Mister Brummell appealed to my subversive side. Blanche wouldn't hear of it, so I saved the name and later gave it to my dog.

Days at sea tend to run together, so to help keep track, I tore the back off a pack of matches and wrote down the number of days until I would get back home. I kept it in my wallet and each morning I would update the number.

One day word swept the decks and berths that the next night we would enter Vietnamese waters. We were to rendezvous with a US Navy escort to ensure a well-protected arrival.

After sunset the following day, the ship suddenly fell silent for the first time since we left Pearl. The intercom system—over which announcements, music, and news were the constant background noise—fell silent. I could feel the vibration of the engines throttling back. Far away on the horizon I saw occasional flashes of light, like firecrackers exploding in an open field at midnight—like the flicker of Nelson's shiny lighter.

"Sergeant Brummell," a voice said, slightly above a whisper.

"Yeah?"

"I wonder what's going on over there." A muffled boom reached us now and then, like thunder. But was it thunder?

"Private Thacel, how are you?"

"Fine," he said propping his right foot on the bottom rail. In the shipboard silence I could hear the water hissing against the ship's hull. I glanced at Thacel's thick frame, bent over the rail in such a way that he appeared weary, much older than his twenty-one years. His deeply-set dull blue eyes were, like mine, focused intently on the flashes of light.

"It looks like there could be a lot of action going on way over there," Thacel said in his slow, Midwestern drawl. "I know I don't want no part of combat." Thacel was practically a conscientious objector. He often said he couldn't kill a man. I wondered how the hell he ended up on that rust bucket. Did he have a death wish?

Absorbed in our own thoughts and fears, we watched the water and the flashes of light in silence. Somewhere above us I heard a clicking sound, and a beam of light shot out into the darkness—the ship was communicating by Morse Code with another vessel. The device made a machine gun-like sound. A short pause, then a light furiously flashed in the distance in reply, like a winking Cyclops.

"Know any Morse code?" Thacel asked.

"Nah. I was never in the Boy Scouts. I don't think they even had Scouts for us Coloreds in Federalsburg."

We parted, he to his bunk, me to the bow to think some more before hitting the sack.

———•••———

"DROP YOUR COCKS AND GRAB YOUR SOCKS!"

I woke with my heart pounding. The guard was screaming orders. "GET UP, YOU LAZY FUCKERS! This is our last day aboard this miserable tub! Get up and see what hell lies ahead! We're entering the harbor!"

I sprung up like a jack-in-the-box, careful not to hit my head on the bunk above. I pulled on my fatigues and laced my boots.

The intercom crackled to life. "Attention! All military personnel! Attention! All military personnel! Stand by your assigned troop quarters until further notice!"

The next voice was Sergeant Jade. "These quarters have got to be cleaned! We're going to have an inspection by the company commander!"

We were glad to be cleaning for the last time and dove into stripping our beds, mopping the decks, and making sure a life preserver was tied on the end of every bunk.

"Get into your field gear! Stand by your bunks at parade rest!"

Minutes later, Captain North and his executive officer descended the steps and inspected the quarters. The company commander made a few comments and chatted briefly with the first sergeant, and then hurried back up the steps. Later, the first sergeant released the platoons to their sergeants. I was among the last of the GIs to reach main deck.

The sun glowed hot like the cherry-red potbelly stove in school, and without a breath of air to cool things off. A bustling coastal town lay off the bow with a beach that would have looked beautiful anywhere else. It was crowded with military hardware—trucks, tanks, jeeps—and camouflaged uniforms scurrying about.

The heat was intense and my forehead seemed to explode with sweat that ran stinging into my eyes. The harbor echoed with the concussions of outbound shells from two nearby battle ships supporting another combat unit miles away. Each salvo unleashed a cloud of smoke and the giant ships visibly lurched and rocked from the recoil.

"Hey, Brummell!" Traver said, tapping my shoulder. "Wanna see something really nice?"

I followed him around several stacks of lifeboats to the other side of the ship. Close by, docked among the gray and camouflaged and stained hulls of military and cargo vessels, was a huge, gleaming, utterly white ship, with USS *HOPE* written in tall black letters on the side—a hospital ship.

"Man, that is beautiful!" I said. "Have you ever seen anything as white as that? That's whiter than you Traver."

Traver smiled. "Yeah. Belongs on a postcard."

I wondered how they kept it so white and clean looking. What sort of cases did they have on board? How long had the ship been docked there? The sight of it was both reassuring and disturbing.

We glided past the *HOPE* and finally dropped anchor. The crew scrambled to the railings and let down enormous rope ladders. Our amphibious training was about to be put to the test. A landing craft approached, drifted in place beside the ship under the ladders. When we were fully geared-up, we watched as another company started the long descent down the rope ladders.

"Don't look down!" the platoon sergeants yelled. "Look up! Keep moving! Move it, soldiers!"

Down in the landing craft, there were photographers, television crews, and reporters interviewing GIs. When it was our turn, my heart began pounding. Sergeant Jade yelled, "Okay! let's go!" I hugged the shaking, dancing ladder, keeping my eyes fixed on the hull of the ship. Boy, was it hot, almost unbearable, hotter even than Hawaii.

Slowly, I worked my way down. I tried not to look, but sometimes I couldn't help it. As I got closer to the bobbing watercraft, I saw and heard the reporters. I hoped one of them would ask me a question, so I could be seen on TV back home, but they didn't come anywhere near me.

"Why do you think you're here in Vietnam?" one was asking. "Where's your home town? How long do you have to stay?" I tried to shuffle near, but it was too crowded to move, like a fully-suited football team crammed into a station wagon.

The landing craft filled and finally the big diesel engine thundered to life and we sprinted across the harbor. The shoreline was visible and before the pilot reached maximum speed, he backed off his engines, drifted through muddy waters and we bumped the bottom. The ramp slowly dropped onto the wet sand and we double-timed to a waiting convoy of trucks, past a group of pretty Vietnamese girls handing out fresh flowers to some of the GIs, mainly officers up front. I had arrived in Vietnam. It was April 29, 1966.

"Vietnamese look darker than Koreans," I told Traver.

"Yeah. Remember, I was here before."

Traver had served as a machine gunner on a helicopter for ninety days. He already had the Combat Infantryman Badge (CIB) and other combat citations. Sometimes Traver bragged about confirmed kills—kills he knew he had committed, kills he bet his life was done by his own hands or trigger finger.

"Brummell, I've seen Congs pushed out of helicopters at fifteen hundred feet and watched 'em bounce like a flat basketball." He chuckled. "We once saw a man and his water buffalo in a rice paddy. We used 'em for target practice—fired a few warning shots and watched them run, until we mowed 'em down."

Traver had a sick sense of humor. I never knew if he was telling the truth.

"Any of them out there on the streets could be our enemy," he continued. "That one over there looks a little suspicious." He pointed to a feeble-looking old man in faded brown shirt and pants. The little tan man walked faster than everyone else, and then broke into a run until he was in a group of other old men and women standing in front of a little store that looked like it was made of mud. The man stopped and turned, his back to the wall, looking furtively from side to side. Was that the enemy?

"We're beginning to move!" a voice yelled from up ahead.

The convoy lurched into motion like a sluggish snake emitting clouds of diesel smoke. Sergeant Jade yelled, looking back from the cab of our truck, "Pass the word to assign air guards!"

A machine gunner from the weapons squad was assigned as our truck's forward guard, so we could keep an eye out, maybe on the sneaky-looking man. I decided I'd rather be exposed and see something than make this trip squashed down with the others.

"I'll take the rear!"

I pulled down the retractable tri-pod on my AR-16 rifle, and positioned it on top of the folded back canvas. Only a few vehicles followed us but to my front there was a long line of trucks that seemed to stretch to the horizon. When our truck reached the top of a small hill, I looked back and saw the reconnaissance jeep way out front, a place I would not choose to be. The gossip about Vietnam included horrible tales of point jeeps running over land mines.

The scenery looked familiar, like Korea. Skinny, hungry-looking kids, some bare-assed naked, approached trucks begging. Villages we passed through bore signs of heavy fighting. Some huts half blasted away, others just piles of rubble. Large craters appeared here and there in the road, slowing our progress to a makeshift airfield.

The runways were built out of metal sheets, laid on the ground. Huge Air Force transports idled, their ramps opened for loading. Our trucks pulled up to the ramp of one plane. A member of the crew hustled beside the ramp in front of us and assumed the position of parade rest.

"Stand by!" Sergeant Jade shouted, running up ahead for a briefing with the company commander. Other platoon sergeants followed with maps in hands.

When the briefing was over, Captain North pointed in the direction of the aircraft and the sergeants dispersed. Sergeant Jade, stepping briskly, signaled the driver with a wiggly thumbs up. The driver got out, ran to the back of the truck, unfastened and dropped the tailgate.

"Let's go! Grab your gear. Load that plane over there."

"Let's go for an airplane ride!" Traver yelled, springing from his seat with much more enthusiasm than I was feeling at the moment.

The men shuffled toward the rear of the vehicle, jumped to the ground, double-timed up the ramp and into the plane. Nylon webbing seats along the plane's walls were down. We pushed forward, sat, and buckled our seat belts. A couple of three-quarter ton trucks were strapped down in the middle.

"Squad leaders! Take head counts!" Jade yelled.

Traver reported, "All present and accounted for!"

Jade disappeared back down the ramp to the first sergeant. Soon he reappeared with a crewman.

"Buckle your seat belts," the airman yelled.

The ramp slowly closed and the aircraft's engines powered up until we were moving. I was near a window so I watched the big propeller blades whirling until they became a blur. The fuselage began to vibrate, making a deafening noise.

"Hope this sucker gets off the ground!" Traver shouted.

The wheels made a huge racket as they rolled across the cut holes in the metal runway. Groaning, the plane angled up and was airborne. High above grass roofs, mangrove and mountains, the metal bird gradually climbed. Out toward the tip of one wing, specks of greens and blues showed throughout the rice paddies. I thought about how miserable it had been working on the farms with Uncle Noble, but those people and water buffalo down there must be really miserable.

My body tensed as I coached the plane skyward. Finally, when I sensed we were safely up, I settled back into the nylon strap seat, closed my eyes, and tried to relax. I slipped into a brief snooze, and woke to find we were flying through gray clouds. Tiny glimmering specks of silver penetrated the fluffy stuff—fighter planes that were escorting us. Sometimes they drifted so close I could see the pilots.

Finally the "Fasten Seat Belts" sign lit. As soon as we hit the ground and exited the plane, Sergeant Jade pointed to a convoy of trucks and shouted, "Load those vehicles over there!" We drove down dusty roads, through several small villages until the truck in front of the convoy came to a halt. The lead driver was talking to an MP at the gate.

We began moving slowly into the division base camp. Squad tents erected on wooden frames were scattered about. Through some of their opened flaps, I saw wooden floors. Trucks continued grinding forward, kicking up heavy clouds of dust that clogged my nostrils. I wished I hadn't volunteered for air guard. I dug a T-shirt out of my pack and tied it over my mouth and nose.

We passed mortar crews who were busy adjusting gun sights and firing rounds toward the front. Farther on, we passed artillery with their crews hustling about, feeding the guns their rounds and closing breeches. First one gun fired, then another and another, down the line. Each of the big weapons sat behind a huge wall of sand bags, but still the noise was deafening. The lead truck made a right turn. Up ahead was a sign—Company A.

"Welcome home, boys!" Traver yelled. "Let's unass this heap of junk!"

Chapter 14

latoon! Atten-HUT!" All chatter ceased. Captain North positioned himself front and center.

"Alright! Stand at ease, men!"

I had never experienced an earthquake, but I could imagine what it might be like. The ground shook tremendously as the big guns fired almost without a break. The noise was so intense I only caught bits and pieces of what the company commander said.

"Men, we have our job cut out for us, a very serious mission to cut down Communist aggression. If we let Communism dominate South Vietnam, then before we know it, it'll spread to back home. Our objective is sweep and destroy.

"Let's face it. We're in a combat situation and some of us are not going to make it."

That got my attention, and everyone else's, which was what we needed. He was being frank, confirming what we already knew. We respected that.

"Platoon sergeants, dismiss your men." The company commander walked away.

The first sergeant yelled. "At ease! Platoon sergeants take charge!"

I threw my heavy duffle across my shoulder and moved toward the NCO quarters. Sandbags surrounded each of the tents. Inside were fourteen folding cots with mosquito nets stretched across two metal T-shaped bars at each end of each cot. The quarters were tight, but I was accustomed to close living after spending fourteen days in the lower section of the *Walker*.

The tent was like an oven, dusty. Dripping sweat, I sat my bag on the wooden floor carefully, upright, near the head of the cot. The first thing was to see if Blanche's photograph made the voyage okay. It was in great condition. I kissed Blanche and hung the frame on a strap that tied a flap back for ventilation.

There were no wall or foot lockers. We had to live out of duffle bags. I blew up my air mattress and laid it on the wobbly cot. There was no sheets, so I stretched my sleeping bag across the air mattress.

Because Traver was the only one in the tent who had been in Vietnam, the rest of us bombarded him with questions.

"Is it this hot all the time?"

"Yes, sometimes hotter," he said, bent over with both hands deep in his duffle bag. "It ain't unusual at all for the temperature to hit a hundred twenty." I knew how hot it could get, growing up on the stiflingly humid coastal plain along Chesapeake Bay. But it was only like that for a few months in summer.

"I have to put up with this hot shit for thirteen months?" I yelled from the other end of the tent. I looked out the door and spotted a mouse racing past in the dust with something in its teeth.

"Wait until we have one of those damn downpours. It rains like hell here," Traver continued, "especially during the monsoon season. All those sandbags you saw when you came in are to keep water from flooding the tents."

"One thing we don't have to worry about is passes, 'cause there ain't gonna be none," Sergeant Jade chimed in. "This is a hostile area. The advance party took it away from the VC (VietCong). There's a lot of unfriendly activity going on in Chu Chee, so no GIs should go there on pass."

I groaned. It would be a while before I had a chance to sample the local beer and entertainment.

I finished organizing my bunk and got the hell out of the hot tent. Traver followed. Tents were scattered all around. Near the center of A Company, a generator hummed. A hundred feet away was a small, underground ammo bunker. The officers' tent was opposite the ammunition stash, another hundred feet from the generator. Across to the left and in front, the cooks were preparing the mess tent for our first meal.

"Sergeant Brummell!"

"Yes, Sergeant."

"Where's your weapon?" Sergeant Jade asked, frowning.

"It's in the tent."

"Go and get it. While you're here, keep your weapon glued to yourself. Every move you make, you'll carry your friend with you. Sleep with it, eat with it. You'll want to know where it is at all times. Remember, we're in a combat zone. It shouldn't take long for you to understand that."

Jade had seen action in Korea and World War II. I couldn't think of anyone else I'd rather be in combat with. We all respected him. In Hawaii, our platoon often came in first place during battalion competition because of his expert strategies in the field.

I ran back to the tent and grabbed my rifle. Traver was still there. I took the pack of cigarettes from my jungle fatigue shirt pocket, lit one, and he and I left the tent.

"I'm worried, man. A little scared too," I said drawing deep on the Pall Mall. "This is serious business."

"I know. If you wasn't shook up, I'd think something was wrong with you. I'm scared, too."

Staff Sergeant Caballo, a short stout Mexican, interrupted. "You amigos like a beer?"

"Yeah, a beer wouldn't be bad. Where the hell did you get beer?"

"From the PX," he proudly replied. Caballo had seventeen years' service, and was third squad leader. He and Jade were old war buddies. Each wore the Combat Infantryman's Badge with pride, but I never heard Jade talk about it. Whenever one of us brought up the subject, he would change the subject.

Caballo was a member of the advance party that arrived two weeks before we did. They secured the area and prepared it for nearly five thousand of us.

"Battalion commander authorized us to have beer after sixteen hundred. Some NCOs, they got coolers and ice. I buy the beer, you pay me back. We get the money straight later. Now let's drink 'em up. The cooler's 'round there." He pointed to a shady spot on the side of the tent, "Only shade there is."

The cooler was filled to the top with beer cans around a huge chunk of ice. Traver clapped his hands. "Man, that looks good!"

Jade warned us not to ingest any of the ice water. "This ice came from the village and you don't want to catch hepatitis."

Standing around drinking beer took me back home, like hanging around Big Frank's Beer Garden drinking under the shade tree. The constant roar of artillery was like the bass thump of the jukebox on Saturday night. When rounds landed, though they were at a distance, they reminded me of backfiring muscle cars.

Suddenly, the ground shuddered several times. It stopped as quick as it started—a barrage of incoming fire.

"Hit, baby!" men shouted, clicking their mortar sights, trying to pinpoint the enemy. Toward the road, several tanks rushed past kicking up a big cloud of dust. When the tank commander, half out of the turret, pointed to the right, the tank drivers quickly wheeled in that direction.

"I wonder what they're up to," I said. The surface of the can was cold from the ice, but the beer was hot.

Before Caballo could answer, a gust of rifle fire broke out, followed by the crackle of machine guns, automatic rifles, grenade launchers, and what sounded like artillery rounds.

"That sounds pretty close!" Traver shouted.

"Shore do!" Caballo said. "Bunker line only thousand meters maybe, behind the weapons platoon tent! C'mon! Let's go see the action."

The three of us took off running in the direction of the intensity. Just as we got behind the weapons platoon tent, a couple of enemy mortar rounds dropped about fifty yards in front of us.

"Hit the dirt!" Caballo yelled, flopping to the ground.

I was down seconds before he was. As soon as the debris had scattered, I looked for something to hide behind. Nothing in sight but a small mound of dirt about fifteen meters to my left. I pushed up and went for it, following Traver's boot heels. I tried to beat him to that pile of almost nothing, but he got there first.

"Damn!" I mumbled. I peeped around Traver's boots and saw tanks rumbling beyond the bunker line, blasting pellet rounds in all directions.

An enemy round lobbed in and crashed close by. I dropped my head closer to the ground. Dirt struck my face and neck. I thought my ear drums would burst. It was like experiencing an explosion under an over-turned tub. I prepared to make a run, but another round hit near me, so I stayed put with my two friends.

Each time a tank fired, its powerful rounds blasted a clearing in the forest. They pounded vegetation while their tracks crept up inch by inch to the wood line. The enemy fire subsided, but the tanks continued pulverizing the forest. A couple of minutes later, everything was almost quiet.

Then, cautiously, the armored vehicles proudly moved back and behind the perimeter, to bunkers built especially for them.

"Ees really close," Caballo said. "You ain't safe no place here."

"You guys ready to move?" Traver asked calmly, lying back like he was enjoying a day at the beach.

"Yeah," Caballo answered. Beads of sweat made dark trails in the dust on his forehead.

Traver got up, brushed off his pants, and we all started back toward the tents.

"There was activity up on the bunker line," Sergeant Lantz said. "Where ya'll been?" An almost blood-red head from Kentucky, he was the weapons squad leader, a good soldier who cared about his men, but one of the sloppiest in the company. His clothes always looked as if he had slept in them.

"No kidding," I said. "We were over by the weapons platoon's tent. God-damned rounds almost fell on top of us."

"Okay. I'm just glad you guys made it back. Listen, I went over to the mess tent a few minutes ago. They have some of the biggest steaks I've ever seen. Oh, yeah, Sergeant Jade gave us our duty details for tomorrow—a lot of sandbagging. Then, in a few days, they're moving us up to take over Ann Margaret. You heard of Ann Margaret, right? She was here in a USO show a few weeks back, so we named the bunker line for her."

"Chow time!" a voice boomed from the mess tent.

We all bolted, like schoolboys at the recess bell. "Hold the fuck up!" Lantz yelled. "Break out those mess kits. The only guys who get to eat off trays are the company commander and the rest of the officers."

"Ugh!" Traver grunted. "I shoulda known we'd have to eat out of those nasty mess kits."

We doubled back to dig them out of our duffles, then hot-footed to a spot just outside the mess tent where there were three thirty-five gallon galvanized trash cans filled with water. We needed to wash the dirt and travel dust out of our kits before we used them. Two barrels were heated by diesel oil burners with tall stove pipes puffing sooty, greasy smoke and ash that rained into the wash and rinse containers.

The first can was filled with hot, soapy water. A long handled scrub brush, attached by a rope, hung from the rim. The second can was filled with hot rinse water. The third was for a cold rinse. It was, by now, a familiar ritual. When I was done, I fell in at the end of the line, fanning my mess kit to make it dry faster.

Finally, I reached the steam table. "Which one of these steaks you want?" asked Sonny the roly-poly, ruddy-faced cook.

"That big one in the right corner."

Sunny Sonny, the men called him, because he was always bright and clean looking. He served me a sizzling slab of beef that dwarfed my mess kit. I positioned it to make room for the mashed potatoes and peas, trying to keep my rifle sling from slipping off my shoulder. No room for the sliced peaches so I lifted the steak and had the cook slide them under.

In the dining tent, there were no seats. Everyone stood, feeding with the urgency and fever of hogs at a trough. Burdened by our weapons, ammunition, and steel pots—the tent rang with a chorus of metal scraping against metal, pot banging against pot—half the battle was getting the food into your mouth without dropping it on the filthy floor.

Sergeant Jade walked past with his meal. "Pass the word, Brummell. Everyone's to report to the supply tent for bullet proof vests." Jesus, I thought. This is the real deal. Hawaii, even shipboard life, suddenly seemed like quaint memories of some long-extinct world.

I wolfed down my dinner, washed my kit, and

went straight to get my metal life preserver. I wanted to give myself time to get accustomed to its stifling weight. It might just save my life.

On the way back to my tent, an immense, fiery-orange sun was setting behind a tall, round mountain. I paused, mesmerized by the spectacle of being able to see the sun descending, bit by bit, faster and faster until it was a puddle of color, then gone. I felt a surge of emotion. Something major was happening to me. I had never paid as much attention to the sun, moon, or life in general as I had since we'd left Hawaii. I thought about Blanche and the baby, and, for the first time, muttered a little prayer.

Although I was brought up in Grandma's Negro holy-roller congregation, I never went to church after joining the Army. I did no praying. But I thought now might be a good time to practice. I asked God to spare me and allow me to go home safe, the same prayer five thousand others were saying at about the same time.

Back on my cot, I stared at Blanche's photograph while I searched through my duffle bag for writing paper. The paper was wrinkled, but it was dry. I started a letter to Blanche. I was deep in thought when another familiar face showed up.

"This A Company, ain't it?" asked a voice outside the tent. "First Platoon?"

"You got it," someone answered.

"Sergeant Brummell. You in there?"

It was Corporal Melvis, who had been a member of our squad before he was transferred to the Thirty-Fifth Infantry to beef it up. His unit had arrived ahead of ours. "Hey, Brother Mel. How the hell are you?"

Melvis stepped into the tent, flashed a big, toothy smile and embraced me.

"I'm livin'. I'm still around. I guess that's something, especially in this shit hole." Melvis chuckled, but his face fell. "That's more than I can say for some others. I seen a lot of bad stuff. You remember Wilbert and Frederick? They were in our squad. No more." He shook his square head. "Gone. You seen Ann Margaret, the bunker line?"

"There was action there today."

"Yeah, they're always having action down there. There's a little bridge that crosses a narrow stream before you get to the bunker line. One night, some VC swam up the stream and mined it. Wilbert and Frederick were in the lead APC. Just as they got in the center, the mother-fucker blew all to hell.

"The APC caught fire. I was in the third APC back. The ramp on the carrier took forever to open, and the guys trapped inside were screaming for all it was worth! When they finally came out running they looked like fuckin' human torches.

"Man, it was a terrible sight. Then the ammo Wilbert had strapped on exploded and he just broke up into pieces. Frederick was screamin' and fell down wiggling like a charcoaled worm. It's a fuckin' hell hole."

It was hard to hear what the Cong had done to our buddies, but Melvis had to get it off his chest. I felt a rush of vengeful rage.

"Come on, Brummell. Let's find us a quiet spot. Shit gets so bad here, you gotta do something. I got some local whiskey. Tastes like shit but it does the job. Nobody cares about gettin' caught. The stockade is a damn sight better than this mess. You have to drink or you'll go crazy thinking."

As we walked he told me about others I knew who had been killed or injured soon after they arrived. The more Mel talked, the more I felt like I was in a nightmare.

A slice of moon popped out from behind dark gray clusters of storm clouds gathering overhead. It looked like we might get one of those monsoon rain storms. Throughout there was the occasional pounding of outbound artillery.

"Those guns. They fire all the time, don't they?" I said.

"Wait 'til dark," he said. "That's when they get to rockin' and rollin'."

"How the hell do you sleep with all this racket."

"You'll get used to it. I had the same problem at first. I hate to think what would happen if they stopped. We'd probably be dancin' with the VC. I'll take the noise any day." He stopped, and looked behind us. "This place looks as good as any. Let's duck behind these tents here."

We sat down in a patch of tall grass. I lit a cigarette. Melvis handed me a tall, skinny bottle. I took a long pull. He was right. It tasted nasty, like grass.

"Be careful, Sarge," he said. "This shit'll knock you on your ass. I picked it up in one of the villages on a mission. Two bucks. You want the rest of the bottle? I can get more tomorrow."

"No, thanks. I want a clear head when I meet the enemy." I pulled my shirt over my head to cover my lighter as I quickly lit another cigarette. It was dark. I wanted to make sure I didn't give some lucky sniper an easy target. After a few drags the whisky took hold. My head was floating apart from my body. The moon peeked through the clouds. I peered into Melvis' black, barbaric face.

"Man, you look like Wily Coyote with those big, fiery red eyes."

We burst into riotous laughter.

For a moment, I forgot about being in a combat zone. I saw Blanche at the airport, tears flowing from her brown eyes, down her soft cheeks. Suddenly, the skies lit up in the direction of the nearest village, Chu Chi. It was an air assault.

Helicopters circled with machine guns and rockets blasting. It looked like the enemy was pinned down in two huts that were visible between the tents. I climbed on top of some sand bags to get a better look. The scene was eerie, the sky pierced by tracer bullets, and huts illuminated in the flash of the explosions. Three choppers dove in formation, pounding the huts with rockets and bullets until they had been leveled.

The rain finally let down and began pouring. Bright bolts of lightening lit the clouds, with thunder that rolled seamlessly through the concussions from the big guns. The rain intensified and we were getting soaked, but Mel seemed oblivious.

"I'm used to the rain now. I just want to forget the war. Getting high helps. Here, Sarge," he said, reaching into a pocket. "Take this joint and fire it up when you're down and out. It's a vacation in a cigarette."

I tucked it in my shirt pocket. He acted as if he wanted to linger a while longer, but it was time to part.

We hugged and shook hands as if it would be the last time.

"I hate like hell to go on this big maneuver tomorrow," he said. "I've had a coupla close scrapes, and every time I go out, I wonder if I'm gonna catch a body bag."

"Think positive, Mel. I know I'm gonna see you soon. Nothing's gonna happen to me or to you. We're supermen, invulnerable." I watched him move off, stumble in a puddle, then disappear into the dismal night.

I went straight to my bunk, took off my wet clothes and hung them on the support bars for my mosquito net. I wanted to lay down, relax, process the first day's events. But thoughts of Blanche interfered. Did she have the baby yet? I closed my eyes and whispered, "Please, God, help Blanche deliver our baby safely. And let me live to see him."

Chapter 15

After breakfast and chores, we formed up for an equipment check. The men were hopped up, full of bravado. "I'm gonna get me a confirmed kill." "I'm goint to inscribe my name on the bullet, so I can prove I killed one." "Well I'd like to hang one by his fuckin' Cong nuts."

I too wanted revenge but it didn't seem as personal for me. It didn't have to be me that took it. I didn't need to know that I had killed. Just that the enemy, the people who killed our friends, were dead.

After inspection, we marched to the road just outside the company and boarded waiting trucks. We crossed the line of departure forward of Ann Margaret on time. We were now in enemy territory and everyone was on high alert.

The trucks sped down dusty roads, past rice paddies, and along neatly arranged laid out rubber plantations. Miles from Margaret, the trucks halted. We disembarked quickly into a line of fire teams.

"Let's get some distance between you guys! One round'll kill you all!" the platoon leader yelled. "Get down, soldier! You think you're someone special?"

After everyone was on the ground, we slowly moved off, through a long, water-filled rice paddy. In a few minutes I was soaked with sweat. Never had I been so hot. My bulletproof vest was like a coiled heater, and heavy. We trudged forward, through muddy trenches, over mounds, hills, and toward a distant, heavily vegetated area.

The countryside was quiet except for a stray water buffalo here and there and a few chickens and pigs rooting about. We encountered a small village and surrounded it from a distance before entering. We met no resistance, and we found only old men, women, and children who regarded us with direct, passive stares.

"Gonna be a long hot one," someone yelled from the front.

I took a big swig from my canteen.

"Better ration that water!" Sergeant Traver yelled back at me. "Could be awhile before we get any more!"

We left the rice paddies and open daylight to enter a dense, dark jungle with a solid green canopy and a forest floor of flowering vegetation, so thick we often had to use a machete to clear a path.

"Keep a little distance between you the next guy," Traver instructed. "But maintain visual contact. This is a perfect place for snipers. No talking! Scan the area well, from top to bottom and left to right. Weapons at the port arms position. Let's go."

As we probed through the thick understory, I realized that the few birds we saw were silent, as if the forest was listening to us, instead of the other way around. There were plenty of bugs, mostly flies, and lots of mosquitoes.

I kept sweeping the area with my eyes from the ground to the tree tops, hoping to spot a sniper before he spotted us. I made sure to place my feet in the same spot as the guy in front of me. We assumed the area was mined, and there were the punji pits—deep holes, camouflaged by forest debris, with sharp pointed bamboo stakes stuck in the bottom, pointed ends up. The VC would smear feces on the points so that even if the puncture wounds didn't kill you, the hepatitis or God-knew-what-else might.

"Step light and keep a sharp look for 'Charlie.'" I repeated the instructions we'd received, over and over. We approached a large tree covered with red ants that had neatly stripped it of every scrap of foliage. A couple of ants dropped onto my sweating chest as I gazed up. One nearly landed in my mouth. Several dropped down my back. A few sharps stings instantly propelled me off to the side of the path. I laid my rifle down, unsnapped my harness, dropped my pack, unbuttoned my shirt, and wiped away the stinging pests. Fast as I could, I redressed, got back into my equipment, and caught up with my squad.

"Punji pits ahead!" yelled a voice from the front.

"There's one over there!" the soldier in front of me called out.

The spiked pits were just as I visualized, except one had at least a hundred snakes in it, tangled like a ball of loose shoe laces. Big black and yellow ones were wrapped around stakes, but not for long. We dropped grenades and claymore mines in them, so those low crawlers died hungry. Our movement slowed almost to a snail's pace. The point squad was very careful not to lead us into a mine field or a pit. We made it through day one without any contact or incident.

2

The next day was our turn on the point. I was glad to be a sergeant because a noncommissioned officer was not expected to precede his men. He was where he best controlled them, and that was somewhere other than in the lead position.

We stopped inside a small abandoned village to eat lunch. They must have known we were coming. The only beings left were two water buffalos, some pigs, and a few chickens scratching in the leaf litter. After the break, we continued north for five hours, until we reached an open area of scattered trees, below a large hill. From there we saw a river below and a smaller, less vegetated hill farther on. The small river meandered north to our left, and on the other side were a few mud hooches.

We continued the grunt across the rice paddies over two hills, until we reached the quiet stream and halted. The company commander sent a squad to search for a bridge or a place where the stream narrowed, but they had no luck. So we sat along the river for an hour or so more, biding our time, waiting for word from higher up to solve the problem of getting all of us to the other side.

"Looks like we're gonna be here awhile," Traver said quietly, looking at a drawing of a woman's head he made on the ground with a little piece of weather beaten bamboo. "You know how long it takes the army to make a decision. We'll probably sit here the rest of the fuckin' war trying to figure out how to get over there." He pointed, moving his hand like a bridge crossing the water. "Now, if I was running this show—"

"Oh, boy," Sergeant Lantz interrupted, "If he was

running this show, the Army would go to hell."

"Listen, Lantz. If I was running this show, I'd have you, with your red head, take your squad and check out the stream. You all could walk, swim, or whatever across. Just lay a safe trail for the rest of us."

"Sergeant Jade," Captain North summoned. The war-hardened veteran quickly trotted ahead. When Jade returned, he told Lantz to take his squad to the other side.

Traver looked across at me with a smirk, then yelled to Lantz, "Make sure that red head is well covered! I wouldn't want Cong to use it for target practice!"

Lantz's squad moved up to point and reluctantly stepped into the river with rifles above their heads. About halfway across, in water up to their chests, a couple of men stopped. "It's really nice and cool in here!" one yelled. "The water feels good!" Another yelled, "There must be a lot of fish in here! I feel 'em bumpin' up against my legs!"

"I feel 'em too!" one of the others said.

"Brummell, you and your men can start across," Traver ordered.

The water did feel great. The strong undercurrent made walking difficult, but we moved quickly. By the time we got half way across, Sergeant Lantz's group was ashore.

"Help!" One of Lantz's men was sitting on the bank, wildly kicking his legs.

"Leeches in the water!" yelled another.

"Get 'em off me!" the kicking one yelled.

We picked up speed and as soon as we got ashore, inspected for leeches. I didn't have any of those suckers attached to me but Lilly, from the weapons platoon, had several stuck to him. One was glued to his skinny butt. Lilly rolled on the ground kicking and screaming. "Jesus Christ! Do something! Gitum offa me!"

Salsado, of Philippine descent and a member of Lilly's squad, calmly asked, "Anyone got a lighter? Put fire to the leech."

Lantz searched his water-filled pockets and produced a butane lighter. He managed to get it working and pointed the flame toward a leech until it turned Lilly loose. One at a time Lantz tortured each leech until all of them dropped to the ground. Our squad rushed past Lantz's squad and formed a temporary defensive position.

Just as Sgt. Caballo's squad was getting out of the water, a shot rang out. One of Caballo's men splashed face down. The green water turned a lumpy red. Everyone crawled for cover. Several more shots whizzed overhead.

"Anyone see where the shots came from?" Sgt. Jade called out.

"Left of that hooch over there!" Traver shouted.

The sniper accommodated us by firing a few more rounds, enabling us to get a fix on his position.

"Sergeant Traver! Brummell!" Jade shouted. "Get your people together! Brummell, your men lay down a base of fire. Traver, your men assault! Go leaps and bounds until you flush that bastard out of there!"

My team and I crawled on line with Traver's men. I was scared sick. Sweat ran into my eyes. My legs wobbled and my heart was racing, but I thought about all the training that prepared me for this moment, hoping it was going to save my life. Those aren't blanks he's shooting. Those are real bullets. I could get killed. That sniper might not like the way I run or look, so he may fix his sights on me.

"Let's go," Traver yelled.

I began squeezing off rounds, laying down a base of fire—covering fire—while Traver and his men ran in the direction of the shooting. Thirty meters on, his team took cover behind some paddy dikes. Then it was our turn to move under cover of their fire.

"Come on, fellows! Let's get up there!" I screamed above all the shooting. We took off, running low at top speed, while Traver's men covered. The sniper fire intensified. Bullets hit all around us but we kept moving, like John Wayne charging a hill in a World War II movie.

Traver yelled, "Brummell! Next move, fan your men a little to the right! We're gettin' closer! Lay down a heavier base of fire!"

We were getting winded, and closer to the enemy rifle, so we sprinted shorter distances. I was exhausted and hot but I couldn't slow down. I had to keep moving. I was a leader. I had to make it to the objective, even if no one else did. We darted out again across a muddy rice paddy, getting closer to the sniper. The objective became clear—the sniper was in a giant ant hill. Again and again, our squads leapfrogged forward.

"I didn't hear any firing the last couple times we moved!" Shark said, his head so close to the ground that his breath kicked up dust.

"We're almost in grenade range!" I yelled. "Shark, Sieber, toss a couple of grenades on that ant hill! Soon as they explode, the rest of us'll assault! Let's go!"

Shark and Siebert tossed grenades where the firing came from and the explosion propelled everyone up and on line for the assault.

We swept up on the anthill. No rifle fire. The sniper had vanished.

I got down on my knees for a closer look—the ant hill had a hole dug in the back, an opening large enough for a VC rifleman to kneel and take aim. The small cavity had a tunnel dug through the back wall and into the ground. No telling where the tunnel ended.

"Okay, keep it spread out, you guys! Brummell, seal off that hole. The rest of you keep moving!" ordered Jade.

As soon as the platoons were a safe distance away, I tossed a hand grenade into the hole, ran, and dropped to the ground. After the explosion, I went back to inspect. I wasn't satisfied so I threw another one in, then ran to catch the others. We continued the march across the rice paddy and into another dense area.

Finally, just before sunset, A Company—hot, sweaty, stinking and tired—halted. Words I learned to hate: "Dig in for the night." We broke into two-man positions.

Shark and I started digging out a square large enough for both of us to assume a prone position below ground level.

"I hate the idea of digging foxholes every night," I told Shark.

"Might as well get comfortable," Shark said, yawning as he lay down. I pulled off my boots, and massaged my feet. It was a pleasure to sit. We had covered a lot of

Vietnam that day.

"I'll take the first watch, Shark. You get some sleep."

The night passed quietly, no rain or sniper fire. But the mosquitoes feasted. At dawn, two helicopter gun ships arrived, dropped off fresh water, and skipped back into the air. One man from each position went to the drop-off point while the other maintained the watch. We filled our canteens and our steel helmets for shaving and washing up.

The company took turns, half at a time, cleaning their bodies and weapons. Some stood, some sat, some squatted, working fast because we were to leave soon. Some of the careless were visiting others, meters away from their weapons and positions.

Suddenly, a burst of rounds ripped through the woods. Everyone immediately dropped and scrambled for cover. Those whose weapons were disassembled for cleaning broke reassembly records. I grabbed my rifle and plunged into my shallow foxhole. I looked around and saw Price, who had been cleaning his rifle on a stump a couple of positions away, writhing on the ground. He was hit, lying on his side in the bush, trying to crawl to his rifle parts. We blasted hundreds of bullets and grenades in the direction of the sniper fire.

"Come out of the woods, you sons of bitches!" Shark shouted, slamming a fresh clip in his rifle.

"Somebody help Price!" I yelled. "He looks like he's in bad shape!" I fired at the invisible enemy.

Once again, none of us got so much as a glimpse of the shooter. A couple of squads swept through the woods but the only thing they found were some odd-looking shell casings.

It was a demoralizing way to start the day. Everyone wanted a kill, hungry for a dead Cong.

A medic ran past me, face low, toward Price, who was moving in slow motion. Articulate Andy was having trouble communicating with the Medevac team. The volume on his radio was loud, but I still couldn't understand the responses to his calls.

"Wish they'd get a helicopter in here quick, and get Price out."

"Yeah," Shark said. "Looks like he's in a bad way."

The company commander ran over and patted Price's shoulder while the medic injected Price's arm with a second shot of morphine.

"Prepare to move out! Prepare to assault!" the company commander yelled.

"Here we go again, Shark."

"Okay, everybody up on line!" Sergeant Jade yelled, his mouth twisted in disgust. "We're gonna form a perimeter and move about a hundred meters, so the chopper can touch down."

Anger flooded through me and I sprang up with my rifle held hip high, blasting along with the other squad members, firing bullets through the brush at an enemy that might or might not be there. We moved forward fifty meters, and by the time we settled we could hear the happy sound of a HU-1-B. It was a relief to know help was on the way for my buddy, Price.

A detail of several men was formed and, without wasting any time, started whacking a clearing for the helicopter with machetes. Someone tossed a smoke grenade to mark the makeshift helipad. The chopper circled a couple of times, then the bolted butterfly dropped, drawing sporadic sniper fire.

Medics put Price carefully on a poncho stretcher and ran him to the Medevac. A crew member rushed to the door and helped pull the litter inside. As soon as Price was secure on board, the helicopter shook for a minute, and lifted.

———•+•———

By the end of that two-week adventure, Cong had killed five of us and wounded seven, and none of us saw a damn thing. When we got back to the compound, Private Mac Ray cheered us up by presenting the platoon with an iced cooler of beer. Ray was an old soldier. He wore the Combat Infantryman's Badge with a star, which meant he had served in two prior wars. He was in Vietnam over a month, so he was entitled to yet another star.

Mac, as we called him, had over twenty-one years in the military and was only a peon, demoted all the way from sergeant first class down to private. He never said why but the old warrior's age showed. He was almost fifty, ancient for an infantryman. He was pale and wrinkled and skinny, his hair gone all gray. Why Mac was still in the Army was a mystery, but there were a lot of men who shouldn't have been there. Still, the old man wanted to see some action but the company commander wouldn't let him go out, and we all agreed. He had already paid his dues.

I had survived my first taste of combat and it

changed me. Nothing bothered me much after that. My bony cot was a feather bed, and the tent a luxury hotel room. Those big guns no longer fazed me. I was initiated and I could sleep. I began to think that if anybody could make it home in one piece, it would be me.

We attended hastily arranged ceremonies to honor our dead and wounded friends, and for medals to be awarded. But otherwise we soldiers tended to keep our minds on the business at hand. There wasn't much time for reflection, and it didn't pay very well.

Shortly after we got back, I tried my luck at poker. It wasn't my game and I lost a month's salary and the part of my check that was Blanche's allotment. I left the game in a foul mood. I wanted to try winning my money back, if I could just borrow some money for a stake.

"Brummell! Over here!" Sergeant Jade yelled, walking toward Captain North's tent.

A formation of helicopter gun ships chattered past overhead, so I couldn't hear everything he was saying. He yelled again, "Go down on the bunker line and relieve Sergeant Lantz. He's waiting."

"Yes, Sergeant. Right away." But I had to get at least Blanche's allotment back. I looked for Big Green, finding him in the shade of a tent eating a jumbo, melting chocolate bar. I borrowed a few dollars and returned to the game. Before I realized it, two hours had passed. I had just three dollars left and had to get going to the bunker line. I was depressed. I wanted to stay, but I grabbed my gear and fled the tent.

As soon as I was out of the hot canvas, the first person I saw was the last person I wanted to see, Sergeant Jade.

"Brummell, goddammit! You're supposed to have relieved Lantz! He's been waiting over an hour! Come over here." The tone of his voiced changed and he had a strangely crooked grin. He headed for the back of a tent, looked around, turning his head quickly from side to side. Then he lifted his voice just a little.

"Listen, nigger boy. I made you sergeant." He stuck his index finger an inch from my nose. "And I can take it away. If you aren't careful, I'll put your black ass forward of Ann Margaret alone as an observation post. You'll be a cinch to get knocked off. Now get your fuckin' ass down on that bunker line. Do you hear me? I mean now."

"Yes, Sergeant!" I turned and double-timed to Ann Margaret.

Jade's racist remark ran off me like water off a duck's back. I respected him and I had to take what was dished out and deal with it. Besides, remarks like his—in the context of battle and shared purpose—were probably more affectionate, however clumsy, than racist. He wanted me to succeed and in a way he was reminding me I had a higher standard to meet. I vowed to never let him down again.

I felt terrible, especially about losing all that money. We were only paid once a month, less than three hundred dollars, and Blanche's allotment was one hundred and fifty. I borrowed fifty bucks from a friend and sent it home with a letter telling her what happened and apologizing.

A week later, we got word we were going on another mission, a battalion-sized movement. Members of the

South Vietnamese Special Forces were to participate in the maneuvers. The little soldiers began showing up in our mess tent, so we knew something big was about to happen. The night before our departure, the ten South Vietnamese troops were separated and assigned to the Company's five platoons.

Next morning, after an early wake-up and quick inspection, we were off. We marched down dusty roads to the airfield a mile away and boarded large banana-shaped helicopters. The ride lasted longer than I expected. Wherever we were going, it was far from base camp. I was one of the lucky ones. I was near an open door and had a good view of the rugged land. Wouldn't you know it? Traver was near the door opposite me. I couldn't hear what he was saying, but I read his lips, "Rough-looking terrain!"

I was thinking the same thing. I hoped they didn't put us out in any place looking like that. The egg beaters finally slowed over a large rice paddy, descended, made a couple of wide swings over the surrounding trees, and touched down in a tactical formation, propellers whirling impatiently. The troops jumped and scattered to the paddy's edge. When the helicopters had emptied, their engines roared back to full power and cleared the area. We organized quickly and started to move.

The First Platoon spearheaded a search and destroy mission. Our platoon followed. Twenty minutes into the brush, the jungle quiet was broken by the crackle of automatic rifle fire spraying all around us, and grenade explosions. I hit the dirt and scrambled for cover, but I was caught in a small clearing.

The nearest cover was a bush. I hugged it as tightly as I could, even though it was nearly dead and the size of a large pencil. My nails dug into the dirt. I was in a bad spot. I scanned the area, searching for my men. All of them were trembling but safe, with the exception of Pfc. Thacel. With his usual bent profile and expression of bewilderment, he wandered around as if he were wearing a suit of armor, his rifle held slack in his hands.

"Thacel!" I yelled," Get down! You're gonna get it! Find cover!" But he wandered up and over a knoll, and out of sight as bullets smashed the ground all around him. He seemed to be in a trance.

"Medic, Medic!" someone shouted. "Get a medic up here. Lloyd and Derek are hit." I crawled in the direction of the downed two, toward a small mound of dirt. Two medics ran fast and low, toward the unlucky ones, pulling first-aid packages from their pouches as they fled. Someone pulled Lloyd over a hill and out of sight of the enemy.

Derek was out of it, no doubt dead. Blood and white tissue spewed from a gaping hole between his eyes and the back of his head. His last sad expression is what I will always remember. Also his bruised face, his lips formed as if he was saying something beginning with an "o." Derek's platoon sergeant examined him and slowly pulled the poncho over his head.

The rest of the weapons platoon hurriedly set up their mortars while the rifle platoons prepared to move forward. But Cong had us pinned in an area inconvenient for an offensive move. We had to climb over a hill. Cong could have picked us off like ducks in a shooting gallery.

Jade, sweating like he'd just gotten out of a sauna with his clothes on, pounded the ground with his fist. "If they'd only let up! If they did, maybe we could move back around and attack the flanks!"

Bullets and grenades continued pouring our way. "We've got to sit tight for awhile!" Jade yelled.

Dirt stung my cheeks as rounds hit near my face, penetrating the earth just beside my head. I scraped the front edge of my steel pot into the dirt, keeping my face close to the ground. An unexploded rifle grenade dropped and rolled near my left foot. For seconds all I could do was stare in frozen terror at the Chinese markings. Then I leaped, quickly grabbed it, and threw the grenade as far as I could. It was a dud.

Another grenade dropped almost into Specialist Fourth Class Dragavitz's pocket and exploded. It blasted the rifle out of the big Polish-American's hand, opened his pant leg up the seam, and blew his backpack completely apart. Miraculously, he was unscratched. I pinched myself hard to see if I was dreaming. If I was, it was time to wake up.

Another grenade exploded near Shark. He dropped his rifle, cupped his hand in front of his face, and yelled, "God DAMN!" A chunk of Shark's left eye fell to the ground and lay there, staring at me.

"Let's get the hell out of here," Jade yelled. "Move back! Move it back!"

We crawled back for a while and, as soon as we could, got to our feet. Shark refused help, crawling until he was able to slowly stand. He staggered some but still didn't seek aid. He continued pressing his first aid bandage over the wound. As soon as we were a safe distance back, a medic ran to him, gave him a shot of Morphine and tied a fresh bandage around his head. Then he disappeared, to call for a helicopter.

Our squad retreated further and assembled in a small clearing away from the enemy's defensive position. I went for cover, toward an old tree stump. The enemy barrage diminished, and only a few grenades found their way into the area. Just as I began to unwind, Williams and Kolby from the Third Platoon approached my position, carrying a stretcher.

My heart fell. Another one! Whoever it was, he was dead—a poncho covered his face. Who was it this time? Will it be me next?

The grim-faced stretcher-bearers grew closer with the corpse. A slim, white hairy arm dangled from beneath the poncho. On the wrist was a big fancy watch, the one I'd bet on with Articulate Andy. I was paralyzed. I had won the watch. Tears flooded from my eyes. "It's Andy, isn't it?"

"Yeah," Kolby said. "He got it through the back of his head. An ant hole sniper. Fuckin' Cong crawled out and shot him with a thirty caliber. Last thing he said was, 'I'll be alright.'"

Williams was crying. "Sergeant Bosi got it too!" Bosi was the Hawaiian who'd left seven kids on the dock in Pearl. Jesus!

"What happened to that fuckin' Cong?" a voice yelled from the other side of the woods.

"We fixed his ass! We tried to killed him twice!" Williams said, as they laid Andy under a tree.

"Sergeant Traver! Brummell!" Jade yelled. He

wasted no time telling us Thacel was missing. We had to go back and look for him. I was horrified. Shock zapped me like lightning. Why me and Traver?

As if he had read my mind, Jade said, "You and Traver are some of my best men. It's a dangerous mission but somebody's got to do it. Traver, you're in charge. Pick whatever men you want. Good luck."

After I recovered from a stunned state of immobility, I left with Traver to assemble our men. Traver picked ten men from the platoon and twelve of us left, all trembling, back into the bush, looking for Thacel. We penetrated deeper than we had before. A few minutes later we stopped. I got into a prone position and peeked around the side of a heavily vegetated hill. Thacel was laying in a clearing. My buddy from the *Walker*. It was obvious he was dead and just as obvious that the Cong had dragged him there as bait, knowing we would be back to rescue our ammo bearer.

Siebert, our point man, made a quick step toward the edge of the hill. An enemy machine gun cut loose. Siebert was hit, several rounds ripping through his left arm. The arm lifted up, fell back down, dangling by a little bit of muscle. He dropped hard to the ground twisting to his good side. I grabbed Siebert's foot and pulled him back. A medic and someone else from the rear came forward with a poncho litter and quickly carried him back to the rear.

Parker, the new point man, had a grappling hook. He threw it out and tried to grab Thacel, but Parker only made himself vulnerable to the machine gun fire. Bullets and grenades came at us from every where.

"This shit's too sticky!" Traver yelled.

"We can't get Thacel," I said. "He's dead anyway! Pull back that grappling hook so we can get the hell out of here!"

As soon as the hook was retrieved, we made an about face and sprinted away from the enemy's nest.

"I'm sure Thacel's dead," Traver reported to Jade.

Jade left to report to Captain North, and returned with a sour look on his face. "Looks like we're gonna have to come back another day for Thacel. We've been ordered to move out."

We moved east, around the enemy's defensive position, then probed north, into more Cong-infested territory. The enemy again cut us up, and we again pulled back. When the Cong weren't harassing us, we had to watch for friendly fire. Navy jets providing air support dropped a bomb so close to us that shrapnel hit some of our own men.

Before the mission was over, we'd lost seven men with four more wounded. Company trucks picked us up at the rendezvous point. I rode back to base camp in a deep funk.

Sergeant Bosi's seven children and wife were going to be a sad family. Articulate Andy didn't have a chance. Thacel, still laying there. Was he dead? All great guys. What a waste. Shark and Siebert. Would they survive? Would I?

Chapter 16

A month dragged by and we found ourselves in more and more skirmishes. On our next big mission, we captured ten Congs and buried twelve in the field. One day we discovered tunnels leading to large cavities stocked with bags of rice, hundreds of bottles of cocaine, heroin, and other narcotics. We sent in Tunnel Rats, which were South Vietnamese special forces trained to explore tunnels because the Americans were too large to enter the cramped spaces. After the tunnel rats pulled the supplies from the cache, we grenaded the tunnels, and continued sweeping forward.

Nearly two hours after that big discovery, we drew a hail of rifle fire from an isolated village ahead of us. We assaulted the huts, but by the time we got into the small village, the fighting population had fled into the woods. Only children, old men and women remained.

While the Third Platoon rounded up the residents, we continued forward, outside the village's perimeter, and started digging in for the night. Soon after I settled my men, I went over to Traver's position.

"Did you see all those chickens, ducks, and hogs running loose back there?"

"I sure did."

"One of those birds sure would taste better than

C-rations. Let's catch a couple. We could cook and have a feast before nightfall."

"Consider it done, Brum," Traver agreed. "Let's get started."

We took off our packs, laid them on the ground, slung our rifles across our shoulders and walked back to the village. Two brown hens, larger than most of the others, strutted around near a muddy water hole. We separated the proud-stepping two from the rest of the flock, and the chase was on. Traver ducked around a hut in hot pursuit of one feathered runner.

I chased my fat fowl down a hill, around several huts, and into a clearing. The hen stopped. Desperately, I dived to catch her, but I missed. She screamed bloody murder, flopped up, fell back down, and ran like crazy away from my clutching fingers, leaving only a few feathers behind. Recovering fast, I continued the pursuit. My frightened, future feast led me, frustrated, to a clump of skinny trees and into a briar patch, where she finally trapped herself.

The hen frantically flapped her wings while I calmly reached down, pulled her legs out from under her, and ran back to show Traver my catch.

Traver was already plucking his chicken. He speared his hen in the neck with a long, sharpened bamboo stick. "West Virginians are great white hunters," Traver said with his half grin.

I stepped on the head of my chicken and twisted its body away, and watched her flop to death. I plucked and gutted my catch, dug a hole for the fire and made a cooking rack out of two parallel rifle rods. Before long, the smell of our roasting chickens permeated the defensive positions.

Big Green was the first to arrive.

"That chicken shore smells good. Looks good too," he said, rubbing his chin.

"We're trying to get it ready before dark so we can put the flames out," Traver said. "I should have known you would be the first to bring your big ass over."

"As soon as it's done, I want some of that bird," Green said, licking his chapped lips.

"Five dollars just for you," I said.

Green reached in his pocket, pulled out a big paper knot, and shook it at me. "No sweat. I don't have nothing else to spend this money on. I may not be living tomorrow."

While the chickens roasted, other hungry soldiers came by to place orders. Chicken parts grew in demand, so we increased the price, doubling it to ten dollars and then to fifteen dollars apiece. We sold out of everything but four pieces—two breasts, a drumstick, and a wing. While Traver and I ate, I counted and divided a hundred and five dollars. The chicken was okay too. Not as good as Grandma's, but a treat in the field.

We were finishing up our banquet when Jade showed up.

"Traver, you and Brummell are taking out an ambush patrol tonight. Get your gear together, select your men, and prepare to move out in twenty minutes. As soon as you're ready, come over to where the Captain is."

We smeared our faces and hands with ashes from the cooking fire, in my case to take the shine off my dark skin, and hustled over to Captain North. He and

Jade were poring over a map with a compass. We were to set up an ambush at a road junction marked on the Captain's map. Intelligence reported the area was a major enemy supply route. If contact was made with Cong, we were to destroy and search for important documents.

The four of us went over the route three more times, to make sure Traver and I had directions to the ambush site memorized. Before we left to collect our men, Captain North told us the directions again. We took off just as the sun dropped below the trees. We walked for two hours, near a narrow road, until we were miles away from the others. We stopped for a break in a small area of big trees and thick brush, keeping the highway in sight.

Traver made a radio check with base camp, then crawled under a poncho while I lit a match so we could check the map.

"Okay," I said, snapping my compass shut. "Let's go. Shouldn't take more than another hour to get there."

We took off again through the eerie darkness, hardly able to see the man in front of us, except for the little white piece of tape we placed on the backs of our helmets. The point man was so far in front of me, I could hardly see the white dot. I hustled closer to the dot as my eyes readjusted to night vision, carefully following him through the bush.

Dark clouds blew in, obscuring the quarter moon. It started to rain. First a little, then a little more, and then a major downpour. But here it was welcome. Rain made it difficult for Cong to see or hear our movements. As long as I kept my illuminated-dial compass on course, we were all right.

It took two hours to reach the ambush site, but it was no good. The terrain was too level and too naked. We would have been too easily detected. We moved a hundred meters down the road.

"Brummell, take your team and set up on the other side, on that knoll over there," Traver said, pointing to the other side of the road. "Fifty percent security. Plant a claymore at each end of the ambush site. When Cong gets in the middle, let 'em have it. That'll also be the signal for the rest of us to start shooting. Since you're closer to the road, you search the dead bodies." I could see his white teeth grinning. "Listen to your Walkie Talkie. I'll let you know when to stop shooting."

My team and I slid down a muddy hill, and crossed the road. We set two claymores along the road facing each other fifty meters apart, with one firing device. The rest of us climbed up the little hill. I assigned each man a position and pointed out sectors of overlapping fire, directed toward the road below.

"I'll wait until most of them little suckers get inside my killing zone and I'll squeeze the trigger," I told the four others. "When you hear the big bang, I want everybody to cut loose, the other claymore, too. Rifles on automatic. All of us will serve as search team. All of us quickly search the stiffs for documents. Then we'll meet Alpha team at the rendezvous point, the old big tree I showed you. We'll force-march back to the Company. Make sure everyone stays close together. Lopas, Haynes, get some sleep, while we watch."

The rain got worse, beating the soil like a butcher's

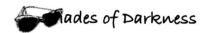

mallet. Somehow I drifted off.

"Sarge! Sarge! Wake up." I was instantly alert. Lopas was shaking my right arm. "Somebody's coming down the road," he hissed.

I jumped from under my wet poncho and crawled through the mud, alerting the others. "Get on your weapons. We got company."

Emerging like specters out of the darkness, three men wearing dark pajamas with rifles strapped across their shoulders approached, riding bicycles in a column, headed in our direction. As soon as the three rode within the killing zone, I got ready to squeeze the trigger.

My Walkie Talkie crackled. "Hold your fire!" Traver's voice whispered. "Don't wanna reveal our position over those three. Maybe more'll come later."

We waited the rest of the night, but nothing happened. The next morning we met at the rendezvous point and moved back through the woods a different way than we had come. While we hurried, Traver radioed headquarters, to warn our defensive positions that we were coming.

I prayed they got the word to everyone. As we approached, the outpost yelled, "Halt! Who goes there?"

"A Company patrol," Traver shouted back.

The outpost yelled, "Where is the ship going?"

Traver said, "To the lighthouse." That was the password and we safely re-entered the friendly zone. Traver reported to the company commander while I took the men back to their positions.

Base camp looked better than ever. Tents looked

like palaces, and our cooks felt like mothers. I first cleaned and oiled my rifle, and then showered. At lunch, Traver and I grabbed our mess kits and showed up early for the first hot meal I'd had in a long time. I was third in line before Traver got there.

A cook's helper scooped a big spoon of stewed tomatoes and dropped them on my mess kit. I happened to notice the cans the tomatoes had come out of and burst out laughing—Donaldson's Brand Tomatoes! Canned goods from the very factory I had worked in, back in Federalsburg! I pointed to the 303-size tins.

"Traver, I might have packed or labeled those cans. I used to do dumb shit when I worked at Donaldson's. Like mislabel a whole palette of corn with tomato labels instead."

I told Traver about sloshing through tomatoes on the floor and being ordered by the owner to shovel it all into the cans.

"If you think that's gross, I have something else to lay on you. The peelers wore large rubber aprons, but they couldn't help getting drenched because of all the steam and squirting juices. Sometimes the peelers, mostly women, didn't want to leave their positions, especially when the tomatoes were large. I heard tell of women pissing on themselves at their work stations 'cause no one could tell the difference. Here, you can have my stewed tomatoes!"

Traver made a face. "I don't think I'll ever eat canned tomatoes again!"

For the next few days we sandbagged. Then A Company began preparing for another operation. I could tell it was going to be big—all support units were to participate. As usual, the infantry had to blaze the trail. From our staging area, we took off for a destination known only to the top brass and God.

The afternoon of the second day out, all hell broke loose. The enemy directed massive firing on us. The company commander was near the front with the Third Platoon. He ordered everyone to take cover in a large trench.

The Third Platoon was the first to enter the trench. We followed but before everyone filed in, the mortar platoon—still above ground—found itself in trouble and suffered casualties. Cong intensified the assault. They bombarded us with everything: rifle grenades, machine-gun fire, mortars, and rocket launchers.

Specialist Nelson, point man for point platoon, squeezed through coming from the front, crying, holding his bloody left shoulder.

Night fell. The mortar crew quickly put their tubes together. "Ready! Fire!" a gunner yelled.

The round landed so close that the concussion knocked me back onto the wall of the trench. Screams of pain and frustration filled the air. Everyone started yelling, "Tell the mortar platoon to cease fire!"

"Cease fire! Cease fire!"

But before the word got back to the mortar crew, another round came whistling through the air. Two of our mortar rounds had fallen on top of the point platoon, sending more casualties with multiple injuries fleeing back through the trench.

"God damn it!" someone yelled. "You'd think we have enough problems already. Now here comes the rain!"

Without any warning, like pulling the plug on a tub of water, the rain pounded down and so did enemy fire. Helpless frightened minutes passed, and the trench was beginning to turn into a small blood-stained stream.

"Private Percell and two others are dead!" one of the injured men said, wading past in ankle high mud. "We can't get to their bodies!"

We waited for C company to assault Charlie's flanks. As soon as they did, and got control, we were ordered out of the trench trap. "VC on the run!" Sergeant Jade yelled. "Traver, take some men and bring those three bodies over there to the rear!"

Six of us moved fast as we could over the wall of the trench through the darkness, to cut six tree limbs into three litters. We moved low and slow back to the trench and pulled the corpses into the trench with us. Haynes and I placed Percell's body on our improvised poncho carrier, but my dead friend kept falling off, face down into the mud. Each time we returned his body to the stretcher, it seemed as if he had gained weight.

His lifeless eyes were open, wide with amazement. I tried not to look at his face, struggling to carry our fallen friend through the rain, mud, and wet bushes. All the while, I heard groans and grunts, as if Percell was still trying to communicate. It was the air in his lungs escaping with each jounce.

"Put the bodies over there," Captain North said, pointing to a space beneath four trees, beside another litter. "Then get some troops back there and make a clearing for the chopper. It should be here soon." We set Percell down, making sure he wouldn't roll off the litter.

Just as Haynes and I turned to leave, the man on the other litter yelled, horrified, "Ahh! Get him away, get him away from me!" I recognized the voice—Sergeant Humble of the weapons platoon, a Black GI from Athens, Georgia.

"What's wrong? Where'd you get hit?" I turned toward him.

"No," he moaned, "I slipped and hurt my back and I can't walk."

"Lucky you. You'll probably get to go home."

"Is he dead? Get 'em the fuck away from me!"

I couldn't blame him. We moved Percell and the other corpse a short distance away.

We hacked out a clearing and two helicopters approached in the rain. Sporadic enemy rifle fire broke out. One chopper managed to land, while the other circled, hovered, and attacked every flash of rifle fire. In minutes, both helicopters whirled back out of sight with the dead and wounded.

The next morning, we swept a path north by northwest and found more casualties from scattered mines and booby traps.

"Step light," I reminded myself. "You've seen guys lose their limbs and their lives today. Please, God," I begged, "don't let me die. Lead me in the right direction."

"Incoming!" someone yelled.

Mortar rounds dropped all around me, followed by automatic rifle fire. Bullets ripped the ground all around. The enemy was in a nearby hamlet, in a sparsely vegetated area to our left front.

We organized into an inverted "V" formation and launched an assault. The Second and Third Platoons moved in from the flanks while the weapons platoon pounded with the heavy stuff. We soon over-ran the village, searched the grass huts, but found only cooking gear, clothing, and a network of tunnels. From a nearby hooch, a voice screamed, "There's someone in there!"

Sergeant Ketchum from one of the other platoons yelled, "Don't let him get away!" Ketchum finished off a partial clip into the hut's door and walls, then expertly slammed in another clip and emptied it as well.

"Ketchum, cease fire!" Captain North yelled.

Ketchum lowered his rifle, grinning.

When the noise subsided, from the hut came the cry of an infant, followed by a woman's voice pleading in Vietnamese. We rushed the door. A frail, half-starved woman came out limping, dragging her left leg, weeping, holding a tiny baby soaked with blood. The infant was hardly breathing. It had been shot several times.

A younger woman emerged, took the baby from the older woman, then dropped to her knees, and held the infant, as if offering it to us. Ketchum, stunned, rushed to take the baby. Tears streamed down his cheeks.

"Oh, fuck me, fuck me!" He looked around frantically. Medic, medic!" he yelled, taking the baby and pulling it close to his chest. "Don't just fuckin' stand there. DO something!" Tears ran down into his thick black-mustache. He spotted an approaching medic and ran to him, placing the baby at the medic's feet and dropping to his knees, sobbing.

A few minutes later, a dust-off chopper landed and rushed the barely living baby and both women away.

After we searched all of the huts, we plunged into the woods like bloodhounds on a fresh scent. How I wished I was back at base camp that day! I even thought of shooting off one of my little toes, but I was too much of a coward.

After searching and destroying a third hamlet, we stopped. I found a shade tree off to one side of the road and flopped under it. I rummaged in my ammo pouch and retrieved the photograph of my son Blanche had sent me, admiring his tiny profile for the hundredth time that week. I pulled out a roll of assorted Lifesavers and stuffed it into my fatigue shirt pocket.

"Wait a minute Bro. Give up some of those Lifesavers!" Traver crawled up beside me. I broke off a quarter of the roll and handed it to him.

Lopas was re-reading a letter from his brother. "Hey, my younger brother's over here. Two Lopases in Vietnam. Those Cong are going to catch hell with the two of us!"

"Sergeant Traver," Jade yelled, "You guys spread out over there! What are you two, lovers? Come here, Traver!"

Traver and Jade talked. I threw an orange Lifesaver into my mouth and leaned back, easing the weight of my back pack off my shoulders. Soon Traver came running back on his short legs, dripping sweat.

"Brummell, come on! Let's go! Mines in the area! Grab your men. We're going to the rear to pull security on a 'dozer. It's going to run over the mines and clear a path so we'll make better time and get to the night

George Brumm

sight sooner. Come on!"

I sprang to my tired, sore feet. We followed the long, narrow, dusty road back to where the support units were bringing up the rear. The engineers had gotten the word we were coming—a bulldozer stood idling.

"You from Alpha Company?" the driver asked.

The name tag read Brady, Specialist Fifth Class. The tanned, black-haired GI sat on the machine like a king, relaxed like it was peacetime, scratching and pulling at his balls.

"Yep," I said.

"Well, I'm your man. Ready when you are," Brady said, putting his helmet back on his head.

"We've been walking a long time," said Traver. "We're gonna ride with you for awhile."

"That's alright with me, Sarge."

Ten of us crowded on the huge earth-mover and Brady slammed the 'dozer into gear and built up speed, tracking down the road at a good clip.

"I'll let you know when to let us off," I shouted at Brady over the diesel roar. "Wouldn't want the company commander to see us bunched up like this."

A short way up the road, we drew some enemy rifle fire, so all of us quickly "unassed" ourselves from the 'dozer. Traver ordered Alpha and Bravo teams to each side and we proceeded cautiously down the road. Everyone up ahead had taken cover, firing to their fronts. We kept moving and Traver trotted low ahead to report to Captain North and Jade.

I halted the 'dozer and men, and left to join Traver and the Captain. The engine stopped as I passed. The big blade dropped slowly with a hydraulic wheeze.

Captain North approached, stepping fast in my direction. "Take the men back to your platoon and prepare to move out."

"Let's get moving!" I yelled. I looked right, at where the blade was just hitting the ground. A deafening concussion knocked me off my feet. I felt myself whirling and flying, floating in a strange bubble of silence for what seemed like minutes. A flash of red cut through the grey darkness. Confused, bent over, I reached the peak of my flight. Then I started my descent, just as I was hit by a second, equally forceful explosion that slammed me to the ground with a jarring impact.

For a long moment, everything was still and dark. Was I dying? Dead? The face of my grandmother popped into my head, in her red head-rag and green-flowered dress.

Then chaos erupted. Crumpled in the midst of it, I was unable to move even a finger. "My God! I've been hit. Help me! Someone!" I felt like I was yelling, but the sound seemed to be trapped inside my head. I heard screams for medics, bootsteps pounding past.

Why wasn't anyone stopping for me? They couldn't let me die like this!

"The Captain! Where's the hell's the Captain!" someone shouted nearby. "Oh shit! He's fuckin' blown away!"

It was the voice of our medic, Carson.

Then I heard Traver's voice. "Brummell! Where's Brummell?"

"I'm here, dummy!" I screamed, but no sound.

"Lopas is out of it," Carson's voice yelled. "Forget

about him. He's dead! Get some first aid pouches over here!" Hands grabbed at my clothes, ripping cloth and equipment away from my body.

"Bring me more first aid pouches, all you can find and quick! Damn!" Carson said, lowering his voice. "Who are you? Your dog tags were blown to smithereens. Lucky you had that flack vest on. There's another hole! Hey, bring all the first aid pouches you can find! This guy's shot to hell!"

"Hey, Doc, get those fuckin' red ants off him," Traver yelled! "They're crawling all over him! Who the fuck is that? Brummell?"

I must be really messed up. Traver doesn't know who I am?

Every sin I had ever committed came rushing back. "Oh, God, I know adultery and stealing are two serious evils. I am guilty of both. Please forgive me for the quarters I stole from Grandma's purse. Let me live. I'll even quit smoking, stop drinking, stop all my vices."

I heard the pop of a smoke grenade. Someone was marking a landing zone. My whole body started to ache. Numbness was followed by tingling and then the hurt intensified, like I was being stabbed. I felt the sharp jab of a needle in my arm. Morphine.

The heat of the sun seemed to be blistering my skin like a swarm of hostile bees. The smoke from the grenade seared my nostrils. The morphine began to kick in. It felt so good I sighed with pleasure.

"Hey, somebody! Get me out of this fuckin' sun and smoke!"

"That's Brummell bitching," I heard Traver say.

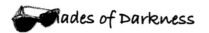

"He'll be okay!"

I felt myself being gently lifted and moved into the coolness of shade. I lay motionless in a state of euphoria, waiting for my ride out, for the moment pain-free. Soon I heard incoming propellers.

I'll be all right now, I told myself. Soon I'll be in a hospital. But I heard someone say it was not a medevac chopper but the colonel, inspecting casualties.

"Sergeant Brummell, you'll be alright." It was Colonel Smitz, the battalion commander. "You'll be stateside before you know it. A medevac is on the way."

The battalion commander left and was talking to one of my wounded comrades, but I couldn't hear well enough to tell who. Then he was gone. As the sound of Colonel Smitz's helicopter faded, I could hear a second one landing. Traver, his voice shaking, was telling Jade about the casualties. At least Traver was all right. Lopas, North, and Web were dead and several others injured.

"Hang in there, Bro," Traver said, squeezing my right hand.

I could feel him trembling. I tried to respond but I was unable to speak or move.

"You can make it, man," Traver said, sniffling. He let go as a flurry of footsteps came running and went past.

"Don't worry about those!" Jade's voice shouted. "They're dead! Get those injured out first! Get Brummell and the others out of here!"

Hands slid me onto a stretcher and I was bouncing along toward the sound of the idling thump of the rotors.

"Take care of yourself, Brummell," Traver shouted. "Hang in there!" said Big Green's voice.

A cool breeze from the chopper's wash, a thump as the stretcher hit the floor, and we lifted, wobbling, off the ground. We were hardly airborne when I heard the ping of bullets hitting the chopper's skin. The door gunner opened fire and, after a long string-like burst, I heard the gun swivel to a new target. The gunner screamed: "Fuck you, you motherfuckers!"

I could hear the pop of rifle fire and visualized the camouflaged enemy below, shooting back, trying to down the dust-off. Cong was trying to finish me off, put a round through my back or blow us out of the air. Instead, the shooting fizzled. I tried to speak but only bubbles came out. I tried to move my head but it wouldn't budge. My spit ran back into my nostrils.

"Help! Help me, somebody!" I screamed, but the sound seemed to be trapped inside me. Finally, straining my vocal cords, I managed a muffled sound.

"Clear his air passage!" a deep, foreign-sounding male voice ordered.

"You do it!" another male replied.

"Okay! Okay! I'll do it!" said the deeper voice, moving in my direction.

He yanked my head to one side, put a finger in my mouth, and pulled away something obstructing my throat, just like we were taught during first-aid training.

"Thanks," I murmured.

"You're welcome," he said, stroking the top of my head. "You'll be alright. We'll be in Saigon soon."

The chopper bounced and swooped. I felt overwhelmed, floating with the breeze of the open door, until the morphine started to lose its touch. Pain began to pinch all over. I moaned and immediately felt another injection. Then I lay still, enjoying the currents of cool air flowing over my naked, bruised body.

I tried to move my arms but they were heavy as concrete. I desperately wanted to pull the bandages from my eyes, to see how badly I'd been hit.

Chapter 17

Brummell! Sergeant! Wake up! I...I have a shot for you." A woman's voice. She was crying. Jesus, I must be a mess. She was a nurse. She'd seen plenty of wounded GIs. Was I so different? Was I going to die?

"I have a shot for you," she said again, her voice bucked up a little.

"Nurse! Nurse! Help!" A man's voice cried out nearby.

"Where's my fuckin' leg...and my fuckin' arm!" yelled another.

"Mommy...Mommy...Mommy!" another chanted in an almost child-like voice.

"Oh, God, my arm! This goddamn war."

"Help me somebody!"

"That one's dead," a man's voice said with authority. "Get somebody in here to take him out!"

"Yes, doctor," a woman's voice answered.

"Old Charlie has had his fingers up our ass today," the doctor said. "This is the fifth slab this morning."

My heart pounded. "Nurse, will I be alright? Did the Cong get my penis? Am I going home?"

"You'll be alright, Brummell," she said, her voice brightening. "And you'll be able to use that *thing* before you're able to use anything else." She made a sound between choking and laughing. "And you *will* be going home. You're scheduled to leave for the States later today."

"What about these bandages on my eyes? I can't see anything. Can't you get the doctor to take them off? And how come my arms are strapped up in...what are these, slings?"

"Your hands and arms were injured, but you'll be alright."

She gave me a shot of morphine, and I drifted off on a cloud as I heard her move away with the sound of a squeaky, rattling cart.

A little later I woke up to a man's voice. "Sergeant Brummell, I have good news for you. You were promoted to staff sergeant a couple of days ago. I have the orders right here. Congratulations, Staff Sergeant Brummell. You've served your country well."

Before I could respond, the voice continued, "Also, I have your Purple Heart." He cleared his throat and began making a formal statement I assumed he was reading off a sheet of paper. "On behalf of the Department of the Army and the President of the United States, for sustaining a wound which necessitated treatment by a medical officer and which was received in action with an enemy, resulting from a singularly meritorious act of essential service..."

Between the pain, frustration, and fear, I had lost all patience with bullshit. I'd been blown to hell. Half my Army buddies were dead or mangled. My tour of duty was done.

"'Scuse me, sir," I interrupted. "I don't give a damn

about the Purple Heart or being promoted. I just want to get the hell back to the States. I want these bandages off my eyes, too! My wife just had a baby boy and I want to go home and see them. You can take that certificate and...shove it. Sir!"

"Calm down, Sergeant. Calm down" he said gently. "I'll take the certificate and the orders and have someone put them with the rest of your belongings. Good luck, young man." His shoes scuffled and he began to repeat some of the same words to the next GI.

The nurse came by and gave me another dose of morphine. I drifted off, hoping I'd wake to find the bandages off my face. I couldn't even claw at them because my arms were immobilized in the damn slings.

A sexy women's voice was speaking as I entered a cave on an island somewhere between the Philippines and Vietnam. "Welcome, George," she purred.

The air was thick with the sweet fragrance of rose and a musty, earthy scent. The cave was dimly lit, almost hazy. I stepped closer to see who was speaking.

I couldn't believe my eyes. The woman's body was skinless. Her slender mass, nearly as tall as I, was a pulsating glob of red corpuscles. Her small blue eyes danced every time I moved. As I reluctantly drew nearer, I could feel intense heat, like a wood stove, radiating from her body.

Her bald head was slightly pointed, her nose was missing, and her mouth and chin stretched all the way down to her navel. Nevertheless, with an elaborate gesture, she opened her arms.

"Welcome to your new home on this peaceful island in the Pacific," she said. "You will never see your family again, but do not worry because you have friends here. We are all alike. The United States Government put us here because our injuries are too massive and grotesque for us to mix with normal society. We've been cast out."

I stared in stupefied silence, and then broke down. Bitter tears soaked my cheeks. I fell to my knees and pounded the earth with my fists, screaming, "Take me home! Take me home! Please take me home!"

"Brummell. Wake up! You're having a bad dream." A woman's voice interrupted my nightmare. My bed was shaking and there was the roar of aircraft engines. My head ached and my left arm was throbbing with pain.

"Where am I?"

"You're flying over the Pacific, Sergeant. You had an operation in the Philippines, and now we're headed for Brooks Medical Center in San Antonio, Texas."

"I'm in pain."

"I have a shot for you," she said, rubbing my right arm with a cool fluid. I smelled the alcohol.

"Morphine?"

"Yes."

"Thank God." I enjoyed my morphine shots and looked forward to the tranquil feeling and euphoria. I listened for a few minutes to the cries of other wounded men and the whine of the aircraft, then drifted back into blissful sleep.

The next time I remember being awake, a nurse told me I had undergone an operation on my left hand at an Air Force Base in California, and was flying over the United States. Opening my eyes and finding it still dark, I asked for another morphine fix and fell asleep again.

"What are we gonna do with *this* one?" A voice, exhausted or disgusted, or both.

"Put him in the ear, eye, nose and throat ward." A second voice, efficient. "The poor fellow's blind. We can treat all his injuries from there."

Another voice, slightly higher than the first, concerned. "He's got burns over sixty percent of his body. Why don't we treat him from the burn ward? What's your opinion, Doctor Artis?"

A deep voice with a European accent, clipped, authoritative. "Orthopedics, I think. That left hand looks as though it might have to be amputated."

Some poor soldier was in bad shape. I'd hate to be in that bed. The higher-pitched voice approached, speaking.

"Well, hello there, Sergeant Brummell! Welcome to Brooks Medical Center. You're in a bed in a hallway, in Admissions. We're trying to decide which ward would be the best one for you."

A jolt of recognition coursed through my battered body. "You mean you were talking about me just now? Am I blind? I'm not blind, am I? I could see if you'd just

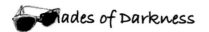

take these damn bandages off."

The voice hesitated. "You...you don't have any bandages on, Sergeant. We don't know yet how badly you're injured. We're going to try to restore your vision. Let's hope, anyway. Just stay calm and everything'll be alright. We'll have you out of here before you know it. I'm leaving now. Good luck, soldier."

The voice moved away. Rubber soles chirped on linoleum. The three voices resumed chatting, just out of range.

Blind! I couldn't be blind. How would I be able to see my son, and Blanche. What the hell had happened to me! I felt tears flooding my injured eyes, flowing down my face like the deluges of Vietnam. At least being blind hadn't robbed me of my ability to weep. My arms were bandaged up and tied down. I couldn't even scratch my nose, if I still had one. I was falling, falling, plunging into a black, bottomless abyss.

This can't be happening. Wasn't it bad enough to be sent to fucking Vietnam? The doctors must be wrong...got to be wrong! God could have picked anyone! There's supposed to be a God watching over us, right? So, after all, it turns out to be just a bunch of bullshit. What God would blind me when I've a wife and child to care for? Fucking restraints!

Chirping shoes approached. A gentle woman's voice came close. "Hello, Sergeant Brummell. I'm a nurse's aide—Miss Sanchez. I'm going to roll you over to the Orthopedic Ward."

I lay in numb silence as she maneuvered the bed down the noisy, hot hallways. I could feel the gurney bump over the threshold of a doorway.

"Dan Zuck, you have company," Miss Sanchez announced. I heard rustling, a phlegmy cough. "This is Staff Sergeant George Brummell. He'll be joining you guys in your corner."

A groan. Or was it a greeting?

Over the next day or two I learned about my invisible hospital-mates. Private First Class Dan Zuck was white, from Jackson, Mississippi. He was blinded when a phosphorus grenade went off in his hand. His nose and eyes were missing and his mouth twisted. I was glad that I didn't have to look at him, but wondered just how grisly I must have looked.

Pfc. William Fisher was a black guy from Georgia who had been temporarily moved for some surgical procedure. A bullet entered one side of his head, severed both optic nerves, and exited the other side.

Shortly after I arrived at blind man's corner, a Red Cross representative came to help me write letters and contact my family. I needed to talk to Blanche like a tree needs bark, but she had been staying with her mother and I didn't have the number. Shirley Staples, the Red Cross worker, took the address. The number turned out to be unlisted but Shirley returned and placed a phone receiver in my hand. "It's your wife," she whispered. "Mrs. Brummell." With my good hand I held the receiver to my ear and heard Blanche's tinny voice frantically calling my name.

"George? George? Is that you, honey? Are you alright? Are you there? George?"

"Hey, Blanche," I croaked. "Sure, I'm alright," I lied.

"I got a telegram that said you got hurt." A sob.

"What's wrong? I'm going to the doctor to see if it's alright to come out there. Mom said she would take care of Junior."

For a moment I debated, then said more brusquely than I intended, "Blanche, I'm fine. I just can't see. I AM BLIND."

Blanche burst into uncontrollable wailing. I listened for what seemed like minutes until she regained her composure. "George, I'll be out there soon. You'll be alright. I love you, baby. I miss you so much."

"That's what everyone says, I'll be alright." I was beginning to believe it. Maybe I would be all right.

She hung up and the nurse took the phone from my hand. I couldn't get my mind around being blind. I would never see again? Now what? How could I keep my beautiful wife interested in me? How could I help raise my new son? What can a blind man do? I'd seen blind people and how vulnerable and pathetic they seemed, tapping their way down sidewalks, needing someone to guide them through airports, unable to drive, or read, or play catch with a child, or look into a wife's adoring eyes as they kissed.

Fuck! I'd have been better off had I been killed over there. Why was I spared, only to suffer so much? Maybe, I thought, I'll get lucky and die of my wounds. After all, what was there left to live for? I couldn't even get a job shoveling tomato slush now.

For hours I lay there wallowing in self-pity, withdrawn from everything but my thoughts, until Miss Sanchez returned.

"You're scheduled for an operation on your hand and stomach, first thing in the morning. So don't eat anything tonight, okay?" Was she joking? My lips had been so badly burned by the heat of the explosion I couldn't eat a damn thing without help, and then only through a straw. My arms were immobilized by bandages and slings, I was blind, I ached all over, and now I couldn't eat.

"Can I at least get another shot of morphine?"

The next morning, I was wheeled out of the corner, upstairs, and into an operating room. Another blissful injection of anesthesia and I was being awakened by a male voice in a recovery room.

The next afternoon Major Artis, the orthopedic surgeon, stopped by during a routine ward check.

"How's my left hand?" I asked. "It hurts like hell under all of these wraps." My hand was larger than a boxing glove, resting above me, on a hanging contraption.

I heard the doctor fumbling with the masonite clipboard that hung at the end of the bed—my chart. "Mmmm... It's too early to tell. You'll need several more operations. I have to tell you up front, it may be necessary to amputate that hand."

"Oh, man! It just keeps gettin' worse!"

"As for your eyes, we believe there's hope you'll regain your sight. Whatever happens, it'll take time." I felt his hands gently examining my bandages and wounds, on my face, my chest, my legs—everywhere it seemed, I had been damaged. Then I heard his pen scratching, the clatter of the clipboard being hung on the bedstead, and the squeak of his shoes as he turned and left.

My roommates were arguing over which television program they were going to listen to. William hollered across the room, "How'd you get hit, George?"

Before I could reply, Dan chimed in. "I was really stupid, man. Fuckin' idiot, man. You wouldn't believe what happened to me." It was the second or third time he'd told the story.

"We were on a patrol and stopped for the night. I had a couple of claymores, so I set both of 'em forward, fifty yards. You know Cong. I heard the little fuckers'll sneak up to a claymore and turn it around, facing you. Well, I heard some noise. " Dan cleared his throat as if he was going to cry.

"Anyway, for insurance, I pulled the pin on a phosphorous grenade and set the claymore on top of it, so it wouldn't fire. If Cong messed with the claymore, the clip would fall and the grenade would blow the bastard to kingdom come.

"Nothin' happened that night. So next morning I got the grenade and stuck the pin back in and hooked it on my bullet-proof vest. But stupid me, I forgot to bend the damn pin and it fell out. It happened so fast, I couldn't get rid of it in time."

He choked a long moment. He continued, voice tortured by grief. "I'm fuckin' screwed up, man. My wife says my mouth is all twisted and my chest looks like a fuckin' gorilla. I've already had two operations on my eyes but I still can't see. The doctor said one eye's lost but he thinks he can save the other one. You know, the second operation I had was to get the pieces of phosphorous that were still in my body. They haven't got it all yet. I sure hope none of that shit ignites."

If there's a hell, I thought, I'm in it, stuck in a hospital room with a bunch of medical freaks like myself who can't see how bad they're messed up. I dreaded having Blanche see me like that. I tried to remember what it was about a gorilla's chest that would resemble Dan's wounds.

Shirley Staples, the Red Cross representative, returned the next day.

"Want me to help you write a letter?"

I did, but what if I wanted to get personal? I sighed. I didn't have a choice, about much of anything anymore. "Okay, sure. Let me know when you're ready."

She laughed, as she often did, and pulled a chair, scraping, near my bed. She sounded nice enough. Was she laughing out of nervousness, or trying to cheer me up? I knew this much: I would never laugh again.

Dictating to a stranger felt as awkward as being in public with an open zipper, but it was the best I could do.

Dear Blanche,

First and foremost, I love you desperately, and need you more than ever especially after what happened. I already told you I was blind, but there's more. I took a big hit to the gut, my left hand is in a sling and some damage to my legs. But I feel fine. Thank God none of my vital organs were touched. The big thing is I cannot see, but I'm fine.

I'm just trying to prepare you that I may not look like myself and you may not want to be bothered with me.

I heard Miss Staples stifle a sob, so I thought maybe I'd better change the pace.

I'm sure though everything will be all right but it will just take time. I also feel very lucky because a lot of the others did not make it.

I can't wait until you arrive; I miss you so much, and don't worry. I'm okay. We will talk soon.

Love always,

George

The Army had sent Grandma a Western Union telegram so she knew where I was. She called, but I had gotten a morphine shot and was out of it. I would have written her a letter, but she couldn't read. I would have loved to have gotten mail from her, but she was too proud to ask for help in writing one. So I had to go through the early days of my hell alone.

One day a nurse's aide rolled me in my bed into Doctor Artis's office where the Major unwrapped my dressings. The more he unwrapped, the more intense the pain until it became so unbearable I was screaming. He had to call for an attendant to hold me still. Then he hollered for another, and the two pinned me down. I begged for morphine, but the doctor kept pulling the wraps off, telling me it was best for him to check it without my having any pain killers.

I howled in protest. "God damn it!" he shouted. "If you persist in acting like a six-year-old, I'll have them strap you down! You're supposed to be a man. Just because you're blind, damn it, I'm not cutting you any slack. You're not the only casualty in this hospital, you know. In fact, you're in pretty good shape compared to some of these guys. I'm going to take this bandage off and if you act like a man, maybe I'll give you a reward."

He lowered his voice. "A little shot, maybe."

I didn't want to be strapped to the bed and I craved the sweet release of the morphine, so I forced myself to control my movements to a stifled cry and a squirm.

I heard no cruelty in Doctor Artis's voice. He was doing his job, putting me on notice that life was rough and I had to take what was dished out. Was he trying to tell me not to expect too much? I began to weep, and kept on weeping until I was back in the ward.

Chapter 18

A soft tissue blotted tears from my eyes. A warm, dry hand gently squeezed my right hand. I licked my parched lips. "Nurse, let me have a glass of ice water, please."

"I'm not a nurse."

It was Blanche. Tears flooded my eyes. I felt her breath on my face, and then a long light kiss on my scorched lips, and a gentle stroking on my left shoulder. I sighed heavily, ending in a sob.

I felt the weight of her head on my chest. Then dampness as her tears soaked into my pajama top. She lay like that, crying in silence, for a long time. Finally the weight lifted. "I love you, George" she breathed in my ear. "You'll be alright. I'm here for you, baby."

A rush of elation. Then I felt Blanche touching me here and there, inspecting my bruised body. Suddenly, I was agitated again.

"Whattaya mean, I'll be alright? Who you tryin' to fool, sweetheart? I'm messed up for life. This miserable, goddamned Army! I shouldn't have joined. Look at me now. I'm screwed, ruined, useless. I should have stayed in Federalsburg and finished high school. We didn't have any business in Vietnam, anyway. Who's gonna want to be bothered with me? Even you. Maybe not right away, but I'm no good for anything."

Blanche choked back a sob. "Don't say that, George. You're the father of our child. I love you. I want to be with you. We'll figure it out somehow."

"You're just sayin' that. Wait. You'll see later. I'm nobody's fool."

Chair legs scraped. I heard pouring water.

"Here, drink this." I felt a straw on my lips. Blanche sniffled. "I'm staying with my cousin Martha here for three weeks. Then I'm going back to pick up Junior and bring him here."

Blanche did what she could to calm and comfort me, constantly asking, did I want this, did I need that, was I comfortable, hungry, thirsty, tired? We talked for hours, about our baby, the news from home, anything but the future, until visiting hours were over.

She was back first thing the next morning, excited. She saw Doctor Artis in the hall and he told her she could come and go as much as she wished. So every day she arrived at seven o'clock in the morning, and stayed until ten o'clock at night.

I had another operation to remove shrapnel from my stomach. Two hours of surgery and a few hours in recovery, then a nurse rolled me back to the blind corner where Blanche was waiting. The operation was a success. Blanche would be going home in a few days. I dreaded being alone again. It was so much easier having her there to share my ups and downs.

On the morning Blanche was to depart, she arrived out of breath. "I called Mom and told her I wanted to stay another week and she said it was okay! By the way," she continued, "I have some other good news.

The doctor said they're going to get you out of bed and into a wheelchair and I'll be able to take you outside. Maybe next week. Isn't that great?"

I breathed a long sigh of relief. "The doctor did say a few days ago that I was making progress, but I didn't think I was doing *that* well."

I was anxious to get the hell out of that bed, so every morning I asked impatiently, "Is today the day?"

I had a lot of time for thinking, and although my lost buddies weighed on my heart, my head was full of anxious thoughts about how my life was going to turn out now. Would I see again? If not, how could I maintain my family? What would the folks at home think when they saw me again, in my condition?

Finally, two days before it was time for Blanche to leave, Dr. Artis reluctantly said, "Okay, if you think you're ready for this. Think you can stand long enough to get into a wheelchair?"

"No doubt about it. I feel fine."

"Morning, Brummell. How're you today?" The familiar voice of Doctor Adophy, the ophthalmologist.

"Where've you been, Doc? What's the deal with my eyes? When are you gonna work on my eyes?"

"Would you lie back on your bed? I have some drops to put in your eyes."

"Am I gonna see again? " I was pestering him, but they *were* my eyes.

"Well, Sarge, this takes time. I don't know about your left but there is a possibility you may regain sight in the right eye. It still has a little light perception, and where there's light, there's hope." I'd heard all this repetitious, vague optimism, or bullshit, before. Finally he was done. "Okay, Brummell, I'll be seeing you next week."

"Are you ready, Blanche?" Doctor Artis asked. "Ready Brummell?" "Let's move out!" I shouted.

"Okay, slowly now. Very slowly, I want you to see if you can get yourself sitting up on the side of the bed." No problem. I did it without hesitation.

"Now, drop both feet to the floor." I felt him take my right arm and drape it around his neck. Then he grabbed me around my waist.

"I'm not a cripple," I groused.

"Well, let's do it then!"

I started putting the full weight of my body down. I felt as heavy as concrete. My legs buckled. I was falling. Doc grabbed me around the waist and lifted my hundred-twenty-pound frame. I felt Blanche shuffle to my left side and she grabbed me, too. I dragged my leaden feet a few steps and they eased me into the wheelchair, like a fragile piece of cargo. Doctor Artis strapped me in the chair. I was completely helpless.

Well, I thought, I'm alive. That's something. That's more than I could say about Captain North, Lopas, Bosi, Thacel, and so many others.

"Okay, Mrs. Brummell, he's all yours. Don't keep him out too long, and stay on the porch."

"Alright," Blanche replied sweetly. Then I was rolling down a hallway, amazed that, in spite of being a sack of shattered bones trussed up in a wheelchair like a Thanksgiving turkey, I had such an intense rush of liberation. I was finally out of that bed!

The door to the porch swung open and I inhaled a lungful of fragrances—freshly mowed grass, hot asphalt, flowers, cologne, auto exhaust. It was a relief from the stifling odors of alcohol, germicide, and shit.

"Don't you worry 'bout nothin', honey," Blanche said. "Just you think about getting better. One step at a time." I heard her pull a chair close and sit down. We just sat like that for a long time, holding hands, thinking.

The next morning we spent crying. Blanche was heading home. She hugged and gently pulled me close. I soaked up the warmth and smell of her body. Her firm chest pressed against me. I wanted to hold and make love to my wife, and here I was with my left hand in a sling and my right arm with a needle stuck in it, attached to a tube.

"Now don't go anywhere," she joked. "I'll see you later." She slowly broke away then squeezed my big toe and was gone.

I sat there wallowing again in self-pity. The plan was for Blanche to return to Akron, where she'd been living with her mother, to get the baby and return. I had no idea how long I'd be in Brooks, but it was already starting to seem like forever. In my dark, brooding mood, I remembered something Grandma liked to say when she was scolding me for whining or moping: "Quit your belly-achin', child. Lords knows, there's plenty o' poor souls in worser shape than you."

It sounded like Dan was in worse shape, but in spite of it, he'd managed to keep his sense of humor. His wife was around, so maybe she kept his spirits up, or maybe he was trying to keep her spirits up.

A sailor a few bunks down had no wife and he was in the dumps. He'd been a flight deckhand on a carrier when the steel arresting cable that grabs the incoming jets to slow them down snapped, flailed across the deck, and ripped off his buttocks. He had his sight, but it wasn't much consolation.

A week later, I began occupational therapy. Miss Sanchez wheeled me outside and into the therapy "shop." She introduced me to Captain Harper and Captain Cabrara, a woman. Captain Harper had a British accent. He had attended a school in England to learn the long cane technique for blind people to get around. He had worked with the blind before the military.

Captain Cabrara was second in charge, and she ran the Arts and Crafts Department. By now I was getting accustomed to asking people to be my eyes. "So, how tall are you folks. What do you look like?"

"Well, I'm six feet two, forty years old, and not as beautiful as Captain Cabrara, who looks to be about five feet six inches, with short black curly hair, and a prize of Spanish descent." Cabrara laughed, and I surprised myself by joining in. It felt good.

Captain Harper gently pulled me out of the wheel chair, supported my weight, and began showing me around. As we walked, he explained that he was going to teach me cane travel. He showed me how to find the soda machine and the latrine, and where the lathes were that I was going to learn to use. Then he turned me over to Captain Cabrara.

She showed me how to operate a loom and told me I was going to make a rug and a belt. I had no interest in making a rug. It sounded like woman's work, but I kept my mouth shut. I didn't want to seem unappreciative.

Next, Miss Sanchez pushed me to physical therapy where a colored buck sergeant and therapist named Lee greeted us. "I been waitin' on you, brother! I heard you're from Federalsburg. I'm from Dover, Delaware, and I've been to Federalsburg."

Lee and I talked for two hours about home towns and people we both knew. We didn't get any work done but we agreed to make up for it at the next session. I was starting to re-connect with the ongoing world.

The next day I went to rug making but I was in no mood for it. "Girls make rugs," I complained.

"Listen, George," Captain Cabrara said. "It's therapy, okay? You're in a hospital and nobody's going to give you a hard time for anything. It's good for your arms and improving your dexterity. Give it a try. At least complete one rug, okay?"

"Okay, I'm convinced. Where's the loom?"

I followed Captain Cabrara's instructions to a "T" and, within a few sessions, I completed a small rug. I didn't enjoy it, and it was slow and frustrating feeling my way through tasks with one hand. But the reviews of the rug were pretty good, so I kept it as a souvenir.

When I wasn't making rugs or belts, I got mobility training and physical therapy. Most of the mobility sessions were spent alone with Captain Harper, but there were times when William was there as well, learning to use canes. We walked sidewalks, swinging our "skinny sticks" right and left, like two confused toy soldiers, trying to master that Long Cane technique the Captain talked so much about.

He told us the technique originated in England as a safe method of travel for the blind. Whenever the left foot hits the ground, the cane is supposed to sway right and vice versa. Sometimes William and I collided, crossing our canes like dueling swordsmen.

The Captain had a sharp wit and teased us about our lack of orientation. "There's a street sign in front of you, Brummell. What are you, blind?"

One day I almost walked into traffic and he grabbed me as a car zoomed by. "You can only do that if you're Superman, have bumpers on your ass, and a paid up insurance policy, okay?"

He was persistently encouraging, never critical, and had me walking independently in a week. The Captain was delighted, so proud of me that he asked me to show off the long cane for the hospital staff. I was feeling great, on a roll.

The three of us in the blind corner gradually talked about battle experiences, explaining how each of us was injured and about our friends who'd lost their lives. I never dreamed of Vietnam, but the other guys talked of dreaming about their injuries, especially William who caught a bullet in the head. He occasionally shouted in his sleep.

Besides Blanche, I had almost no contact with family and friends. Chris wrote me from time to time until Blanche put a stop to it. An aunt, Susie Mae, would let me reverse the charges so I could talk to her and find out what was happening with the family. I loved her a lot for that.

In addition to walking and getting around without bumping into everything, I was also working on building my strength, using a treadmill and then graduating to a leg lifting machine. I began sit-ups and later added weights behind my neck, held with my good right hand. I worked hard and developed a strong bond with my therapist, Lee, the black buck sergeant.

A month after Blanche had returned home, she called to let me know she and Junior were arriving in three days. I was elated. Sergeant Lee offered to drive me to the train station, but needed Major Artis's okay.

We went to see the doctor. "Sir, I'm George's physical therapist," Lee began.

"I know. Get on with it, Sergeant! I'm on my way to surgery."

"Sir, George's wife and new son are arriving tomorrow at the train station in San Antonio. I've never seen anyone gain their strength back as fast as George. I was wondering if I could have your permission to take him to meet his wife and son."

"You've been doing rather well," Doctor Artis replied, tapping my shoulder. "Okay, go ahead. But be careful with that bandage on your left hand. Don't bump it. You still have a few operations to go."

I could have done a flip. I would finally get to ride in a car again. I hoped it was air conditioned. The hospital wasn't, and the weather had been oppressive.

The next morning, I woke to the usual clanging of bedpans. After a bath and breakfast, I was ready and jumped up when I heard foot steps finally approaching my bed.

"I'm ready Lee."

"Hello, Sergeant." It was Dr. Adophy, the eye doctor. I sat back down. "I have Dr. Rachett, an eye surgeon, with me and he's going to have a look at your eyes."

"About time," I grumbled. It had been weeks since Adophy even bothered to visit. Maybe I could take

Blanche some good news.

"Lean your head back a little," Dr. Rachett said. He pulled open my eyelids and dropped some cold stuff in. I heard the click of his flashlight. He drew my head closer to him until I was breathing his breath. He'd just had a cup of coffee.

He spoke to Adophy like I wasn't there, throwing around technical terms. Then Adophy had a look.

Finally, I asked. "Well, doctors, what do they look like?"

"Dr. Rachett?" Adophy asked.

A long pause. "Your left eye looks pretty bad," he said clicking his light off and on. "To be honest, I don't think there's any hope for it. Your right eye, I don't know. You still have a little light perception. Maybe. But don't build your hopes too high. I'm going to make an appointment for you to come to the clinic for further examination. It's doubtful though. We'll let you know more after your visit to the clinic."

"Well, I guess I just shouldn't worry about it, right?" I said, annoyed, sarcastic.

"Don't," Ratchet said. His bag closed with a sharp snap.

Lee arrived and we wasted no time getting to his car. He said it was a beat-up 1956 Ford. "I'm sorry but the front passenger door doesn't open, so you'll have to slide in from the driver's side."

Then the engine wouldn't start. I was anxious to be on time, when Blanche stepped off the train. I wanted to be standing there ready to greet her. I shifted in my frustration and tapped my foot.

"Don't worry, George. I have a set of jumper cables

in the trunk. I'll just see if I can get someone to jump me. Don't go anywhere. I'll be right back."

Fifteen minutes passed before Lee returned with a man who gave him a boost. Finally we were rattling and squeaking through the streets of San Antonio.

We were twenty minutes late. Lee insisted I stay in the car while he went to find Blanche. I was aggravated but understood—a blind man would slow him down. The longer I sat in that hot car, the more abandoned I felt and a wave of sadness passed over me. I was too helpless to meet my wife and child on my own.

I tried to think more rationally. "Brace yourself, George. This is the way you're gonna be the rest of your life. Might as well prepare for the frustrations of being a blind man."

I listened intently to the sound of passing foot-steps until finally I sensed someone next to the car and a bundle was passed through the window and placed gently on my lap, followed by a pair of lips on mine.

"There he is! There's your son," Blanche said, her voice smiling.

It took me a moment to determine which end was up, then I lifted him and drew him closer. Junior start-ed screaming and squirming. "You sure make a lot of noise for such a little fellow. I have a funny feeling you don't like me."

"He'll get used to you," Blanche said. I kissed him gently on the side of his little face. On the ride back to the hospital, I petted and stroked my son's tiny body. He seemed healthy. All his fingers and toes were intact, and his skin was smooth and soft as satin. He had a full head of hair and I could tell he had some muscle potential.

"He's perfect!" I cried out, tears of joy stinging my unseeing eyes. He was fussy, so Blanche handed me his bottle and I held it while he sucked away. Finally! I was a real father.

Lee dropped us off in front of the hospital so I could ask Dr. Artis for permission to walk with Blanche to the guest house where she would be staying. He wanted me back in the hospital in three hours, so we hurried off. Blanche carried the suitcase with her right hand and Junior in her left arm. I followed the sound of her footsteps, proudly swinging my cane as we walked across the parade field.

A guest house attendant led us down a narrow hallway with a creaky floor. He pointed out the bathroom. "You can have the room a couple doors away, so it's easy to find it." He unlocked the door and handed Blanche the keys.

"Hope you have a nice stay while you're here," he said, fading down the hall.

The room smelled musty and sounded small. A single bed filled the wall to the left. I followed along side it. Almost touching the headboard was a small desk and a wooden high-backed chair. Above the desk hung a lamp. I followed the wall around, and found the room's only window, blocked by an oversized air conditioning unit. A sheet of paper covered the vents.

"What's the paper for?"

"It says, 'For an additional dollar a day, the air conditioning will be turned on,'" she said.

I passed a metal locker jammed in the corner and was back at the door where I started. Blanche parked

Junior in the carrier on the dresser. I tried to sneak up behind her but suddenly she was in my arms. I pulled her close, then closer and closer, just standing and pressing our bodies together as if trying to merge. I could feel the pounding of her heart. I gently stroked her soft, lean body. It was heaven being back in her arms.

My joy blocked the nagging pain of my left hand. I was only aware of the need to get closer to her, my wife and friend. Blanche started to cry. He tears saturated my shirt but we continued caressing one another. Finally we dropped to the bed and nourished our love-starved bodies.

Later we slowly walked, arms locked, back to the hospital. She showed me where the elevator was, then she left because babies were prohibited on the ward.

In the days that followed, Blanche visited when I was able to go to the lobby to sit with them. Later she made friends with Yvonne Brown, a soft-spoken, young colored girl from Birmingham, Alabama, whose husband, Frank, had lost both legs from an enemy mine. Yvonne sometimes watched our son while Blanche came up to the ward.

Then Doctor Artis released me as an out patient. I only had to return for bandage checks and physical and occupational therapy.

When Captain Cabrara found out Blanche and the baby were back, she insisted they come to therapy with me. Junior was an instant hit. While Blanche attended my sessions with me, Cabrara insisted that Junior stay in the office with her. Blanche sat and watched while I made another rug, and helped me when I made a mistake.

Captain Harper thought it was important for Blanche to know about the cane technique so he invited her to tag along during my mobility sessions. She followed me, sometimes pushing Junior in a stroller, under the blistering sun, encouraging me when I was low with frustration, and praising me when I was high with accomplishment.

It was hard for her to watch in silence as I stumbled off curbs, smashed into walls, or got lost within an arm's length of my goal. Gradually I learned to take Captain Harper's instructions to an objective several blocks away, and actually get there. My ability to move more independently improved as the weeks zoomed by, and eventually I was able to walk back and forth from the guest house to the hospital alone.

Four more months passed and I had the last of my surgeries. The boxing glove bandage came off and the doctors declared that my left hand looked good. I slowly reached with my right hand to feel it. It was strange, exploring this misshapen appendage that was almost boneless and had four stainless steel rods sticking out of it, to stabilize my bones while they healed. The beginning of my left wrist felt as small as a broomstick, missing a plug of flesh the size of a quarter. The back of the hand was smooth, from tightly stretched skin grafted from my thighs.

The doctors declared it a masterpiece and decided it was about time for me to start therapy to try and regain finger movement. Just two weeks more, and I'd be done.

Chapter 19

I spent endless hours in occupational therapy trying to enhance my finger movement. The effort
was ineffective, but not unproductive. I learned
to manipulate the wristless limb and to appreciate the
hand even if it was a bum one.

For drinking, I found I could wedge a glass or can
between the thumb and index finger, and could squeeze
the thumb just enough for holding small objects. Thank
God for thumbs. Otherwise, my hand would have been
useless and I would be unable to grasp or carry.

To my surprise, my hand and blindness created a
new sense of awareness. I noticed the big bandage had
affected my mobility and balance. I moved more gracefully without it. Now, when I was outdoors, I could feel
the air flowing like water over my skin. Without that
bundle on my left hand, the days speeded up, sweeping by.

In November, Captain Harper suggested that my
next move should be to go to the Hines Blind Rehabilitation Center, a Veterans Administration facility in
Hines, Illinois, a close-in suburb of Chicago, home to
Loyola University.

"The VA's mobility training is more extensive
than what I can offer here," he explained. "They teach

Braille, typing, wood work, and daily living."

"Sounds almost like being back in the military, but I'll go."

"Okay!" Captain Harper clapped his hands together. "Now, more good news. We can have you out of here in three days."

I hustled, in slow motion, back to the guest house to tell Blanche. We were both relieved to finally be moving on. The next three days we prepared for the long bus ride, first to Federalsburg and then on to Akron, Ohio, where Blanche's mother lived and we would make our home.

I wanted to live in a town bigger than Federalsburg, so I'd have access to the resources I would need and wanted the challenge of living in a city were I knew almost no one. I did know that Andy Miller, my suave black buddy from Korea, lived in Akron and I looked forward to putting my good hand in his.

The following day I got my orders to clear the hospital. I was still officially in the military so I went to supply and was issued a Class A uniform, complete with ribbons and brass. I was given travel pay, met with my doctors, had a meeting with a Veterans Administration contact person, and it was time to go.

At the bus station, Blanche pushed her left elbow lightly into my side, as she'd learned to do. "We're going to go up two steps. Be careful."

"Blanche, sweetheart. I do remember how to get on a bus. You step up and I'll follow."

We found a seat near the center of the smoky, cold, crowded bus. I slid in next to the window, sat Junior in my lap, and reached for the button to recline the seat but found Blanche's hand already there. My seat tilted back. I handed Junior to her, settled down, and thought about what an ordeal it had been just making preparations for the trip. I was exhausted. For almost five years, I had been accustomed to an energetic military life. Now I felt physically inept.

Blanche and I spoke little during the ride from San Antonio to Jackson, Mississippi. She entertained Junior while I mulled the future. We negotiated the chaos and confusion of traveling as a woman with a helpless child and a nearly helpless husband, and it seemed to bring us three closer together.

After a couple of days on the road, we pulled into the Philadelphia bus station—familiar territory. I surprised myself by remembering the layout. As we passed the information counter, baggage check and snack bar, I pointed them out to Blanche. She was impressed. When I showed her the coffee shop, she insisted on stopping to eat. I was starved, too, but our budget was tight. We could only afford their dried-out cheeseburgers. Blanche picked up a carton of milk which Junior quickly downed.

Most bathrooms are arranged in a similar pattern, so I felt confident when I entered the men's room in the depot. I followed the interior wall, stumbled a bit, but found the urinal. That was one place where a sense of smell was helpful.

Someone took the urinal next to me, and I could sense he was very close. I could smell his foul breath, a combination of onions and diseased gums. I felt like he was leaning toward me.

"Hello, handsome," he whispered, his breath on

my ear. Startled, I jerked away. I felt his hand on my leg, trying to push me away from the urinal, then reaching for my penis. I was shocked, but not finished. I grasped the plumbing fixture tight and pulled myself closer.

"Leave me be!" I said. Jesus, I couldn't even piss in peace! If I'd been sighted, I'd probably have decked him then and there. Blind, I was essentially helpless.

"Come on, man, let me feel it," the strange man begged, trying to work his hand between the urinal and me.

I smacked his big rough hand as if he were a child. "Get back, Jack!" But he was determined, shameless.

"Would you like to be done?" he hissed. "I could give you a blow job in the bathroom across the street. No one's never there. I'll give you five dollars."

"I don't go that way," I growled, zipping myself up, turning, and heading toward the sound of running water—the sinks. He followed and as I washed my hands, he kept jabbering.

"Okay, but you can't blame a man for trying. Here, let me help you find the door."

"That's okay," I said, but he insisted on pushing me out to where Blanche waited. Our bus was about to depart so we walked straight to our platform while I told her what had happened in the bathroom.

"Oh, George! That's disgusting! We should tell the police, or somebody."

"Forget about it," I said. "Let's just get the hell out of here."

"All points south! Wilmington! State Roads! Harrington! Seaford and Norfolk!" A man's voice called out from a speaker above my head.

"That's us," Blanche said.

Three hours later, the bus rolled into Seaford, Delaware. I phoned my brother Donald in Federalsburg, ten miles away, but no answer. So I called my Uncle Noble.

"Pie! My God, boy! It sure is good to hear your voice! Sure, I'll come after you. I just bought a new deuce and a quarter (slang for a Buick Electra 225). Wait 'til you ride in this baby. I'm on my way, Pie!"

Twenty minutes later, Blanche announced, "I think this is your uncle. It's a new big car."

We gathered our suitcase, portable record player, and Junior and walked toward the idling motor.

"Pie! How you doin'?" Uncle Noble asked heartily.

"Your voice still sounds the same, Unck!" I stretched out my right arm and grasped his small, calloused, sharecropping hand for a firm but gentle shake. He quickly grabbed the luggage and put it in the trunk, chattering about last summer's crops, which had been bad for tomatoes.

"Okay Pie," Uncle Noble said, slamming the trunk. "Let's go."

"Is that liquor store still across the street?"

"Still there."

I turned to Blanche. "The men I used to work with in the canning factory stopped there, because it stayed open later than the liquor store in Federalsburg."

I listened to the sound of the tires, and enjoyed the luxurious new-car smell. "We're crossing the bridge on Stein Highway. We must be near the DuPont plant."

"For goodness sake, Pie, you're right," Uncle Noble said, his voice full of surprise. "We're coming along side of it now." We continued outside of town, down the almost car-less two lane road, into Maryland.

"We should be making a right soon, onto Reliance Road."

"Not quite there yet, Pie, but we should be making the turn in a few minutes."

Suddenly, all the energy in me drained away. The long bus ride, the new burdens I faced, unsure what I was going to do with myself the rest of my life—it all had taken its toll. I settled back, pulled the armrest down, and leaned toward Unck.

It was calming to be back home, in a slick new car, rapping with Noble and, best of all, away from Vietnam and alive. With each rotation of the tires, memories unfolded. The mental game I played, trying to calculate our position, was stimulating. Turns in the road, shaded areas where the warming sun was blocked, stands of pines smelling of sap, all helped me pinpoint my location. Bumping across railroad crossings and humming across bridges were especially reassuring.

"Cody's Bakery should be coming up on the right real soon. Blanche, Mrs. Cody sometimes gave me doughnuts when I bought day-old bread for Grandma. Next stop should be Central Avenue and then Brooklyn Avenue."

Finally the car turned off the pavement onto sand, and stopped. I heard Grandma crying out before she got to me. Almost as soon as my foot hit the sandy turf, she was on me with a big warm hug and kiss.

"George! God bless you, son. How you doin', boy? It's been a long, long time since I seen you. Lord be praised." She put her hand on my right shoulder and shook it gently.

"I'm just fine, Grandma. I can't see, is all."

A pause, then Grandma's sad voice. "I'm sorry, George. You only had a touch o' light, and now it's dark." Then her voice brightened. "The Lord works in mysterious ways. If'n it's His will, you'll see again."

I grabbed Grandma's fulsome arm, pinching it gently through her heavy sweater as we walked toward the back door.

"This is something new," I said as we mounted the two steps before entering the inside. There was a floor where there hadn't been one before. "I don't remember a back porch."

Grandma laughed. "Now how did you know that? You sure you can't see? I've had it for a few months now and I just love it!"

I felt Grandma turn. "I'm sorry, child. I don't recall your name, honey. You know how it is when you get old. My memory just ain't what it used to be."

"It's Blanche, Grandma," Blanche said.

"How you doin', child?"

"Fine, Grandma," Blanche said.

Grandma opened the door, slowly moved down the short hall, passed through the small kitchen where I could smell her beef soup, and into the living room, smelling of kerosene from the heater stove. I heard her drag her old rocking chair closer to the stove.

"It's a little chilly in here," she said. "Bring in a kitchen chair. Hand me the baby, honey. Come on and get close to the heater."

"That's okay," I said. "I'm plenty warm. I'll sit in my favorite chair, by the phone."

"No sir," she said, standing. I could hear her lips smack as she kissed the baby. "You come and sit down in my old rocker."

It was an honor to be offered Grandma's rocking chair. No one was allowed to use it but her.

"I see, or smell, we're having beef soup."

"Boy, you got a nose like a bloodhound! I threw on a couple old bones for you. I hear blind people can smell better. Is that so, George?"

"Maybe I can smell better than some sighted people, but it's not better because I'm blind. I just depend more on my nose than other people."

I heard Uncle Noble stand up. "I'd like to stay longer but I gotta be goin'."

"Noble, you always on the go!" Grandma chuckled. "You gonna work yourself to death. Can't you stay and have some soup?"

"I'd like to, Mom, but I can't. I got a boxcar of chicken crates I got to move." Uncle Noble made his exit, and Grandma got up to go to the kitchen. "Betty, you wanna he'p set the table?"

"Okay, Grandma. But my name is Blanche."

"I'm sorry, Honey. You know how it is with us old people."

While they prepared the table, I had a chance to examine the cluttered room. Everything was the same. In front of me to the left was the door to the front porch. To the right of it, a small couch. In the opposite corner, a stand with an old radio on it. To the right sat the squeaky recliner, and the big console television was still shoved in the corner.

"Soup is ready, boy," Grandma said, tapping me

on my left shoulder. We settled at the table and I had slurped only a couple of spoonfuls from the bowl of steaming, fragrant broth when a familiar voice yelled from the back porch.

"Hey, Pie!"

"Is that my man Fox?"

"You got me!" Fox said entering the kitchen. I stood, meeting him with a big hug. "What's happenin', cuz?"

Fox got his nickname from the reddish tint in his skin. He was clever like a fox, too, although his formal education ended with the sixth grade. We had always lived next to each other, except for the one year I stayed out in the country. We remained the closest of cousins.

"How long before you're finish, Pie? I got a bug to put in your ear. Hi, Grandma! Hey, Pie, you sure got a good lookin' wife."

I gulped down the remainder of the soup and stepped into the hallway with Fox, closing the door behind me.

"What's wrong with your hand, Pie?"

"Old Charlie tried to do me in. It's the after effects of an explosion."

"Charlie? Charlie who? Man it must been hell over there. You'll have to tell me about it sometime." Fox stepped closer and whispered, "I got this bottle, man. You know we can't take a nip here. You know how Grandma is about whiskey in her house. Pie you got a couple dollars?"

"Maybe."

"We can walk down to the beer garden. Buy me a couple o' beers, I'll give you some of this whiskey."

"Sounds like a winner, Fox."

I had considered walking over to the beer garden alone, but couldn't muster the confidence. I was afraid of making a mistake. I didn't want the home folks to see me fumbling or getting lost. If there had been sidewalks, it would have been a lot easier.

Fox grabbed my good hand and tugged me impatiently toward the door. "Come on man, let's go."

"Wait a minute. Blanche, Fox and I..."

"Go ahead George." She sounded as if she really wanted to give me some space. "Have a good time. Just be careful of your hand."

"Let me have your left arm, Fox." He relaxed and dropped his lean, muscular arm. I grabbed it above the elbow, and we darted out the door, my coat thrown across my left arm.

"Better put that coat on, boy!" Grandma yelled.

Fox bragged all the way over about his three girlfriends. When we walked into Big Frank's Beer Garden, I immediately heard more familiar voices.

"Hey, Pie! What's happening."

"How you doin', man?"

"What's goin' on, soldier?"

"Big Frank's tending bar," Fox said, pulling a square stool made of rough lumber and plywood for me to sit on. "He's got his hand out to shake."

Big Frank was a gentle giant, more than six feet tall and over two hundred pounds. I remembered his gut drooping over a thin twisted brown belt. He spoke little but smiled a lot and when he laughed, it sounded like a series of hiccups.

"Sorry about your accident, Pie," Big Frank said,

thumping a can of beer down in front of me. "This one's on the house."

It crossed my mind that he offered me the drink because he felt sorry for me. "Thanks, Big Frank. You know it takes all kinds to make a world. It's time for me to play the role of a blind man."

He chuckled in a sad sort of way and then came from behind the counter and lifted a creaky iron lid. I heard him drop a log in the roaring fire. The heat was intense, but I didn't feel like moving.

"Where you comin' from, Pie?" Big Frank dropped the lid and moved back behind the bar. Glassware clinked.

"An Army hospital in Texas—Brooks Medical Center."

"How was the weather?"

"Warm for November."

A familiar woman's voice chimed in. "Pie, I bet you don't know who this is." I was startled.

"How could I forget my own mother's voice?" Last time I heard her was before I left for Vietnam.

"You're right, son."

I tried to conceal strong emotions as I turned in her direction, casually sipping my beer.

"What's the matter with your left hand, boy? I tried to reach you lots of times, but I couldn't never get through. Lines musta been busy, or maybe you was out. I even tried writing you, Pie, but my letters came back. I musta had the wrong address."

I turned away, toward the bar, took several gulps of beer, then rotated back in her direction.

"There is no excuse for you not getting in contact

with me, your own son who was damn near blown to pieces." I felt guilty delight in letting her have it. "Nevertheless, I survived. I didn't hear from you once. That's okay, because that's the way it's been most of my life. Really, I don't know you very well."

I paused. The jukebox filled the awkward silence with a hit tune by Martha Reeves and the Vandellas—

Jimmy, Jimmy, Oooh Jimmy Mack,
when are ya comin' back?
He calls me on the phone,
about three times a day.
Now my heart's just listening
to what he has to say.
But this loneliness that I have within
keeps reaching out to be his friend.

A cloud of scuffling and stomping shoes, and youthful laughter, moved toward the dance floor. The lopsided, creaky dance floor sagged and bounced beneath my stool. It felt like the floor would collapse any second.

I got tired of waiting for her to speak. "I don't expect things to be any different, now." Having lost my independence, it felt good to be strong in one area of my life.

"I did try to get in touch with you." Her voice trembled.

"I'm not buyin' it. There's no reason for you not finding me for four whole months. No excuse at all. You knew I was on the critical list. Somebody must have told you that. You could have even flown out to see me."

"Where could I have gotten the money to go way out there? Texas somewhere!" she protested. "I ain't had no work!"

"The Red Cross. You could have gotten help from them."

Fox interrupted. "Pie, you want a swig of whiskey."

"Sure, I'll take a shot. Maybe two."

"Give me one, too," my mother said.

Fox uncorked the bottle with a little pop and poured the liquor into paper cups. As he put one in my good hand, he leaned near and whispered, "Atta boy, Pie! That's tellin' her."

"Here, Aunt Elsie," he said, serving my mother.

We drank in silence for a long moment. Her pants swished as she shifted position, crossing her legs.

"I bet I can tell you what you're wearing."

"What?"

"Pants. A pair of men's pants."

"What's it to you! They're mine. I bought and paid for 'em. Everybody's always worried about these pants I wear. It'd be different if they paid for them but, god-damn it, I bought these pants. You know, you don't even seem like my son. You even talk different." I didn't like the feisty tone that was creeping into her voice.

"You know why. It's probably because I haven't been influenced by you. That's why I left this place, and I'm damn glad I did!"

"You got some nerve, talkin' to me like this, all the things I done for you! After all, I AM your mother!" A heavy gulping sound.

"Hunh! After all you did? Well, tell me exactly

what it is you did for me. Tell me one thing you ever did for me? Oh, wait, there's one. There was one thing you did. Almost before I was born, you gave me away!"

I felt a breath of air and then a finger pressed into my chest. "Okay, here's one." Her paper cup hit the bar top with a hollow click. "Remember a few years ago, I loaned you my car, and you was caught drivin' without a license? Now, who do you think paid your fine! I did!"

I tapped my cane impatiently. The Supremes came on the juke—

Set me free, why don't cha babe?
Get out my life, why don't cha babe?
'Cause you don't really love me.
You just keep me hangin' on

"Fourteen lousy dollars. Six or seven years ago. I was only fourteen years old. Tell you what," I said, digging into my pants pocket before I realized I only had pocket change. "I'm gonna give you that measly fourteen bucks back. After that's settled, I won't owe you nothin'! I don't have the money on me now, but I'll get it. Fox, walk me back to Grandma's."

"Okay, dude. Let's go."

I felt Fox's left elbow expertly brush against my chest. I took his arm with my good hand and he guided me toward the door. My mother stormed passed and I heard the door slam before we got to it.

Fox led me across the rain-soaked sand of the parking lot, carefully skirting the mud puddles like it was an Army obstacle course. We stepped onto the main drag and started walking toward my grandmother's.

"Uh-oh!" Fox said. "Aunt Elsie is just up ahead, pulled over in her car. She looks like she's pretty mad. You wanna talk to her?"

"Let's just go and get the money. I'm not joking about this." We continued walking until Fox whispered we were passing her car. I heard her voice from the inside.

"You're a smart ass, Pie!"

"Thanks!" I yelled back. "I'd rather be a smart ass than act like you!"

"You're no son of mine!" she yelled. The engine cranked and roared to life. We kept walking.

"You're right! I'm a son of a bitch!" I called back.

The car frame creaked as it pulled onto the highway pavement.

"Shit, Pie! Here she comes. She's fuckin' crazy!"

The motor raced, the tires screeched. Fox ripped my hand from his arm. "C'mon man!" I was no longer a combat soldier, but I'd been in combat. I followed Fox, hopping as best I could into the darkness, toward his voice. The car roared past, close.

"Man, she just about got us. She coulda killed both of us. She's crazy as hell!"

"I've been through a lot worse." We shared a nervous laugh and continued up the small rise, down the other side, toward Grandma's back yard.

Suddenly Fox stiffened. "Pie, Aunt Elsie is walkin' 'cross the field and...she's got a gun!"

"Oh, yeah. I'll just bet." Fox had a reputation for tall tales and pranks.

"I'm not shittin', man. She's got a rifle. Hang on!

Keep up." I tightened my grip on his arm. His stride lengthened to a gallop, then a trot. It was crazy, a nightmare. My own mother trying to kill me, after all the shit I had just been through trying to survive the war.

Fox kept up a steady, gasping jog until we reached Grandma's porch and we clomped inside, panting.

"Grandma! Grandma!" Fox yelled. "You gotta talk to your daughter. She's got a rifle and actin' like she's gonna shoot Pie."

"What daughter? Shoot Pie! What for?"

"Aunt Elsie!"

From the guest bedroom Blanche came running. "What's the matter, George? Are you alright?"

"Everything's alright, sweetheart. Just a little family misunderstanding. Listen, I need fourteen bucks I owe my mother. It's a long story. Just get me the fourteen bucks."

"That's gonna leave us short, Pie. We need milk and diapers, the bus tickets, and food for ourselves."

"I know all that. Just get the money, please. It's something I gotta do and I gotta do it right now. We'll make it."

I heard Blanche walking toward the guest room and followed. She searched her purse and handed me the bills—two fives and four ones. I smoothed them out, folded the wad, and stuck in my bad hand.

"What's going on?" a new voice cried out. The back door creaked open.

I recognized the voice of Doris, my youngest sister of four. She was fifteen and lived nearby with Mother. I heard her approaching and then felt a warm, wet cheek against my face and an embrace. "Pie! I'm so sad you got hurt in the war."

I felt for and patted her head. "You were just a little girl when I left town. Look at you now!" Doris giggled through her tears. "Look at her, Blanche. She's almost as tall as me!"

"Mama said you were home." Doris sniffled. "She said she was going to shoot you. I just had to see you, Pie. I don't know what's going on." I took a few steps toward the back door.

"Don't go out there, boy!" Grandma yelled. "Elsie's got a rifle. She's crazy as a bedbug. She might shoot."

"I'm not worried about my mother shooting me," I said, opening the door. I stepped outside and off the porch a few feet. I heard Grandma's footsteps following me. "She's just putting up a front, Grandma. Come here, Doris. Take this fourteen dollars over to your mother."

Doris took the money and I heard her footsteps fade as she walked across the field. I stood Army straight and tall, straining to hear what they were saying. I twisted my head this way and that, and cupped my ear. But I couldn't make out a word.

A racing car engine approached, crunched into the yard near me, and stopped. A door opened. A commanding white male voice demanded, "What's goin' on here?" It was one of Federalsburg's three cops. "Is everything alright, Miss Susie?"

"It's okay, Officer Wilson," Grandma said. "Nuthin' we cain't handle."

Voices congregated around the patrol car. I recognized several voices in the crowd, gossiping about our family feud. It was humiliating to be stalked by my own mother, with a rifle no less. It was worse than living in the Wild West, or being in combat. I decided then and there that Blanche and Junior and I needed to leave Federalsburg immediately.

"You see, Wilson, my grandboy here cain't see and his mother, Elsie, has a rifle and she's threatnin' to shoot 'em."

I smelled peppermint, and then a tap on my shoulder. "Could you step over here, sir?" I followed Officer Wilson's voice, maneuvering through the curious crowd, to the rear of the cruiser. The radio in the car crackled. He snorted, and spat.

I explained the situation, and my blindness. "Yeah, that's a real shame," he said. "So, you wanna press charges?"

"She's my mother. What do you think?"

"You can swear a warrant for her arrest, but that'll mean you and she have to go to court in about two weeks."

"I'm leaving town before that."

"Well, that's up to you." He drummed his fingers on the trunk lid and his keys rattled.

I was pretty steamed up, but I was more worried about what she might do to others, like Doris or Grandma. "Okay, I'll have her arrested. She should be checked. Maybe she should be kept away from sane people, even if she is my mother. Maybe she can get some help."

"Okay. We've got to go to the magistrate's house to get the warrant. Hop in the car."

"Hold on for a moment while I get my wife and baby." I forgot where I was in relation to the house. I took a couple of steps and then stopped, listening. The door opened and I followed the sound.

"George, I'm here. Right here," Blanche said, touching my good hand. She'd been there all the time.

"Get your coat and Junior's. We're going downtown to get a warrant."

"You're gonna have your mother arrested? George, why don't we just leave and go to Akron and forget about all this?"

"I'm going to do this. Get Junior's coat."

The three of us piled into the rear of the police car and rode downtown to Judge Thompson's house. Before he was a judge, he'd been the local fish-monger, selling fresh fish and Chesapeake crab off his truck. Grandma had been one of his first credit customers.

"Y'all wait here. I'll git the judge," Officer Wilson said. He returned a minute later.

"What's the story here?" A white man's voice spoke through the open window. Blanche was shivering a little in cold fall draft. "You want to make out a warrant for your mother's arrest?"

"Yes."

The judge went back inside and returned with the forms for my signature. Blanche held my hand and positioned the paper so I could get started. It couldn't have been much of a signature, but it was in my hand. The judge exchanged some gossip with Officer Wilson until Blanche handed the papers back to him.

"Alright, then. Court's scheduled for two weeks from yesterday."

"Your Honor, can we take care of this sooner? I'm on my way to Akron, Ohio."

"That's the procedure, boy. There's no way of holdin' the trial any sooner! What do you want to do about it? Have her arrested or not? I don't have time to be standing out here in the cold! Make up your mind, now."

I let the process go forward and soon after we got back to Grandma's house, word spread that my mother'd been arrested. An hour after that, we were surprised when she roared past Grandma's house in her Ford, her horn blasting away.

The whole shameful episode was too embarrassing to go out in public so, for the next two days, I sat around the house talking to Grandma about old times. When Blanche took a nap the second day, I used the time to call Chris. I was happy when she answered the phone. With so much to say but too little time to say it, we talked fast. I asked about Theresa and Chris said she'd have her oldest daughter bring the little girl up to see me.

I still had no idea whether she was my child, but I felt a connection. I'd told Blanche about that part of my life, so I woke her up so she could meet Theresa. Hilda arrived and greeted me with a quick hello and a fleeting handshake. Blanche sat me near Theresa but the child shied away. I had a roll of Life Savers in my pocket so I pulled it out. "Theresa, would you like a piece of candy?"

"Mm-hmmm," she muttered.

"You must come and get it, child."

There was silence for a long moment, and then Theresa walked into my arms. While she fumbled with the Lifesavers, I inconspicuously examined her tiny body. Gently, I pulled her close and lightly kissed her. As soon as she'd liberated a Lifesaver from the roll and put it in her mouth, she darted away with the roll. I heard the porch door slam behind her. We followed her outside.

My heart felt a little heavy. Would I ever know if I was her father and would I be able to explain to Theresa who I was? Would I ever see her again?

"Well, I think I'll go back home now," Hilda said scraping a shoe on the packed sand. "Mamma told me to get home before dark."

"Okay, Hilda, I understand." I felt rejected. "Maybe you should be leaving. Bye Theresa," I called out. I wanted to hug her again, but she was too far away.

"Bye Mister Pie," Theresa said from far down the hill.

As soon as we were back in the house and in our room, I told Blanche, "I'm not going to court about my mother. I just want to leave for Akron, tomorrow if we can."

"Okay, George. I think that's best. I can have us packed and ready by morning."

"Soon as I find someone to give us a lift to the depot, we'll be on our way."

"Oh, honey. I'm glad." She put her arms around me, squeezed, and we shared a quick, soft kiss. Then she broke away. "I better get busy."

Chapter 20

e're here! Wake up, George! We're here!"
Blanche was shaking me. We'd been on the
road for sixteen hours.

The bus rolled up in front of a hotel where Blanche
reported that a few hard-luck prostitutes eyed us as we
got our luggage and caught a cab to Blanche's mother's
house.

The living room sounded small, smelled of moth-
balls, and was cold. Blanche turned up the heat and I
looked for a phone. When I found it, I dialed information to get a number for Andy Miller, my Korean soul
brother who I knew lived in Akron, but it was unlisted.
Blanche got out the telephone directory and we started
dialing Millers until we found his cousin, who reluctantly gave me his number. I dialed, and he answered.

"I bet you don't know this voice," I said.

"I don't have any idea," Miller said slowly.

I told him a couple of personal details I remembered about him.

"Listen!" he yelled, "Whoever you are, you know
a lot about me! You better tell me who this is before I
hang up!"

"Okay. Prepare yourself for a shock. This is Brummell, and I'm just around the corner from you."

He burst out laughing. "How long you gonna be here?"

"For a while. At least three weeks. Then I got to go to Chicago to a VA hospital."

"I'll be right over," Miller said, adding in a loud whisper, "Soon as I get rid of this bitch."

"By the way, Andy, I went to Vietnam and Cong got me. I'm blind."

"Blind? You're blind? You mean you can't see nothin'? What happened, man?"

When Andy got to the house, he insisted on escorting me to a chair, lighting my cigarette, opening my soft drink. He even offered to help me put on my shoes. If I'd asked, I think he would have wiped my rear. Andy finally calmed down and I told him the story of what happened after the last time I saw him, in Korea.

After listening for awhile, Andy asked, "Can you walk over to my apartment? It's not far."

"Sure. You think I'm a cripple, too?"

His second floor apartment was small but orderly and while he was showing me around, the phone rang in the kitchen and I waited while he had a cryptic conversation about some business.

When he hung up, he said, "I'm going to call a couple of whores I've been pimping." He dialed but got no answer, or a busy signal. "I hope those bitches are out trying to make me some money," he said, slamming the hand set back on the wall phone.

He returned to the living room and put a jazz record on the player. Then he opened a drawer in a table to the right of the couch I was sitting on, and rustled around in the contents. I heard paper. Some sounded like rustling sheets and some sounded thinner, almost like tissue paper. I heard metallic noises too, coins and some plastics. Something light landed on my lap.

"I also got some champagne I been keeping for a special occasion."

It was a piece of aluminum foil, folded with something inside. When I unfolded the little package, my first reaction was to smell it. One sniff and I knew what it was.

"Is this grass?"

"Man, what the hell you think it is, spinach? You been off the set too long. It's the bomb! I'll roll you one."

"No, man, not now. I don't think I can handle it, being blind. I have too much to do to get my life back together. I'm on a mission."

"Wow! I wonder what it would be like high and blind," Miller laughed. "I didn't think of that."

"Do you have a car?"

"Well, yes and no." I heard a match and smelled the first puff of acrid pot smoke. "I missed a couple payments. The finance man came last week and took it." He pulled deep on the joint.

"But if you want to go somewhere, I can get my cousin's ride."

"I want to see what Akron's night life's about."

Miller arranged to borrow his cousin's new Electra, changed into a suit and tie, and caught a taxi to pick up the wheels. The only suit I had was military so I wore what I had on: gray slacks, pink shirt, white sweater, and a black leather coat Blanche bought a few days before. Miller proudly walked me into nearly all the local bars: The Silver Leaf, The Hi De Ho, The Rendezvous, and the It Club.

For the three weeks I stayed in Akron, Miller and I hung out often, sometimes bar hopping and sometimes just at his place drinking beer and listening to jazz. I was grateful for his friendship, especially at that time when I was just starting out my new life.

On days Miller couldn't get a car, we walked from the Westside to downtown Akron like we were in Korea again, humping hills. He seemed to relish being my eyes, taking pains to describe our surroundings, and quizzing me about what I felt as a blind person. One day he told me he blindfolded himself for several hours just to get a feel for what I experience. Miller said it helped. Maybe it did, because I was convinced he saw me as a person and not as a blind man. Miller and I had big fun, but finally it was time for me to move on to Hines and my blind rehabilitation training.

Blanche and I flew to Chicago's O'Hare Airport, where we were met by a Hines representative. At the hospital, after I finished with all the paperwork, we were shown to the Eye Ward. I would stay on the ward for a week for a general check-up and observation.

Blanche gave me a quick kiss goodbye as she left for the return trip to Akron. "Well, you're on your own, now. I can't wait to find out what you've learned."

The next week crawled by with blood tests, x-rays, and other procedures. Finally, Simmons Bradley, the mobility instructor, escorted me to the Blind Center and started working with me.

"With your right hand, grab my left arm just above

the elbow. I'm going to keep my arm down along my side, but when we're in an area too narrow for both of us—you know, like a narrow doorway or a tight hallway—I'll move my arm to my back which will clue you to step to your right, behind me. When there's room again to walk abreast, I'll move my arm back to my side. Got it?"

"Got it. You know, I had some of this kind of training at Brooks."

"Okay, then you're a pro. Let's do it!"

Bradley stepped off with his left foot and, after a few yards, quickly moved his left arm to the rear. I jumped to the right and followed. A couple steps farther and he moved his short chunky arm back to his side. I shuffled like a dancer back to the left without losing step.

"That's good. You're gonna do alright here."

Next he picked up the pace, breezing down the corridors at a gait I was accustomed to in the military. "Believe it or not George, before you leave here you'll be able to travel independently all over these grounds."

In the building that housed twenty-nine other blind veterans, Bradley pointed out the pop machine, public phone, bathroom, classrooms, work out room, and finally, my room.

"This is where you'll live for the next four months. Extend your right arm alongside the wall to about a forty-five degree angle. Make sure your palm is down and your fingernails forward. Most important, curl your fingers." Bradley took my hand and clumsily clenched it half closed, in a position like my left hand.

"Now, fold your left forearm in front of your head

and proceed carefully along the wall."

I followed the wall with short steps until I came in contact with a single bed, then a desk, a cushioned chair, a sink, and a metal locker.

"You can start unpacking," Bradley said. "I'll be back later."

He returned a moment later with two watches. "You want a pocket watch, or a wrist watch?"

"What difference does it make? I can't tell time with either."

"Oh, but you can! Both of them are Braille watches." Bradley wrapped his warm palm around my right index finger and pressed it gently against the winding stem of the pocket watch. The lid popped open. I was impressed.

"Feel the raised dots? Notice the twelve, three, six, and nine have two raised lines and the other numbers have one." He softly eased my finger onto each number. "The hour and minute hands are sturdier than most other watches," he went on, "but be cautious. Approach the hands straight and carefully with your index finger. Try not to move the hands left or right, okay?"

"Okay."

"Now, tell me what time it is."

"It's...it's eighteen minutes after...after five."

"Very good. Now, which watch do you want?"

"I'll take the wrist watch."

When he left, I finished organizing my belongings, checking my new watch every five minutes. What a relief to be able to do something as simple as tell time again. If only I had a radio, my room would be complete. I could hear music from other rooms. I stood in the doorway, listening. Scrambled in the hodgepodge of noises, footsteps approached from my right. Before I could step out of the way, a face smacked into the right side of my face.

"Ooomph!" a male voice said.

"What are you trying to do, make love to me?" I joked.

The other guy burst out laughing. "No, man! I don't go that way." He had a southern accent. "You're in a bad spot. I have the right of way. Name's Dan. I live on the other side of the bathroom, in the corner."

We struck up an extended conversation. He was from Seattle, and told me what to expect in training.

Early the next morning, Ben, the mobility instructor, brought me a small radio. "I'm going to escort you to breakfast. You won't be getting a cane yet."

"I don't know if Bradley told you. I just left Brooks Medical Center where I learned how to walk independently. I have my own cane."

"I know, but try to forget the training you've had," he said. "We're going to start you off new, with a clean slate. We want you to learn our technique because it's the best in the country. Let me have your cane. We collect them. We're impressed with the many types there are. When the time comes, we'll give you one of ours."

Ben disappeared with my folding cane, then returned and walked me to the chow line, where he left me.

"Let me know when you move," I told the man in front of me.

"Okay," the man answered.

"We're moving," someone shouted.

I stepped forward until I bumped into the man in front of me. "We're moving again," he said, shuffling. Ben was waiting inside near the doorway.

"Okay, Brummell," Ben said. "To your right there's a stack of trays. Grab one. Move forward a couple of steps and place your tray on the serving line. To your right again is your silverware and plates. Keep moving, Brummell, and you'll find napkins. Place your silverware on the corner of the tray."

"It's like being in the army again."

"You're right about that," commented a woman behind me.

"How do you want your eggs?" a rushed female voice asked.

"Scrambled hard."

A minute later, a plate hit the steel counter.

"Reach up higher. Higher!" she shouted. "Okay, you got it! Take it down a level."

I placed the plate on the tray and slid it down the line. "Where's the meat?" I asked.

"No meat," the woman said, handing me a carton of milk. "The government's too cheap for that."

Ben was waiting at the end. He backed me up to the edge of the serving line and told me how to find a seat. "Keep your tray up, chin high, so you won't hit anyone's head. Take four or five steps straight forward. There are tables in line to your right and left. Here, you take the second table to your right. This will be your seat, beside Mr. Strong and in front of Mr. Johnson, both World War II vets."

"Hello, there. Name's Strong, Albert Strong. I can see a little. Let me help you to your seat." His throat was congested. "You're a young man. How old are you?"

"I'll be twenty-two in a few days."

"Vietnam?"

"Yeah. Charlie got me good."

"Too bad you had to get messed up like that at such a young age." Strong was legally blind from the side effects of diabetes. He'd lost a leg above the knee and wore a prosthesis.

Mr. Johnson said little, only that he was World War II vet from Chicago, also diabetic with no vision.

Ben escorted me back to my room, telling me that the largest group at the Center were World War II diabetics or had glaucoma. There were only three service-connected veterans from Vietnam, but more were expected when space became available.

My mobility training went into high gear, and graduated to the outside and, eventually, to Maywood, a community near the hospital grounds. Ben drove me into town, gave me directions to a restaurant several blocks away, and said, "You're on your own, buddy. I'll be following at a safe distance."

The wind blew hard at my back. Sand particles blasted my face. The objective took me across a busy overpass, where the wind blew even harder. Cars and trucks zoomed past, creating an air current that nearly pushed me to the pavement. The high volume of traffic noise made finding the restaurant more difficult.

Ben's voice called out, "You're about half-way across, Brummell."

A huge gust of freezing wind lifted me off my feet and slammed me against the guard rail. I dropped my cane. I instinctively tried to grab it before it hit the pavement or blew beneath the rail.

"Damn it! George! You're not remembering the first week of training," Ben roared. "You could've cracked your skull and knocked yourself out! Remember, whenever you drop something, take your time when you go down. Think! Put your arm in front of your face and then squat to pick up the object. Maybe if you crack your head on something, you'll remember! Come on. Let's cross this bridge. It's cold as a witch's tit out here."

I found the restaurant, went inside, sat at the bar and ordered a soda. "Hey, Ben, you want a drink?"

"You don't have to holler. I'm right here beside you. How long are you going to sit there thinking you've reached the objective?"

"You said the restaurant on the southeast corner didn't you?"

"Yes, I did. You're on the northeast corner, in a topless joint."

"And I thought I smelled food in here." Ben started to laugh, and then I joined. I paid for the drink and clumsily walked across the street, ego dented.

The following few days were repeats of the windy work-out. Saturday we woke to snow. My weekend routine was to take a short walk after breakfast, but it was too slippery.

That night Blanche called. "George, are you sitting or standing?"

Oh, boy! "I'm standing by a pay phone in the hallway."

"I don't know how you're gonna take this."

"Take what?"

"The fact that I'm pregnant."

"Again?"

"The doctor figures I'm about six weeks."

I was stunned. We wanted another child, but not this soon.

"George? You still there?"

"I was just thinking. We can hardly afford the one we have."

"You're right, but we'll manage."

I didn't want to just manage. I wanted to get my family into a home of our own. It was frustrating being away from Blanche and Junior for so long. I went back to my room feeling defeated. I was tired of being blind and frustrated by life's challenges. I pulled out my beginning Braille book and started reading a short story, written with only the letters A through M.

The following Friday, Johnson invited me to spend the weekend at his place. I thought a change of scenery would do me some good. I was tired of hospital odors. "I only have twenty-five dollars. You think that'll be enough?"

"You don't need no money! You're going home with me. I'm known all over Chicago. You'll see, son."

Johnson was short, with big rough hands. He told vivid stories of famous Negroes who'd lived in Chicago: Joe Louis, Jesse Jackson, Elijah Mohammed, and others.

"I knew a bunch of great ones," he bragged, dropping a dime in the hall phone and dialing. He spoke with someone, arranging for a ride, then hung up. "Damn that brother of mine! Fred acts like he don't want to come and get us! Said it's too snowy out. But

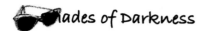

he's coming. He'll be here."

I felt sorry for his brother. The radio said the snow had drifted to six feet in spots.

Chapter 21

Fred arrived five hours late, and landed like a mortar round. Johnson's older brother, like many sighted people when encountering the blind, felt the need to speak to Johnson and me in a loud voice. He yanked my arm as he pumped my hand. Was he a country boy too, accustomed to pumping water?

I tried to retreat, but Fred's big palm was glued to mine. He released it, only to grab it again. Then I felt him press both sides of his rough face against the back of my hand. Next he grabbed my head in both of his hands, like a melon. He jerked my head down and pressed his broad forehead against mine. His mouth was damn near touching my nose, like he was speaking into a microphone.

It was about as bizarre as being propositioned in the bus station men's room, and equally disorienting. I no longer could read people by their expressions, only their voices and actions. And this guy was acting mighty weird. My mother had tried to run me down and then threatened to shoot me, a stranger tried to seduce me at a urinal, and now this guy was acting like a child with a rag doll. Was there something about being blind that made me a target for crazy people?

I kept expecting Johnson to pipe up and rescue

me, but not a peep out of him. Fred laughed and told me repeatedly how glad he was to meet me.

The smell of garlic, wine, fish, and cigar smoke repelled me backward, but my new friend doggedly followed. I tried to wag my head loose from his grip, but his large hands held firm. Finally he let go, then hugged me with one arm, pulling my small frame close. I was a bug to his flypaper.

"Meet my friend, John," Fred said expansively, his thick arm beneath mine, shoving me forward. He turned me loose again, but only for a second. He grabbed my right hand and placed it in John's smooth palm. I was learning that handshakes were an important way to take the measure of some of the people I met—a firm handshake suggested a strong personality. John's hand was moist, slim, with long fingers. His grip was limp but he pumped my arm fast. For a second he covered my hand with his as if saying, everything's okay my friend.

"He-e-ey." John said, slow and smooth. His metal heel plates clinked and scraped on the linoleum. I could smell his leather jacket, and hear it crumple as his arm returned to his side. He was chewing Juicy Fruit gum, rather vigorously for how slow he talked. The two smells fought—the cloying sweetness of the gum and the dark, earthiness of the leather. I wondered if he was standing there looking stunned and embarrassed by Fred's loony antics. But he sounded like he hadn't even noticed.

"My ma-a-an! What's happenin'?" he said.

"Great meeting you Fred."

"Come on man, let's get this show on the road, cut

the bull shit," Johnson said impatiently.

I guessed that both of these guys were soused, but the prospect of excitement was a powerful lure. It might be my only chance to sample Chicago. I might be blind and beat up, but I was still an otherwise healthy, spirited twenty-two-year-old. So I rolled the dice and signed on for the adventure.

We piled into Fred's long Buick, and he played the jocular bus driver, laughing loudly and continuously, talking fast, infusing the car with cheap cigar smoke as he slipped and slid down the snowy highway into downtown Chicago. Happily, I got to sit in the back with the leather jacket, out of Fred's sticky reach.

Fred complained about the slow moving traffic, while I told his friends how I had been injured. Johnson interrupted to tell stories of old Chicago, Prohibition, and working in the slaughterhouses.

I felt the car slowing and descending a ramp as Fred projected his voice right, toward the passenger's seat, where Johnson sat.

"Where you goin', Bro?"

"I thought we'd stay by your place."

I didn't like the sound of that. Johnson had made it seem like we were all set up with a place to sleep.

"Oh no, Bro!" Fred chuckled. "No fuckin' way! You 'member what happened last time. 'Sides, I ain't got room. I'll take you down to Bruno's Place. You can figure it out from there."

"Damn, Fred! I got my man with me, can't you see? You can let us stay one night, can't you?"

"Fuck no! I tol' you the deal! Bruno's!"

John piped up from my left, talking to the back of

Fred's head. "Come on, man. He's your brother, and it's only one night."

"You ain't got nothin' to say about it, shithead," Fred snapped. "This is family business. What you don't know is that the last time Bill was at my house he got all liquored up. He knows he's ain't supposed to, what with his diabetes and all. But he does it anyway. And what happens? He sets my son's bed on fuckin' fire! Almost killed us all. Goddamned fuckin' mess."

"Okay, okay," John said. "Forget about it. We're almost to Bruno's."

The car jolted over several railroad crossings—I could hear train whistles in the distance—slowed, crunched to stop, and Fred killed the engine. "Here we are!"

Before I could locate the handle for the door, Fred had sprinted around and opened it for me. I unfolded my cane and stood by the car. Little needles of cold prickled my face and hands—snow. It was snowing hard, but after the fog of cigar smoke, the fresh, crisp air energized me. I took a deep breath.

I remembered from my blind training to make sure I had a clue where I was, just in case. "Johnson, what street is this?" I had told the folks at Hines I was visiting Johnson and given them his brother's address and phone number. I had enough money to call Hines or to pay for a ticket on the train.

"Cottage Grove," he answered. "Damn it's cold! You've probably heard of it, George. It's the same street Lou Rawls mentions in that song, what the hell was it? Used to be a lot of jazz and blues happening around here, but lately it's died down some."

Fred was stuck to me again, this time guiding me to the bar. Johnson knew the area so well that he took off independently. "You'll be alright, George," Fred said. "My brother knows everybody here. Watch it. There's a big mound of snow here we gotta climb over."

At the top of the mound, fighting for my footing, a sudden gust of Lake Michigan wind came whipping around a corner and nearly slammed me to the ground. I recovered and tottered like an old man across the ice to the door. A cloud of warm, fetid air enveloped me as we crossed the threshold. I instantly recognized it as a dump. The stench was overwhelming—sour, stale, brown. Angry male voices at different ends of the room were exchanging insults—"Motherfucker!" "Son of a bitch!" Even the women were swearing.

We paused near the sound of glasses clinking and kerplunking into water. Fred pulled out a bar stool for me. It wobbled so you could hardly sit on it, and the stuffing had erupted where the vinyl seat was ripped. Palm down, I swept my hand lightly across the bar top—dusting, I call it. I encountered a puddle—beer by the smell—a full ashtray, and a toppled beer can.

"Well, Brother George!" Fred shouted, smacking me on the back. "I gotta be goin'. Gotta pay off my winners. I write numbers, you know." I didn't, but I wasn't surprised.

As soon as Fred left, Johnson yelled, "Bruno! Bruno! I know you're there 'cause I can hear you!" He pounded the bar.

"Whaddaya want, Bill?" Bruno finally answered. I felt a tap on the shoulder. Bruno said, "Could you move your arm, son? Gotta clean up this mess." The rag hit the bar with a slap and the can landed somewhere with a clatter.

"Okay. That's better. Now, Bill? Usual?"

"Yeah. Double scotch with milk."

"And for you, sir?"

"Make mine a single whiskey sour."

A hand came to rest on the back of my right shoulder and an unfamiliar male voice appeared at my left ear. "Hey, man, can you tell me which way to State Street?" He draped his right arm across my back. I got that queasy Fred feeling.

"Sorry. I'm not from around here."

The bartender clunked my drink down in front of me. I reached into my front pocket and pulled out a bill I had carefully folded so I'd know it was a twenty. I had a fiver stuffed in my left front. I had been taught not to carry any bills over a twenty and had a billfold with three sections—one for fives, one for tens, and one for twenties. Singles I carried in my pocket. At Hines they had also taught me about folding bills to tell them apart—twenties in half and tens in quarters.

The bartender moved off without taking the twenty, but suddenly it was plucked out of my hand just as the stranger behind me dropped his arm and his footsteps shuffled toward the door. Fuck!

"Hey! Call the cops! Some guy just ran off with my twenty! Jesus Christ! Are you all blind or something?" I was so pissed off, the unintended joke didn't hit me for a few beats. I shook my head with weary recognition.

"Oh, George man! I'm sorry," Johnson said. "I shoulda warned you. You can't take out big bills down here. I thought you knew that!"

The bartender returned. "Hey, brother. I'm really sorry about that. Goddamned punks, takin' advantage like that."

"Well, call the cops, man! I was robbed! In plain fuckin' sight!"

"Look, buddy, forget about the cops." He leaned toward me, lowered his voice. "Too much trouble. You know what I mean? In a place like this? Look, drinks are on the house, alright?" He gave my shoulder a squeeze. "This shit happens all the time, even to people who are just drunk. Ya gotta be careful, 'specially you."

I needed that drink and downed it in two gulps. A second round arrived. Johnson went to use the phone and see if one of the girls he knew could take us in. "Both girls are gone," he said when he returned. "There's another bar a couple doors down where I know some people."

Johnson was newly blind and this was his stomping ground, so he knew every crack in the concrete.

He killed a third double and then he led the way out. The wind had stopped but it was stinging cold. My ear drums ached. The snow was getting deep, spilling into my shoes, and still coming down heavy. Managing the icy spots was a challenge, two drunk, blind vets holding each other up.

When we stopped for a moment to listen for clues to direction—yes, the blind were leading the blind—I could hear the subtle hiss of the snowflakes landing, a sound I hadn't noticed since I was a kid living in Federalsburg. I would sit in the outhouse listening to the stillness of a snowstorm, thinking how good my hearing must be to be able to actually hear snow fall.

As we scuttled down the street like a couple of clawless crabs, it hit me how bizarre my life had been. In just a few years I went from being a country boy hoeing corn to a battered vet with a cane wandering the streets of Chicago looking for a place to lay his head.

"I could write a book," I said.

"What? Watch it, there's a curb here."

"My life. I could write a book, my life has been so crazy. But nobody'd believe it if I did."

"You got that right.... Here!," Johnson said. "The Easy Club should be right around here."

The old fellow might be tipsy, but he could find his way around. I could faintly hear a guitarist picking strings and fingers squeaking across frets.

"Okay, I got the door open, George. Step in and then stop. There's another door. I'll get it. I know this place like the back of my hand. Hey! That's got to be Mojo Buford. He's got a band, The Savage Boys. Plays with Muddy Waters. Man, listen to that guitar!"

Johnson opened the second door. The band was playing a B.B. King tune, the drummer rolling his sticks on the snares, tapping cymbals, and kicking the bass. Then an alto saxophone began to wail. Musical heaven. We got ourselves settled at the bar with a round of drinks.

I checked my new Braille watch—nine o'clock. In between songs, the club was quiet—not much ambient sound. "It's getting late," I told Johnson. "You figured out where we're gonna spend the night?"

"Don't worry about it!" he snapped defensively. "I got two girlfriends that'll take us in, if I ever find one of 'em. . . . The usual," Johnson told the bartender. I passed.

He gave the ice in his glass a vigorous shake. "I'm gonna have to nurse this. I'm just about broke."

As precarious as the situation may have seemed, I was sure Johnson's brother would take us back to Hines if nothing else panned out.

The band performed one Muddy Waters and B.B. King tune after another. I was transfixed by their talent, and felt like I was rediscovering music, appreciating it in a different way, now that I wasn't distracted by images. I was hearing every note, every lick, every pluck.

"Could you move your stick down?" a male voice said, low and sullen. My back was leaning against the bar. He was standing in front of me.

"Sure." I moved my cane where I thought it would be out of the way. Heavy paper crumpled, like a grocery bag being rolled up. The man sat on the barstool beside me, brushing his leg against mine as he twisted himself into place.

"You blind?"

"Yeah, about a year."

The bartender interrupted. "Can I get you something?"

"Give me a whisky, straight." Again the paper bag crumpled, and my nostrils filled with an unfamiliar, cloying odor, reminiscent of a barnyard. There was a brief silence and then a thump. I reached for my drink and my hand brushed against something sticky, stringy, hair-like.

"Give this guy a drink, too," the man added calmly. "I'm payin'."

"Oh, my God!" a voice on the other side of me shouted in horror. Then others chimed in.

"Put that fuckin' thing back in the bag!"

"Holy shit! That's fucked up!"

The bartender chimed in. "What the... Roy, call the cops! This idiot just laid a goddamned hog's head on the bar!"

My heart began pounding—a rush of terror, not of the head, but the man who brought it. I snatched my hand off the bar. My watch band snagged on something—the hair on the hog's severed head! "Jesus Christ!" I tugged to break away. The head dragged with me.

"Damn!" I yelled, hopping off the stool. The head followed. My watch band stretched and snapped back as the hair untangled itself. Then, I heard a sickening thud at my feet.

Johnson had his hand on my arm, tugging. "Let's get the hell outta here!"

Tables and chairs were scraping and tumbling as patrons fled. Music from the trio moaned a slow death, as if someone had pulled the plug on a record player. Johnson and I left as fast as two blind men could. Once outside, the crisp air was like a glass of ice water in the desert. Sirens wailed in a distance.

"Okay, Johnson. Now what?"

"If that was a hog's head, I don't know why they're sending an ambulance. The Jillstone! That's it! The Jillstone Hotel! Come on! It's about two-and-a-half blocks straight up this way."

Johnson held his cane horizontal to my left side so I could tell the direction he meant. "We'll cross a couple side streets and, just like mobility training, we'll be at the objective."

I pulled the ear flaps down on my Russian cap, turned up the collar and buttoned up my coat. The air got colder, the wind increased, and I could feel it was still snowing hard. I trailed Johnson, trying to keep my cane above the new snow. The two of us drifted with the snow down Cottage Grove. Johnson whistled an old jazz tune, pausing to reminisce about winters past.

"I remember when snow was as high as a giraffe's ass. I'm going to move over to the right. There should be a wall up here."

There was, and Johnson tapped along it, testing for the doorway to the hotel. His taps changed from the rough sound of masonry to the sharp raps of glass. "Bill Johnson!"

"Lester? That you?"

"It's me, alright. You looking for the door? Over here."

"Les, that's George watching my rear."

I followed him through the doors, and into a large space filled with the smell of new carpeting. There seemed to be people all around, talking and laughing—a festive mood. "Bill Johnson! How the hell are you?" a woman asked.

"Cassie, I been tryin' to call you. Meet George. He's my friend from Hines."

"He's sorta cute." She pulled my head down into her chest and rubbed my neck. This time, I didn't mind being molested. "I'm not that tall, but I AM wonderful," she said in a honeyed voice, planting tender kisses up and down my neck. She was short, buxom, and wearing a lush fur coat that smelled like the real thing. Her body was warm and soft, and she was wearing a perfume that smelled like coconuts. She straightened up and said close to my face, "I gotta go. You guys gonna be around a while? I gotta turn a trick."

"How long you think you'll be?" Johnson asked

"Won't take long to polish this one off. He's a regular. I know his style."

"Cassie, I'm in a bit of a jam," Johnson half-whispered. "We need a place to stay tonight,"

"Hmm. Hang around. I'll talk to you about it later."

Johnson told me she had been a prostitute most of her life. "She used to be a beautiful woman. Not bad now, for her age. She must be around fifty, but you'd never know. She and I go way back."

We hung out in the hotel lobby, in a couple of battered easy chairs. Cassie returned an hour later, pulling up a chair and sitting between us. "Now, what was that you were saying before I left? I'm finished for the night. I'm tired. Can't turn 'em like I used to. I'm gettin' old."

"I need a place to stay tonight," Johnson said.

"I thought that's what you said. I'm livin' in this dive. Got a place up stairs, in the back. You know, we're alright Johnson—you and me. But what about...uh... what's-his-face? He's gotta have a place to bed down, too."

"Cassie, he's blind like me. Can't see nothing. Why can't he stay in the room with us?"

"I only have one bed but, well... Alright. But only for the night, Bill. And only 'cause we've been friends all these years. I've had more than one man in my bed before, but no screwing tonight, you guys. I couldn't screw again if my life depended on it. Bu-u-ut, if you've got twenty five dollars, I might try." She yawned.

"How do we do this, now?" she asked, getting to her feet, shuffling in front of Johnson. "I got it. Bill, you grab me and, George, you grab Bill. It'll be like pullin' a train." She giggled at herself. "Okay, let's go."

She carefully snaked through the crowd to an elevator. "Shit! This rat hole elevator never works. We gotta walk up three flights."

I had no trouble with the stairs but poor old Johnson, drunk and diabetic, was wheezing hard by the time Cassie unlocked her door and clicked on the light. Soft music came from opposite directions. The place had a cozy feel, with a living room, kitchen, bath, and bedroom. Her heavy velour drapes and round king-sized bed were impressive. I discovered Cassie had no couch, so I sank down onto the plush shag carpet near several big fluffy pillows.

"What're you doin' down there?" Cassie asked.

"I can sleep over here somewhere."

"Nothin' doin'! You're my guest. You'll sleep in the bed with us."

"Are you serious?"

"Yeah! This bed's big enough for a football team. Here, you sleep at twelve o'clock, George. Bill, you're over here at nine o'clock, and I'll sleep over here at six o'clock. I'll stay as far away from George as I can. After all, he looks dangerous!"

"Only to myself," I laughed.

While Cassie was fluffing the pillows, the phone

rang.

"Hello, honey, what's on your mind?" Cassie adopted her professional tone, low and provocative. A few moments of chatter, and the bathroom door closed behind her. Johnson felt his way around until he located the refrigerator. I took the opportunity to strip to my underwear and hop into bed.

The bathroom door opened and a warm soapy scent permeated the room. Cassie swished past the bed. I imagined her ample, bare breasts softly smacking against her glistening body, her firm, round buns, strong smooth legs, and long, curly pubic hair.

As if reading my mind—maybe I had a look on my face—she hesitated by the bed, softly chuckling. "You should see me now, George," she purred. "I guess I won't be staying tonight. Too bad. You mighta got lucky!"

Chapter 22

About the time I got into the swing of things at the Hines Blind Rehabilitation Center, it was time to leave. In the last week, I met with Dr. Malri, a psychologist. It was April of 1967, a year since I'd been wounded.

"Well, Mister Brummell," he said, standing at his desk, shuffling papers. "I have your test scores here somewhere. While I'm looking, tell me your plans when you go home."

"Plans?"

"Have you thought about going to college, or vocational training? Anything?"

"Well, I always wanted to be a disc jockey, or a truck driver."

"I think you'll have a difficult time driving a truck," he said with a chuckle. "Disc jockey? It's possible, but improbable. Disc jockeys run a tight schedule, you know. How would you manage? Oh, here are your records. Let me review your evaluation sheet." A pause, with pages turning.

"You mentioned college," I said. "Think I might be able to do that?"

"According to these scores, I'd say no. I think you'd probably need to find something else. I understand you're going home next week. I wish I'd gotten a chance to talk to you sooner. Maybe we could have planned something. But all is not lost. When you get back to... um...where are you from?"

"I'll be living in Akron, Ohio."

"When you get back to Ohio, check with Cleveland Veterans' Administration." He was now all business. "You have access to the GI Bill. When you get home, don't just sit. Stay busy. Do something. If you ever get back this way, stop in to see me. Have a good day." He showed—gently pushed—me to the door.

"Yeah, you too," I said, as ironically as I could. "As a matter of fact, have a good life."

Discharge day rolled around and a Red Cross volunteer met me at The Blind Center's front desk to drive me to the airport for the flight home. When I got out at the airport with my luggage, a black man's voice greeted me. "Sir, I'm a Skycap. I'm going to walk you to the ticket counter. The lady took care of it for you." The skycap loaded my three bags onto his cart and I held on to his long skinny arm.

"It ain't open yet," he said after a short walk. "There's seats over there," he said, moving about twenty-five feet away from the counter. "The seat's here, sir." He bent and touched the chair. I followed his hairy little limb to the arm rest.

"I'll put your luggage over here."

I felt for the bags but couldn't find them. "Where are my bags? And which way's the ticket counter?" No answer. "Hello?" He had walked away before I had a chance to ask. I flipped the lid on my watch. It was six o'clock in the morning and quiet where I was sitting. I heard people walking, but a distance behind me.

I had learned a lot at Hines and had much more confidence in my ability to get around. But my graduation was jarring. After fifteen weeks of trained professionals watching my back, correcting my mistakes, protecting me from myself, I had suddenly been dropped back in the real world.

I stood and unfolded my collapsible fiberglass cane. I swung a circle, making contact with some chairs to my left. I followed them, swinging my cane. The chairs were arranged in an arc. Just inside the bend, I bumped into one of my three suitcases. I sat beside it and found the others. I pulled the bags close so that each made contact with my legs.

A squeaky metal cart slowly headed in my direction. It stopped every few feet and I heard sweeping and the sound of metal and glass tumbling into a metal container. A janitor's cart.

"Sir," I called out. "Could you tell me where the American Airlines counter is, and when it opens?" No answer, so I repeated myself, a little louder, straining to hear an answer.

"Are you talkin' to me?" a young woman answered. I nodded. "Lemme check." She walked away, leaving a light, sweet scent. She was back in a few seconds. "They'll be open in about forty-five minutes. If you want to be first, you should get in line early. It's right over to your...let's see...to your right front, about thirty feet."

I heard her resume sweeping, then she turned a corner, and was out of hearing.

As I waited, I thought about what was next for me.

How much did the training help? Would it translate into a job? Could I get to a job? Could I keep notes well enough in Braille, and what could I really do with one hand?

A half hour later I heard a couple discussing their children's report cards. The ticket counter must be opening. Now, how was I going to get three pieces of luggage over to the counter? I decided to risk taking one at a time. I grabbed the first one and managed to find the counter.

"Good morning, sir," said a smiling female voice. "Looking for American Airlines?"

"Yes."

"We're not open yet. My co-worker and I have to go to the main office. We'll open in about fifteen minutes."

I dropped the suitcase, turned and stepped off in the direction I'd come, making wide swings with my cane. When I realized I'd walked too far, I stopped and tried to figure out which direction I should turn.

"Sir? Sir, can I help you? Are you looking for something?" An older man's voice, croaky but kind.

"Only my suitcases."

"You're well away from them. They're over here. Come on, I'll help you." He guided me to my bags.

"Thanks," I said. "I think I can manage from here."

"Well, I'm not leaving for awhile, so I'll just stay here and make sure you get on alright."

"That's not necessary."

"Forget about it. I see by your tags that you're a vet. I assume you were in Vietnam."

"Yes, I was in Vietnam and proud to have served. I was hit back in June of '66 by a landmine and now I'm on my way home from blind rehabilitation."

"This war's turning out to be a mess, don't you think?"

"I never really questioned why we were in Vietnam," I said. "I volunteered for the Army and I'm not bitter. That'd be a waste of energy. But I do wish the troops were back home."

We chatted until he helped me to the counter to check in, and then stayed with me until I was on board.

"Good luck, soldier," he said as we parted.

Blanche met me at the Akron airport. "I left the top down so we can just throw the luggage in the back seat." It was the same little white Chevy we'd had in Hawaii, in which we'd taken so many romantic drives around Oahu—before babies, before blindness.

"You came alone?"

"Sure did. I wanted you all to myself!"

"So you got your driver's license?"

"Um...well, I'm working on that. I was supposed to go down to..."

"Blanche, it's no good to be driving around without a license. What about the registration? Did you take care of that?"

Silence. I could just about hear her pouting. I wondered if she could tell from my face, scarred eyes hidden behind sunglasses, how annoyed I was by her irresponsibility. As a sergeant, I had learned to always be prepared and to set the example for others. As a black man, I knew it would be better to have as little contact as possible with the authorities. Even tickets. Justice, I knew, was not as blind as I.

Once in the car and out on the highway, the wind and sun on my face calmed me and I allowed myself to reminisce about the good old days. Blanche sighed as she wiggled her bottom into place.

"You'll like the furniture," she said, lighting two cigarettes and handing one to me. "I financed it. I put down half the three thousand dollars back pay you got. The rest I put in the bank, like you told me." She described with increasing enthusiasm all the furniture she'd bought for our newly rented Cape. I wondered how much it all cost. I was drawing veteran's benefits and Social Security disability, enough to raise a family in a modest way. I hated to spoil the party so I kept my mouth shut.

The house was a small cape with a narrow asphalt driveway that stopped at a side door. The house faced Hardesty Street, which Blanche said was lined with trees. The neighborhood was working-class black.

As soon as we were inside, Junior was there to greet us, giggling as he toddled past me into his mother's arms.

"Hello George! I'll be there in a minute!" Carrie, Blanche's younger sister, hollered from another room. "I'm on the phone, calling for my ride home! I know you two will want to get BUSY!"

Blanche giggled and squeezed my hand. "Okay, Junior. Say hello to your Daddy." She picked up Junior and held him to my chest until I got a good grip. He was heavy!

He gave me a tentative hug—one tiny arm laid

lightly on my shoulder. With Blanche's encouragement, he shyly pressed his face against my cheek. He smelled of candy and sour milk and soap and diapers. I felt such an odd mixture of joy and longing. I had a healthy son, a child that I had high hopes would never experience any of the hardships I had endured.

But God, how I wished I could cast my eyes on him! To look into his wondering eyes and see him smile; to see who he resembled—Blanche claimed it was her; to watch him grow and learn. I remembered when I'd first seen Chris's daughter—maybe my daughter as well, according to Chris. I remembered sitting in Chris's car—I wasn't much more than a child myself—and being mesmerized by how her tiny dark face looked so alert. Her large eyes glowed inquisitively, almost motionless, hardly blinking, just staring at me.

I would never have that experience with Junior but I could explore his shapely head, his silky little ears, and his miniature feet. I managed to coax a chirp of mirth out of him by tickling his belly. Someday, when he was older, even that joy would be taken from me. The enormity of my new life began to settle on my shoulders. How would I manage?

Carrie chatted with us until her ride came. She clumped down the steps, a car door slammed, and we were alone as a family again. I turned, extended my cane, and was about to explore when I sensed the heat of Blanche's body before I felt her warm, wet lips meet mine, and her big, hard stomach press against my groin. Junior, in her arms, interrupted us, planting a sticky kiss on me as Blanche and I parted. He wriggled happily in his mother's arms, gurgled, and laid a couple more kisses on my cheek.

"Okay, George. Let me put the boy in his crib and then I'll give you the grand tour."

The living room set was impressive. Each chair was different. A high-backed armless chair was covered in a fuzzy fabric. "That's powder blue," Blanche said. The other had a smooth, silky texture, small arms and a firm seat cushion. I favored the single-cushion couch the most. It was covered in a coarser material that felt more durable. The back was high enough to support my neck, with rounded, angled arms. The cocktail table was heavy oak. The end tables had ceramic lamps with raised, winding vertical patterns. Both lamps were heavy. Good. Not so easy for me to knock over.

"Junior's room is down here. I'll show you his furniture. Go on," she said.

"No, you go ahead. I'll follow. I need to get to know the floor plan." A door opened, hinges squeaking. I kept walking and softly smashed into Blanche's back.

"Oops, sorry! I didn't see you standing there." I couldn't tell if she got the joke, but she didn't laugh.

"Junior's asleep already," she whispered, gently pulling the door closed.

I reached and found her waist. She stood still for a second or two, took both of my hands and pulled them further around her expanded waist. "Follow me. I'll show you our room."

"I submit to you, mother-to-be. Lead the way. I'll just follow your rosy scent."

A week later I was bored and restless. I had too much time to think, about Blanche and the pregnancy, my future, our future. I missed the regimented setting of Hines and the Army. From always having something to do—a schedule, a plan—it was torture being idle. A couple times a day I'd get so cabin-feverish I'd grab my cane and walk a few blocks, then retreat home, looking for something to do.

Attempts at reading Braille were half-hearted ways to kill time. It was a struggle, hand reading, and everything seemed to distract me and make me lose my place, even the ticking of the clock on the end table, or Blanche's soft footsteps padding back and forth as she did her chores in the finished attic where I'd hung the rug I made in Texas.

One day when I'd gotten tired of reading, I had laid back on the couch and drifted into a light sleep when a sharp rapping startled me awake. It came from the glass storm door. Wooly-headed, I got up, cracking my shin on the edge of the coffee table. "God DAMN!"

Limping in pain, I opened the inside door, then the storm door.

"Yes?" Silence. "Who is it?" No answer.

But the storm door had hit something short of open. I let the door close. Strange. I could have sworn I felt the presence of someone out there. I made my way back to the couch and settled into a comfortable position to resume my nap.

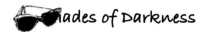

"Rap-rap-rap!"

I thought maybe it was someone playing a joke. I couldn't imagine anything else. I decided to ignore it. But the rapper continued, tenacious. Annoyed, I hopped back up, went to the front door and flung it open.

It hit something with a thump—sounded like a person.

"Who is it?!" I demanded. Silence. If it was a joke, they'd taken it too far for me. I slammed and locked the door.

"Blanche! Would you come here and see who's at the door!"

Blanche came down the steps and peeked through the curtains.

"There's a white guy out there! All dressed up." She opened the door. "May I help you?" Not a peep.

"Oh my God, George! He's a deaf mute. He's got a little card saying he's asking for a donation."

I was sorry the guy couldn't hear me roar with laughter—a deaf-mute trying to get a donation out of a blind guy. I figured that was a story worth a five dollar donation. He gave me a vigorous, "smiling" handshake.

No longer sleepy, I decided it was time I explored the basement. I stumbled through a minefield of debris—boxes, Junior's stroller, two old chairs—and felt my way around the furnace. I stepped on something mushy. I reached down. It was sticky, hairy, and lumpy. It smelled raw, nasty. "Blanche, come here!"

Holding the stuff at arm's length, I asked, "What's this? I stepped on it."

Blanche screamed.

"What! What! What's the matter?"

"It's a dead mouse! The cat must've killed it. The head's chewed off. You've got the guts!"

I flung the mess away. "Gimme a towel or something to wipe this crap off."

Nothing but surprises when you live in the dark.

A few weeks later my Vietnam buddy and pimp, Andy Miller, and I were cruising in his brother's new Olds convertible and I was griping about having nothing to do.

"What about Goodwill Industries?"

"Good who?"

"Goodwill. Haven't you heard of it?"

"Can't say I have."

"Man, you really must have lived way in the back woods! I thought everybody knew about Goodwill Industries. They fix things people throw away. The handicapped fix the stuff and then Goodwill sells 'em. I saw some blind people going in and out of there. Check it out, man. They may have something for you to do."

It sounded like a make-work deal but I was desperate. I made an appointment and got recruited into Goodwill's rehabilitation program. I was assigned tasks such as tearing old electric lamps and irons apart, and sanding furniture. I'd been there three weeks when I was handed a sanding block half the size of a pack of cigarettes and told to sand an executive desk.

"With this?" I chuckled, incredulous. "The whole desk, with this little thing?"

The slow-talking supervisor assured me that others had done just fine, but it was humiliating, like giving a grown man a baby bottle. Five minutes into the job, I decided it was just too ridiculous to continue. I asked the supervisor for an electric sander. I knew they had one. I'd heard someone using it.

"Wa-a-a-l, we aren't allo-o-wed to let you use a sa-a-nder."

"Why not?" I crossed my arms.

"I don't have to give you any explana-a-ation!" he whined.

I unfolded my cane, called a taxi, and left. When I got home I almost tripped over Blanche's suitcase, sitting just inside the back door.

"Oh my God!" Blanche was yelling. "We almost forgot the suitcase. Get the suitcase, Mama. Feels like I'm gonna have this baby any minute!" She hustled past me and out the door.

"George, she's in labor," her mother, Maggie, said. "I'll take care of everything. Just go in and have a seat." She meant well, but it made me feel helpless to be excluded from experiencing the miracle of the birth of my second child.

"Excuse me!" Maggie blew past me, picked up the suitcase, and followed Blanche out the door.

"There's some barbecued ribs and pork and beans in the oven!" Blanche called back. "Junior's in his crib. Aunt Sophie is on her way. Oh! A salad's in the refrigerator."

Blanche's aunt soon came for Junior and left just as quickly. I needed to relax, so I turned the radio to a jazz station, took a shower, and then investigated the kitchen. Blanche had prepared a plate and left it warming in the oven. How had she had time between contractions?

When I finished eating, I decided to take matters into my own hands. I called Andy and got him to give me a ride to the hospital. I wanted to be with Blanche when the baby burst through the birth channel. But at the hospital I found I had to wait until mother and child were cleaned up.

We had another boy and, after some debate, named him Keith. I wanted to name him Mister. Blanche flat out refused, and I demurred.

When I got in to see mother and son, both were healthy and Blanche was relieved and happy. Visiting hours ended and one of the nurses guided me toward the door. Just as I was about to leave, I realized I had no cash.

"I need the bank book, Blanche. I need to go to the grocery store."

An extended pause. "I can't remember where I put it. Umm... Lemme think and I'll call you later."

"Call me as soon as you can, so I can get Andy to take me shopping before he goes home."

Back at the house, I put a jazz record on the player and we had a beer. Blanche called and said the pass book was in one of her winter coats in the bedroom closet. As soon as I hung up the phone and found the bank book, Andy and I were out the door. The bank closed at three o'clock and it was already two-thirty. We made it minutes before the doors locked.

"Yes sir?" asked a middle-age sounding woman at the teller window. "May I help you?"

I placed my passbook on the counter. "I'd like to withdraw two hundred dollars."

"Oh, you're Mister Brummell! Your wife has been

coming in here for quite awhile and I never met you. Did she have the baby yet?"

"Just today," I said proudly. "A healthy boy."

"Congratulations! Can you sign for this or do you want to make an 'X'?"

"I'll sign." I pulled out my military ID card. I asked Andy to line up the top of the card with the signature line, and then I wrote my name along the top edge. It's no problem for blind people to sign their names, but it is almost impossible to write in a straight line. I asked for twenty five-dollar bills, and five twenty-dollar bills. I put the fives in my left front pocket and the twenties in the right. As I turned to leave, I remembered to ask for the account balance.

"There's—let me see—one hundred and seventy-five dollars."

"Are you sure?"

She checked again. "Yes. Yes, that's it."

What had happened to the fifteen hundred dollars in back pay Blanche said she'd deposited in the bank? I went straight to the phone when I got home.

Blanche's mother answered and handed the phone to Blanche. "Could the bank have made a mistake? The teller said we only had a balance of a hundred and seventy-five."

Silence, then a sniffle, then crying. I ran my hand over the arm of the chair. Maybe she lied about the cost of the furniture. Maybe she shouldn't have spent that money in the first place.

"I don't know what I did with it," she finally said, sounding miserable. "I just don't know what happened to the rest of the money." I felt a flush of anger. She didn't remember? That sounded like bullshit to me. I pressed Blanche. "Think! That's a lot of damned money to forget." She started crying again which only made me angrier.

"Don't you get it? A marriage is based on trust. Now that I'm blind, my need to trust you is everything."

She tried to change the subject, but I was a dog with an old shoe, becoming more and more agitated. How the hell was I going to make it with a spendthrift wife who lacked the common sense to get her driver's license and registration renewed? I needed a strong mate, someone who I could rely on absolutely to take care of business and be my eyes. My frustration with life, with being blind, faced with mouths to feed and money being squandered on God knows what—it all boiled over.

"Look, Blanche, right now I don't give a damn about how adorable you think our son is, or whether he looks like me. If I can't trust you, I don't want to stay in this marriage. You tell me right now where that money went, or I'm history. I'll just go back to Federalsburg."

"Go ahead, then!" Blanche snapped. "I don't care! And I still don't know where the money went, either!" Then she hung up on me. I slammed the receiver down, missing the cradle and making a ruckus as the phone clattered to the floor.

"Andy!" I shouted.

"Right here, friend."

"I need a ride to the bus depot."

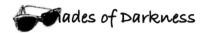

Chapter 23

Three days later I was back in Federalsburg in my brother Donald's home, sharing a room with my five-year-old nephew, figuring my next move.

I had moments of utter despair: I was blind, physically limited, married, father of two young children, with an irresponsible wife who now had her mitts on my weekly VA check, essentially homeless and having to sleep in a child's bedroom.

I had moments of wrenching guilt—Blanche had been a happy, carefree young woman who fell in love with a sturdy young man with perfect eyesight and a lusty appreciation of her. Now she was a weary mother of three, me being the biggest. I couldn't even compliment her on her latest hair style or dress. It had to be tough for her at times, even embittering.

In spite of all the help and support she'd been through my service, injury, and recovery—and all the passion we'd shared—the list of disagreements was growing. She had taken to sniping at times, ridiculing me when I tried to encourage Junior to learn well so he could go to college.

"I don't know why you think a college education is such a great thing," she'd scoff. "It's the college people that're outta work. Better he should learn to drive a truck and get a union job."

We had different parenting styles. I had grown up in a family of kissers and huggers. On top of that, I'd lost the use of my sight as a way to read and communicate emotion. So I couldn't get enough of having Junior sit in my lap, letting me snuggle him and nibble his ears and feel the flutter of his heart and hear the laughter bursting from his lungs and his soft breathing when he slept. I wanted him to get used to me, his blind father with the disfigured eyes hiding behind sunglasses.

Blanche, to my bewilderment, actually resisted showing affection for Junior. Once when he was begging to be picked up and she rebuffed him, I asked, "How come you don't kiss and hug 'em once in awhile? You're his mother."

She sighed. "I don't know, George. I...just can't is all."

I yearned to be a good father and set an example by finding my own way in the world, instead of using my challenges as an excuse to lay around living off my VA checks. I'd seen some of the other men who'd done it and most ended up alcoholics and diabetic. Could I avoid a similar fate?

The perfect antidote for these low moments was being around my family, in a black community where I had history and a little status, and where I could be reminded that the strong can survive just about anything. I had survived my mother, a brush with the law, and now a landmine. Through it all, my grandmother had been there, urging me on to do my best, and scolding me when I wallowed in self-pity.

In fact, Grandma visited my thoughts almost

every day, wherever I was, whatever I was doing. She was an ever-flowing well of emotional sustenance, and a source of anxiety—she was almost seventy years old and I was just twenty-four. She had been there for me my whole childhood. She was even there in my mind's eye at the moment of my disaster.

Now she was an old lady with old-lady health problems, recently diagnosed with liver cancer. I dreaded the inevitable phone call that would mean my anchor line had been cut. I wanted her to live long enough that I could spoil her and make her life easier, the way she had mine.

So my first visit back home was to pay homage and be renewed by her nurturing, and entertained by her faith. She was a church lady. Her life revolved around a Pentacostal congregation in nearby Bethlehem, a village that people came to from all around Washington and Baltimore each Christmas to get their holiday cards postmarked. My grandmother—they called her Miss Susie—sang with the lively choir and helped out with the bake sales and seasoned her conversation with plenty of "Lord knows!" and "Jesus be!" and "It's in His hands!"

She'd taken me to church with her through much of my childhood. What I got out of it was mostly the entertainment value—they sang all the old hymns and gospels. The services dragged on forever, with people giving testimony, and faith healing, and wild hooting and hollering. I never caught the fever, but I enjoyed sharing the experience with her.

It was good to see Grandma again, to hang out at the bar and catch up with old friends. But it only took a week for the glow to fade and I was again bored and restless. I missed my family, my life in Akron, and especially the comforts of home, like air conditioning and indoor plumbing. The little room I shared with my nephew was crowded and hot. It had one window and a screen with holes that let in mosquitoes as ferocious as the blood guzzlers of Vietnam.

Trips to the outhouse were always an unwanted adventure—first trying to find it, then hitting the hole. I found a stray branch was a helpful way to find it without using your hands. One night, I wandered off into the woods in a pouring rain. Another time I got so lost fumbling in the trees it was almost an hour before someone saw me, a neighbor running to the community funk house.

"I'm lost friend!" I shouted when I heard the hurrying footfalls. "Can you turn me back in the right direction?"

"I'd take you all the way, but I'm a little pressed." I could hear him prancing in place. He pointed me in the right direction, and took off to the community outhouse like he was being chased.

Blanche and I stayed in touch by phone. Sometimes it seemed we would be able to get through it, and sometimes she was nasty and threatening. I told her I needed money wired to me.

"I got a lawyer."

"What do you mean you got a lawyer? Why do you need a lawyer?"

"He says you got to pay for the kids, and I don't have to give you the VA checks if I don't want to."

Finally, after about a month languishing in Federalsburg, Blanche and I agreed to try to mend our life together. I returned home determined that this wouldn't happen again. I opened my own bank account and started saving toward the house I could buy using my VA Loan Guarantee privilege. In about a year we moved into a small starter home with a detached garage and finished basement, just a few blocks from a supermarket and an elementary school.

I was trying to figure out ways to entertain and educate myself. I remembered some white kids in Federalsburg had CB radios in their cars with big whip antennas and the call letters stenciled on the back window. I had been impressed and intrigued. Talking was something I could do and nobody would know I was blind. I went to an electronics store, bought a whole setup, and began to spend long stretches in the basement chatting with people all over the country.

The radio became my friend, always there whenever I was ready. My sleep patterns had been irregular ever since I'd left the regimented life at Hines. I often found myself sleeping in the middle of the day and being wide awake at night. When I wasn't listening to talking books and music, or reading Braille books on ancient Greek and Roman history, I was on my Citizens Band radio. I made a lifelong friend who lived just six blocks away from me in Akron.

Three years flew by, but the undercurrent of restlessness persisted. I wasn't doing enough for myself or for my family. We were secure and there was always food on the table, but I wanted more. What could I do to make myself and my family proud? What could I do to encourage my boys to be strivers?

People I knew or met often suggested organizations for the blind so I got in touch with the Summit County Society For the Blind. They operated a "work" program that taught basket weaving, public speaking, and abacus. I wasn't interested in any of that, but they did have contract work and, with scarcely a thought, I went to work packaging light bulbs for a dollar thirty an hour. It was something to do, to get out of the house and test my mobility and other skills. I stood next to a conveyer belt and when I felt the bulbs come by, I grabbed four and stuffed them in a box.

There was a little ironic humor in a blind man packing light bulbs. But there was bitterness, too. How I wished I could screw one of those bulbs in the top of my head and produce light for my darkened life!

The work was constant and monotonous, and the repetitive reaching left me with a strained back at night. I lasted two months.

A co-worker in the light-bulb brigade had encouraged me to check out the Cleveland Sight Center, about thirty-five miles from Akron. I discovered they offered a residential program to learn how to operate a news and candy stand. I was overdue for a change of scenery, so I signed up.

The Center's rehab program was similar to Hines. Lodging was a few blocks from the school, in an apartment I shared with two other men about my age, Larry and Jason. Larry was lazy, a slob. Jason was articulate and organized. Jason and I, the ex-Army sergeant, worked hard keeping the place tidy. It's easy to get sloppy when you can't see the mess.

Having the living quarters apart from the Center

allowed me an opportunity to experience real independence, and independence was something I missed. I started by refreshing my mobility and Braille skills, but I really concentrated on learning the vending stand operation.

The training supervisor started out by handing me a half gallon can of pennies, nickels, dimes and quarters. I had to learn how to identify them quickly and accurately. Then I was taken to one of the city court houses where there was a busy stand owned and operated by two blind men. They were in their late fifties but hustled about their business like a couple of frisky squirrels. They told me to start by cleaning counter tops and making coffee. Later they taught me how to distinguish between brands of cigarettes, sodas, candies, and other items.

The cigarettes were stacked in a rack in alphabetical order with each rack holding a different brand. There were also labels at the bottom of each stack in Braille.

They had me doing everything, including cashier. It was hard work, stuck in the same place all day, having to keep twenty things straight in your head at all times, listening for thieves and worrying about cheats. It didn't take long for me to be cured of any desire to run a news stand.

But I finished the training anyway, then went home to pick up where I left off, doing nothing. I was lying in bed one morning a few weeks after I returned—in November 1970—when I got the phone call I had always dreaded, from my brother Donald.

"Hey, Pie. I got some real sad news. Grandma

passed last night."

The words hit like a thunderbolt, like the land-mine that stole my eyes. First thought: Donald had made a cruel joke. Then—he wouldn't. He couldn't. My stomach flip-flopped.

"But...but she wasn't... Was she... Was she sick?"

"Yeah, she'd been real sick with the cancer, for a few months anyway. I didn't want to worry you, and then she just went so fast."

"Man! You mean she was DYING and I never got a chance to say goodbye? Man! I can't believe it. Grand-ma... Just like that?" My throat started to close. "Later. Gotta go!"

Poor Grandma! After all she'd done for me, and there I had been, sitting on my rump in Akron, absorbed in my misery. I was doing exactly what she'd scolded me for, feeling sorry for myself, when I could have been with her, could have told her some things, could have comforted her, could have... My grief gathered like a tsunami until it broke with a howl of emotional agony. Blanche came running from the kids' room.

"George, what is it? What's wrong? Are you hurt? Did you fall?"

She was frantic, looking for blood. In her terror, she also began to cry. It took me a few minutes to get a grip. "Call your sister to come look after the kids for a week or so. We've got to go to Federalsburg."

We buried Grandma in the cemetery next to the Bethlehem Pentacostal Church, where she could always hear the congregation and choir singing the old gospels and hymns she loved. Her favorite was "The Old Rugged Cross," and we sang it at the service:

On a hill far away, stood an old rugged Cross
The emblem of suff'ring and shame
And I love that old Cross where the dearest and best
For a world of lost sinners was slain

So I'll cherish the old rugged Cross
Till my trophies at last I lay down
I will cling to the old rugged Cross
And exchange it some day for a crown

Black funerals often double as black reunions, and so did Grandma's. Over fried chicken and biscuits and sweet potato pie in the back of the church, I got to visit with family I hadn't seen since I was a kid, like my oldest sister, Ida. It felt good to reconnect. Even my mother was there and we had a polite conversation, recalling the good days and steering clear of the bad.

When the dust finally settled, Blanche and I visited Donald in his newly purchased house. He was proud of the good deal he made. "I only paid seventy-five hundred, and it's got six acres. Pie, If I had more money, I'd buy the house next door, too. It's almost two acres and a newer house. They only want eighty-five hundred."

The houses were in a tiny black neighborhood about four miles from where Grandma lived, in the country along a dirt road. There were a half-dozen small homes, and open fields surrounded by forest.

The more my brother talked about the small house across the field, the more intrigued I became. I had always looked up to Donald, the older, wiser brother who got to do all the grown-up things before I did. If being a home-owner in Federalsburg was good enough for him, it might be good enough for me. It sounded like a clean way to make money.

I tapped Blanche on the knee. "Let's take a look."

"Take a look at what?"

"The house across the field."

"Why? You aren't thinkin' about moving back here, are you? Because if you are, you can just..."

"I know all that. I just want to look. I have an idea."

It was almost a doll-house, a tiny, three bedroom bungalow with wood siding that Blanche said was yellow, with brown shutters. The builder had run out of money so it had no steps, interior doors, kitchen cabinets, baseboards, floor covering, plumbing, or central heat—just a wood stove. The house did have a bathroom, with tub, commode, and sink, but no septic tank or well to hook them up to. What the house had plenty of was potential.

Back in our motel room, Blanche and I debated long into the night. Five hundred dollars down was all we needed. We had about fourteen hundred in the bank and my steady income. So we decided to buy it.

To my surprise, Blanche agreed that we should relocate to Maryland. We would rent out our house in Akron and live in Federalsburg for two years while we fixed up the bungalow. Then we'd do the reverse, rent the Federalsburg house and move back to Akron. We closed on the house in three days and left for Akron to wait a month while the new place was properly wired and a septic tank installed. Then we moved.

The house was even smaller than I remembered, so small that we had to sell or give away some of that expensive furniture Blanche had bought, plus my favorite black reclining chair. Even then, the house was still cramped. Once we figured out where to stash everything, we hardly had room to walk.

We enrolled the boys in the local school, rolled up our sleeves, and went to work. We hired a neighbor and his old putt-putt tractor to cut down all the weeds while we hung cabinets, laid carpets, and nailed baseboard. It took us a year of living in a construction site inside a matchbox, but we nearly completed all the projects.

Once again, boredom and restlessness returned. There was almost nothing to do in town, not even a movie theater. The boys were now five and six years old, and they were complaining, too. They missed Akron and their family and friends. By that time I also felt the urge to go back to the Rubber City. Federalsburg was too slow, even for a home boy. But the Akron house was rented out for another year, and we weren't finished with the renovations.

Blanche's way of dealing with the boredom was to get a job working the night shift at a local plastics factory. I envied her, and had my radar working, hoping something would pop up for me as well.

One Saturday night, my old stuttering friend Nelson and I stopped in at the Beer Garden. Big Frank was long gone and Ethel, the current owner, was fuming.

It was her big night of the week, her popular Saturday Night Record Hop, and the disc jockey was a no-show.

"All that jive you talk, Pie. Too bad you don't know how to deejay. I got all the equipment."

I couldn't believe it—spinning records was one of my dreams. "Where is it?" I jumped off the creaky stool. "Show me."

"What you g-gonna do, P-Pie?" Nelson demanded. "You don't know nothing 'b-bout it!"

Ethel took me by the hand and guided me to a table that held the control board for a public address system, microphone, and two turn tables. Everything but the music. "You know anything 'bout this stuff, Pie?"

"Well, I learned some electronics in my blind training, and working with my CB setup. How complicated could it be? Got any records?" I was dying to fool around with it, see if I could create some excitement.

"I got some at home," Ethel said. "Gimme five minutes." I turned on the system. It popped and hummed. Both turn tables started spinning. I found the mike switch and flicked it on. "TESTING!" My voice boomed in the empty bar.

Ethel brought back a tin box full of forty-fives. She read off the labels. "Marvin Gaye, 'What's Goin' On'!" I cried. "Put it in my hand here." It was a big hit, a protest song that spoke to my soul:

Mother, mother
There's too many of you crying
Oh, brother, brother, brother
There's far too many of you dying

...
Oh my father, father
We don't need to escalate
You see war is not the answer
For only love can conquer hate
...
What's going on in the world today
I'd rather be dead
Than turn my head away
We gotta first world vision too comfy to lift our
Hands in the air and cry for a switch

I swayed to the music as I cued up a second record on the other turn table. Within fifteen minutes, I felt like a professional. One of my cousins, Clarice, came by and agreed to be my eyes. She read me labels, or found a specific tune I wanted to play. One song led to another, the bar started to fill and get noisy, and I could feel the thumps of the dancers through the floor. Soon I had the place rocking, fingers popping, hands clapping, and shoes scraping.

When it was over, Ethel surprised me by pressing twenty-five dollars in my hand. "That was the most fun I ever had making money!" I crowed.

"If you had your own equipment, Pie, I'd pay you 'nother twenty."

"You'd let me play it here?"

"Hell, yeah! I can't depend on 'Spinnin' Simpson.'"

I got home at three o'clock so wound up I woke Blanche to brag.

"Baby, listen. You won't believe it. I have a job!"

"A job?" She groaned. I'd had a few drinks and it

must have showed. "Pie, it's the middle of the damn night! What job? Where?"

"On weekends, at the Beer Garden!"

"Hunh! As what? A *bouncer*?" My enthusiasm that night was immune to her customary put-downs and sarcasm. I didn't care what she thought. I just needed to tell somebody.

It took two weeks to find a decent starter sound system. Then I bought a bunch of the latest releases, two cheap turn tables, and a microphone. Next I bought a used van with low mileage and no extras.

I was ready. Almost. I needed a name, but it had to be memorable, clever. For lack of something better, I decided to use my CB handle, "Monkey Meat," which was a cruel nickname that some of my friends and I called a boy we went to school with because he was very dark and unusually hairy. Instead of Record Hops, I called the dances Monkey Jumps.

Ethel booked me some Saturdays and in between I spun for high school graduations, birthday parties, and wedding receptions. Blanche drove me to most of the gigs, but sometimes Nelson or his brother pitched in. I was able to carry the equipment and had no problems connecting the components myself.

It didn't hurt being blind, black, and musical at a time when Ray Charles and Stevie Wonder were about as hot as they would ever be. The music helped me connect in so many ways.

I took every gig that came along, and did some Monkey Jumps as far away as Wilmington, Delaware. When I wasn't spinning, I rented the PA system to small bands, and to the local day care center.

But just as I was building up a reputation and a head of steam, the last brick was laid on the front steps marking completion of all the renovations on the bungalow. Our two year project was ready to be rented out, so we returned to Akron.

We arrived in Ohio during a brutal August heat wave. As we drove up to the house, we realized we'd packed the house keys in a dresser that was in the moving truck, two days behind us. Blanche drove to the real estate office that collected the rent to get a spare set. We went straight back to the house. I followed Blanche as she unlocked the front door. She stopped short and I bumped into her. Then I got a whiff of garbage.

"Oh my God!" she shrieked. "This place is a wreck! The trash is piled almost to the ceiling!"

Every room in the house had a pile of bulging plastic bags and overflowing paper sacks full of trash and garbage. I was furious, but first we had to figure out how to get rid of it all. We drove to the nearest telephone booth and called the realtor.

"I don't have anything else to do with it! It's your responsibility now! Our contract is over," he shouted.

"Look, I know you didn't put the trash there but I have to deal with it. Just give me the tenants' new address and phone number. He and I need to have a little talk."

I immediately phoned and got him on the line.

"This is George Brummell, and I want to know who the hell you think you are, leaving my house like that?"

"Not mine!" he snapped. "That's *your* shit *now*, Bud."

I bruised my knuckles trying to slam the receiver into the cradle.

When I got back to the van, I told Blanche that he wanted me to bring the trash to his new house. "He'll take care of it," I lied. I was seething, but she didn't question me.

We loaded all the trash in our van, filling it. "Seventh Street," I told Blanche. When we got there, she pulled to the curb and I immediately opened the passenger door and started to get out.

"Where are you going? You don't know where the steps are."

"You're in front of the bastard's house, aren't you?"

"Yeah. It's right behind you. But..." I slid open the side cargo door, reached in, and started grabbing bags and flinging them as best I could in the direction I thought the house was.

"George! What the hell are you doing! No! You can't just throw trash in front of people's houses. Stop that!"

"I am not throwing trash in front of people's homes," I said, flinging a paper sack that burst and showered me with cigarette butts and ashes. "I'm throwing trash in front of the trash owner's place."

I was reaching into the van to find the last few bags when a door slammed and I heard a man, the tenant, bellowing. "What the hell are you doing? Damn blind fool! What the fuck's wrong with you?"

"It's your shit, man! I'm just bringin' it home." I kept tossing bags. The guy sounded truly enraged, so I grabbed the last few bags as quickly as I could, flung them as far as I could in the direction of his voice, jumped back into the van, and we peeled away.

Blanche wouldn't speak to me for two hours. The tenant took me to court. I may have had the satisfaction of ruining the guy's day, but the judge was unimpressed.

"Son, I can appreciate what you did, going to the war and all! But that doesn't excuse your bad behavior! You can't go around dumping trash on public or private property! You either clean up that mess or get someone else to do it. I don't care. But get it done! If it's not done in two days, I'll lock you up, blind or not. Now CLEAR MY COURTROOM. Next!" He smacked his gavel like he was flattening a bent nail.

The next day I hired someone to clean up the mess. It was almost worth every penny.

Chapter 24

The next year passed quickly. We made some improvements to the Akron house, but otherwise our lives settled into a stultifying routine— eating, sleeping, and watching television. I especially enjoyed the morning news shows, and never missed Larry King on the radio. I also had been addicted to sharing "Sesame Street" with the boys, who seemed to get a kick out of telling me what was going on.

One day we were watching and I heard a character cough, followed by a strange noise.

"What happened?"

"A man was smoking a cigarette and he coughed so hard his head came off," Keith said.

I had a cigarette in my hand and I self-consciously stubbed it out in the ashtray. I'd been trying to quit without any luck. Since I'd been blind, smoking wasn't as pleasurable and it was a little dangerous. With my olfactory sense heightened, the smell had become an irritant. I decided to try a pipe and bought a few with all the accessories—pipe ashtray, humidor, the works. But that was a lot of fuss and after a month I gave the tobacco up altogether, donating my pipes to a friend.

It felt like a big accomplishment to quit smoking, but it set off a crisis in my marriage. Blanche was a committed smoker and she ridiculed me for trying to get her to quit as well. We seemed to disagree about everything anymore.

I retreated more and more into my CB radio and reading, mostly nonfiction and especially ancient history and philosophy, like Plato's *The Republic*, and Aristotle's criticisms of it.

That summer, 1974, I upgraded my CB microphone and put my old one up for sale. A young man just out of high school, Jesse Post, came to buy it. Jesse was shy, but bright. He worked in a record shop for his father, who'd retired from a rubber company.

He enjoyed selling records, but electronics was his first love. He stayed late into the night and we drank a few beers while talking about radios, my van, and then how we might make some money. Jesse said that with a truck, we could make good money doing light hauling. Before the night was over, we were business partners. We tried to think of a good name for our little venture and finally came up with The Blind and Associate Light Haulers—me the blind, and Jesse the associate.

I bought a used appliance truck, blankets, ropes, and other moving equipment. Then I ran an ad in the local newspaper. During the day, I sat by the phone scheduling moves and making excuses. I told customers that our regular trucks were tied up until after four o'clock, and the only thing available was a van. Patrons, often in a jam, usually settled for the van.

After Jesse finished his work day at the record shop, we did the moving jobs. If it was too big for the two of us, we hired a third person. They were mostly small jobs but occasionally we moved the entire contents of homes, making numerous trips with my half-ton van.

In spite of my blindness and my injured left arm, I found I could be helpful as the caboose, lifting large objects like a refrigerator, a dresser, a couch or a stove with my good right hand, and following Jesse's lead. Even I was impressed with the weight I could handle.

Customers couldn't figure it out at first. They'd ask Jesse, "Where's your helper?"—like I was invisible.

"George is going to help," Jesse replied. "He owns two thirds of the company." The customers would reluctantly let us in, but then they watched us like hawks. When the job was done, they were impressed and often gave generous tips.

Jesse and I had fun and made money that summer. But he began to lose interest and we agreed to close up shop. I retired from yet another endeavor but I'd made enough money hauling for a down payment on a third piece of real estate, which I immediately rented out. I also started putting money into an annuity, just twenty-five dollars a month at first, but over time I increased it until I had a nest egg I could borrow against.

We moved late that fall, into a white frame colonial. Another year passed and I had enough money for a down payment on a three unit apartment house in a rough part of town. It needed work but I was proud of my progress and the triplex soon made a profit. I was rolling, feeling more needed and responsible, providing shelter for five families.

Once I had my real estate empire under control, I returned to Hines for four weeks of laser cane training. The new electronic cane emitted three laser beams at different angles and gave warning beeps when I was close to running into an obstacle or stepping into a depression more than three inches deep. The upper beam transmitted out and up. When it hit something, the cane made a high-pitched sound, letting me know something was above. The middle beam went straight forward and emitted a medium frequency sound when something was in front of me. The last beam shot out and down and made a low frequency sound when a depression was in my path. The cane was a big improvement, picking up low hanging tree limbs I used to run into and saving me from stumbling off curbs and steps.

When I got back home with my high tech cane I was ready for some action. I took daily walks, but I wanted a destination like work or school—a place to go. Friends had encouraged me to try college, but I never took them seriously—I was a high school dropout and blind. When I heard about a blind man and woman who were attending the University of Akron, I decided to give it a shot myself.

A disabled Vietnam vet I knew, Carstell Stewart, who had been working on his masters degree in communications, was eager to help and guided me through the application and registration process. I started classes in the Winter semester: English, reading and math. All were in the same building on the same floor, so getting around was a cinch. I loved the atmosphere, loved meeting and sharing experiences with new people, and proudly swung my beeping cane around campus, free as a bird. I felt liberated, like I had unbuttoned a too-tight collar.

Home life, however, was in an accelerating downward spiral. One day, as I was getting out of a taxi coming from class, Junior ran by me shouting, "Mister Norwood got on a pair of pants just like yours. Same color and everything." Paul Norwood was visiting his sister Jackie, the charming, cool flirt who lived next door. He was also a vet and we sometimes chatted about our Army experiences.

"Hello, George," I heard Norwood call from the driveway next door.

"Hello Paul. What kind of pants do you have on that are just like mine?"

"These ARE yours—your red ones. Your wife loaned 'em to me a few days ago. Mine got wet. I'll give 'em back to you tomorrow."

Shit! My favorite pants. What the hell was she thinking? "Never mind," I said. "You can keep 'em if you want."

A new chapter opened for me when I was invited to a VA event in Cleveland where I was given an award as vet-of-the-year for my efforts to improve myself at University of Akron. The local media picked it up, and then the national wire services. One of my college professors, who was teaching me geology, wrote an article about how I learned to distinguish different rocks by taste, and he won an award for it.

The laser cane was so new and intriguing that I ended up in an article in a supermarket tabloid, the *Weekly World News,* and was booked to be on ABC's *Good Morning America,* until a scheduling conflict interfered.

The more attention I got, the more surly Blanche

became. I tried to encourage her to go to school and she did take some beauty courses, but didn't get her license. Her habit of speaking disrespectfully to me in front of others became more pronounced. One day our neighbor Jackie said, "I saw you on the tube last night, on the Six O'Clock News. You're a star!"

"Oh, please don't tell him that," Blanche complained. "He thinks he's God now, going to college and everything! Hunh!"

In spite of the media madness and marital discord, I managed to complete the semester with a "B" average, which called for a celebration. We took a family vacation to visit my sister-in-law in California. Blanche drove while the children and I sang, played games, talked on the CB, and listened to the radio. We visited the Queen Mary, Tijuana, and San Francisco before heading home with a van full of trinkets and souvenirs, including a huge ceramic tiger we named Leo that arrived home in pieces.

Blanche refused to attend college functions with me, and declined my offer to enroll her in a business math course because she was having a terrible time keeping the check book balanced. "I'm not college material and I'm not going!"

I wanted Junior to learn to make his bed, but Blanche disagreed. In fact, she often let the boys do the opposite of what I told them, making them promise not to tell me. According to her, I was too strict.

I wanted the boys to aspire to be successful and proud, while Blanche was convincing them they also were not college material and should be happy to grow up and drive trucks.

When Keith, the youngest, was having trouble with multiplication, I had him make three multiplication charts and place one on the mirror in the upstairs bathroom, one on the mirror in his bedroom, and one on the wall in the downstairs bathroom. I thought it would help reinforce his memory.

Blanche was outraged. "My God, George! The boys can't use the bathroom without you cramming them with education!"

I was just not getting through to them or Blanche, and it hurt almost as much as the pain I suffered in combat. I became deeply depressed, until finally one day I'd reached my limit. I didn't know if I could live without Blanche, but I knew, in spite of the hurt and sorrow, that I had to try.

In the divorce we ended up separating the boys. Keith stayed with me, which surprised no one since Blanche openly favored her first-born, Junior. In fact, I often found myself having to defend young Keith from her biting tongue and unfair treatment. In spite of it, Keith loved his mother and would have preferred staying with her, but he knew she did not want him.

Most of the first week apart, Keith and I cried. In the evenings I heard him in his room, wailing to end the world. And I suspect that when he wasn't crying, he could hear me sobbing. As the weeks passed, the tears were replaced by lingering heartache, and then the dull throb of mourning. I tried to avoid self-pity, but I couldn't shake some of the feelings of regret that dogged me about decisions I'd made in my life, all the way back to joining the Army. Where did my love and innocence go, I wondered. Would I ever feel whole

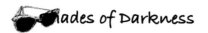

again?

Around this time I got a phone call from another blind, black vet who was traveling the country doing research for the Blinded Veterans Association. Tony Gunter was from Philadelphia and I was impressed to learn that he'd traveled the whole way independently. We had a lot in common, not least of which was that he also had been blinded in Vietnam. Almost on the spot I adopted him as a role model.

The kind of work he was doing, traveling state to state to serve blind veterans, was the most appealing job I could imagine. Tony's task was to find out how much blind veterans knew about their benefits—federal, state, and local—and to spread the word about the Blind Veterans Association—the BVA. When he told me that the BVA had an employment program to help blind veterans find jobs, I became stoked.

"You're just the man I've been looking for. Sign me up! I'll be graduating college soon and looking for work."

"I'll make sure our employment rep gets this information. He'll be calling you very soon." I so admired Tony. He was articulate, smart, and had straight-forward answers to every question I could think of. He left with my hopes soaring.

Keith was sixteen then, old enough to get his driver's permit. A family friend taught him to drive and he passed the test on the first try. We decided to take a drive to Federalsburg to visit the family and check up on the house I owned there. Happy for the adventure as a distraction from our lingering sadness, we rolled off on a hot August morning our two-tone brown Chevy van that Keith had lovingly washed and vacuumed the day before. I even helped with wiping it dry.

I reclined in my captain's seat, adjusted the radio volume, and settled back for the eight-hour trek. We ran into miles of road construction on the Pennsylvania Turnpike and lost a lot of time. When we stopped for lunch, he sounded really tired.

"You okay?"

"Yeah, Dad, I'm okay. Just tired of sitting is all."

"We can stop and take a nap. It might perk you up."

"No, Dad. I'm fine. Really."

After lunch and a short walk, we hit the highway again. We had talked ourselves out so I fiddled with the CB radio while Keith chewed gum in sync with the rhythm of the "bump" of the tires hitting the joints in the concrete. After a while, I noted that Keith's rhythm had changed—there were longer silences between chews and tiny bubble pops. Then it sounded as if he'd stopped chewing altogether. Just as it hit me that he'd fallen asleep, the van rocked violently side to side.

"Keith!" No response.

Plowing ahead at full speed, the van shrieked as it scraped against something and seemed to bounce off. Then it swayed wildly. "Keith!" I shook his shoulder. Tires squealed and horns blasted from opposing lanes. I grabbed the dashboard to brace myself for the inevitable impact.

"Yeah! Yeah!" Keith said groggily. Then, "Oh shit!" He got control of the van, pulled to the shoulder, and burst into tears.

"Thank God," I whispered. "My life has been

spared once more." I stepped out of the van on wobbly legs and breathed in the fresh air. We were in the mountains of western Maryland, on the side of a steep slope.

"Dad, we're lucky!" Keith said when he'd gotten hold of himself. "Wow! We're on top of a mountain. If that guard rail hadn't held... I'm sorry, Dad! I'm really, really sorry!"

"Okay, son. Everything happens for a reason, I guess. I hope this scared the hell out of you. You might remember it next time."

I felt my way around the van, assessing the damage and listening to Keith's description. In addition to peeled paint, the front bumper and fender were twisted, and the head light on the right side hung by its wires. I had a momentary flashback of poor Shark, my Vietnam buddy, who'd caught a mortar fragment in the face. One of his eyes had popped out and landed on the ground, staring at me.

The van was drivable, but too badly damaged to continue, so we turned around and headed back home.

———·+·———

When I was about to graduate from college, I got a long-awaited call from an employment representative with the Blinded Veterans Association. He put me in touch with Roberto DeJesus, who was in line to become the organization's National Field Service Director. He promised he'd consider me for a field rep position when he was officially in charge.

The summer passed with no news, so I decided to enroll in graduate school for social work, at Case Western Reserve University in Cleveland. At the end of my second semester, Roberto finally phoned with news of two openings for field service reps, in Dallas and Chicago. I flew to Washington for the interview and got the job. I was excited and frightened at the same time, but not a bad feeling. My adrenaline was pumping like it had in Vietnam.

"We need a man with a strong personality like yours in Chicago," Roberto said. "There have been some problems with the group in Illinois. I think you could handle them up there better than the other man I hired. I'll send him to Dallas."

I would have chosen Dallas over the miserably cold winters of Chicago, but Roberto made me feel important, confident. I needed time to think about it, to decide whether it was worth pulling the plug on grad school. I only needed eighteen more credit hours to get my masters in social work.

I wondered what Grandma would have said, and decided it would have been something like, "A bird in the hand is worth more than two in a bush, boy." How I wished I could call her and brag about how well I was doing!

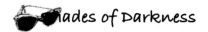

Chapter 25

I arrived in Chicago in the middle of a December snowstorm, exactly the weather I dreaded. I had wanted to live outside the city, but the housing agency that made the arrangements specialized in investigating cases of racial discrimination and they put me in a white neighborhood farther from downtown than I would have liked.

But I was near the Hines VA facility and they were happy to send a mobility instructor to help me get oriented. I had tried to get Keith to move with me, but he decided at the last moment to live with his mother's sister Carrie in Akron. I understood that living with her would be easier than tagging along with a blind father in a strange city, so I agreed when he asked to stay behind. But it was a decision I regretted daily. I really missed my son's company.

After I became acclimated and oriented, I went to work, beginning with a frigid one-hour commute involving two buses, an elevated train, and a two-block walk. I was a bit shaky that first day, trying to find my way. I crossed a wrong street and waited for the bus on the wrong corner. When I finally got to work, it felt great to have made it there on my own. Now I had my own office in downtown Chicago. Those nine years of school finally paid off. Chicago, here I am!

The office was more cramped than I expected, windowless, narrow, with barely room for the two credenzas, a file cabinet and a desk which was for the secretary because she needed space for the typewriter. I sat at the credenza in a corner.

My predecessor, the outgoing field rep, was laid back and unhelpful. He was supposed to teach me the job but only answered questions and left me with no records or veterans' files. I had nothing to work with, not even a secretary since she left when Roman did.

The first phone call was from the president of the Illinois Regional Group, a guy named Yardley. "Welcome to Chicago, Mister Brummell. I'm glad Headquarters cleaned that office out over there. That Roy Wilson, the vice president of the Group, and Roman have been plotting to overthrow me and eventually the national organization."

Yardley laid it all out, helping identify trouble spots. I wanted to stay away from politics. I wanted nothing more than to do a good job serving blind veterans.

I hired a secretary, Jane Moore, from Volunteers In Service To America (VISTA). Jane was short and a single black mother, out of high school only two years. Fresh from Georgia, she had lived in Chicago only a few months. She had a pleasing Southern accent and a tone that smiled.

After some additional training in Atlanta, I started contacting and introducing myself to all the Visual Impairment Service Team (VIST) Coordinators in the states I worked: Illinois, Indiana, Missouri, Michigan,

Ohio, and Wisconsin. They were contacts for blind veterans at VA Medical Centers, scheduling annual physical exams and blind rehabilitation.

In a month I was ready to start the travel part of the job, but my supervisor encouraged me to spend more time organizing and familiarizing myself with the office. It was February before I took my first trip.

When I got to Milwaukee it was snowing hard. The wind roared and it was so cold the cabbie wouldn't even get out of his car to help with my garment bag and briefcase. I threw them on the back seat with me.

Once I was settled in my hotel room and had figured out where everything was located, I called the driver who had been assigned to take me to my appointments. The voice that answered sounded like it was down a well, or under a blanket. "Hello," he muttered.

"Is this Rufus?"

A long pause. "Yeah, who's this?"

"This is George Brummell from Chicago. Remember me? You're supposed to be driving me around town. Will you be ready tomorrow morning?"

"George, I remember. I remember you," he mumbled. He was drunk. Another long pause. "I can't do it! I just can't do it!"

Shit! Nice beginning. "You can't do it? What do you mean, you can't do it? I don't have any other driver!" Calm down, I reminded myself. I hung up and sat down on the bed. Here I was, stuck in a God-forsaken Siberian nightmare and I was blind and helpless. If I couldn't get the job done, my boss would think I was a fool.

I flipped open my watch. Twenty-five past ten. It was too late to call clients to see if they knew someone I could hire to drive me to visit veterans and agencies. I decided to go to the lobby and ask the bellhop if he knew someone who might be interested. I grabbed my cane and headed out the door. Which way was that damn elevator? I almost let the door close but then remembered I had not increased the TV volume, a way of helping me find my way back to my room. I also placed the "Do Not Disturb" sign on the outside door knob. The room numbers were painted on the doors so I wouldn't be able to feel my way back.

I stood outside my room for a few moments, listening for the telltale "ding" of elevators. Hearing nothing, I chanced left. A short hall came to a dead end. I turned, stepped to the opposite wall, and felt my way along until I came to a connecting corridor near my room, apparent by the volume of the TV.

A door closed behind me. "Good evening, sir," a male voice said. "I'm from Room Service and I just delivered food to Room 459. Where are you trying to go?"

I explained my predicament and he suggested I go to the restaurant and ask for Lola, who he thought might be available and appreciate the extra money.

Lola was up for the challenge. "I sure can use the money. Sure, I'll do it. Besides, it sounds like fun and you're sorta cool. There's a lot of snow out there. Can you handle going to them houses in all that white stuff?"

"I was five years in the Infantry, camped out in many places and under all kinds of conditions. I can handle just about anything, and that includes you."

Lola, who was black and had an Alabama accent, chuckled shyly. We made our plans and I headed back to my room. As soon as I stepped off the elevator and turned the corner, I heard music from my door. Next time I'd turn the volume down. At least I didn't get lost.

Lola called at seven o'clock the next morning to tell me she would be in front of the hotel by eight-thirty.

I phoned the first veteran, got directions to his house, and recorded the instructions on my new toy, a microcassette recorder. After a room service breakfast, I went down and stood inside near the entrance. Lola rolled up on time, tooting her Road Runner horn. Her little car was like an oven inside, and smelled sweet from the fruity cologne she wore. "Very comfortable," I said, settling in to the seat. "We're going to National Street first. Do you know where it is?"

"Of course. I know every house on that street." Within a few minutes we were there. She guided me by voice through the drifts to the front door.

"Come on in!" said Mister Brock. The house stunk of dog shit and damp dirty clothing. Brock was a World War II veteran, sixty years old. Like most of the men and women I would meet, his blindness was due to aging—macular degeneration. Also, like so many other blind veterans, he lived alone. His house was paid for, with insurance money from his wife's death, and he received a small pension from the VA.

I stumbled over some shoes just beyond the entrance. Unopened mail, a tee shirt and other objects cluttered the living room floor. He showed me where the couch was by beating on its cushion. I pushed away a shoe box, a pair of underwear, and a thirty-three rpm record.

Brock could barely find his way around in his own home. When I asked for a glass of water, he ended up in the bedroom. I tried to convince him to go to blind rehabilitation. He needed it. If he had gone, maybe the house would have been in better order, and he could have found his chair when he returned with the glass of water.

Brock was impressed that I came into the house alone through all the snow. I continued talking to him about blind rehabilitation, and I felt triumphant when he agreed to go to the rehabilitation center.

I told him that a sighted person could escort him at no charge on the Greyhound bus. I also explained the Talking Book Program of the Library of Congress. He was especially pleased to learn that he was entitled to a thousand extra dollars a year in his pension.

It was time to go. I dug out my veterans' list in Braille from my brief case and asked for the phone.

"It's the kind of phone you turn. I usually call and have the operator dial for me," Brock said.

I assured him that the rotary phone was not a problem for me to dial, and showed him how I did it. I put his right index finger in the zero slot. "Count the holes from the zero forward or from the one backwards." But I could tell he wasn't interested in learning. I guess he liked talking to the operator.

I took the phone back and called the next vet, recorded directions to the vet's house on my recorder and headed for the door.

"Where you going? You're not leaving yet, are you? I ain't told you about Normandy," Brock said, moving slowly toward me.

"I really would like to talk longer, but I got to go."

He took my hand and shook it vigorously.

When I got outside, Lola hollered, "Over here, baby!"

The day went quickly and efficiently. I visited five more vets. One was a retired sailor from the Korean War era who was blinded a decade after he was discharged. "My ex-wife urinated for days into a container, then mixed lye with the stinky stuff, cooked it, and threw it in my face while I was asleep."

"Damn! That's crazy. Why did she use piss?"

"Piss has more impact than water, so I've been told. It worked on me," he replied bitterly. "A ten cent pistol, she called it." I couldn't tell if he was making it up or not, but either way, he was clearly a paranoid schizophrenic.

"Listen," Charles said, crying, "my mother's coming back to get me. Don't you hear her coming through the wall? Don't you hear her? Damn! You gotta hear her!"

There wasn't any one coming through the wall, only sounds of people walking past the front door of his apartment.

"Yes sir, I hear her," I said. "Let's not disturb her. Let her come in." A long pause, then he started laughing wildly, stomping his feet and clapping his hands.

"You're alright! I like you. You understand."

After a day with Lola, and a little bit of flirting,

she returned me to the hotel. I undressed and hung my suit up. The room seemed noisy. People outside sounded like they were in the room with me. I heard their voices and footsteps. I turned on the television just as the phone rang.

"Hello, Mister Brummell? This is Sarah at the front desk." She giggled. "I don't know how to tell you this, but I think you need to put something on or close your drapes." She chuckled some more. "You have quite a few admirers looking in on you."

"My goodness, yes. I'll do something about that." I quickly hung up and turned my back toward the Fan Club. I stood there for a second or two, wondering what to do. I decided to back up to the window. I bumped into a table, then a chair and knocked it over. I nearly fell. By then I was really disgusted, and I could hear people laughing at me. They probably thought I was drunk.

I turned, faced the window, and tapped on it while looking for the draw cord. Someone, a crowd pleaser, tapped back and several outbursts of laughter followed. At least I was wearing my clean white jockey underwear.

"The show is over," I yelled and pulled the cord. I was afraid I would run into some of those spectators in the lobby, so I had dinner alone in the room.

I spent a lot of time that night thinking about Nick Trace, one of the vets I had visited. His condition left me depressed. He had multiple sclerosis and couldn't speak. He could hear and move his eyelids, that's all. Nick had been a paratrooper during Vietnam, highly trained to move gracefully on the ground and in the air, but here he was, motionless.

Nick's mother explained that he would blink his eye twice for yes and once for no. She said Nick smiled at my jokes. I suggested his mother plug a speaker phone in his room so that I could call and tell him what I was doing. I asked if he would like that and, according to his mother, he blinked twice and smiled.

Blind veterans' homes were not the only visits I made that first week in the field. I stopped by the Veterans' Administration Medical Center to meet with the Visual Impairment Services Team Coordinator. I left names of vets interested in attending blind rehabilitation and taking their annual physical examinations. I left her the names of veterans requesting equipment, canes, tape recorders, and writing guides and, of course, told her about my friend Charles, whose mother was coming through the walls to get him.

At the Veterans' Administration Regional Office, I met with an adjudicator to review files of blind veterans with active service or non-service connected claims. I also stopped at other agencies serving the blind in search of veterans not aware of their VA benefits.

Lola and I had gotten along so well, and she was divorced, that we decided to go out dancing. She picked me up at the hotel.

"Well," she said, "I'm not going to keep you wondering what I look like tonight. Honey, am I looking GOOD! I have on a purple suede mini-skirt, with a matching purple low-cut silk blouse—but not too low. So don't let your imagination run too far away with you.

"This skirt is fitting me fine, too. Take a look at

these long, dangling purple earrings." Lola stopped and took a deep breath. "I forgot, you can't see. Here. Give me your hand. You can feel them." Lola pulled on my left hand, but I reached across with my right.

"I got on a fine gold chain, too, with a small purple medallion. Oh, I forgot about my black heels and black fishnets." I wondered if she was going to let me feel the fishnets. I didn't have the nerve to ask if she had on purple or black panties.

"Oh, I got on purple panties, too," Lola said, reading my mind.

We found a parking spot close to the entrance to the club. Lola was already used to me attaching myself to her left arm, so she maneuvered naturally. The speakers were so loud my right side vibrated along with the music.

We found a place to sit and Lola immediately left for the powder room. The disc jockey played popular tunes and I got used to the volume and started to sway with the music.

"Take those God damn sun glasses off!" a loud voice shouted just in front of me, spraying saliva all over my face. I pretended not to hear him.

"You ain't fuckin' blind! Take those glasses off!" he yelled again, closer to my left ear.

Lola returned in the nick of time. "I found another seat away from the speakers! Come on! We're gonna dance! Let's see what you can do! No ballroom! Free style!"

"Okay, just yell my name every once in a while, or put your hand on me so I can keep aligned with you."

"Alright!" she yelled back from a distance.

The beat was excellent and I warmed up with a few side steps and a couple of forward gyrations. Then I spun away. I was in my own vast world, a world where you need to be blind to realize what it's like—dark endless space.

Lola bumped into me a couple times but she didn't say anything, so I figured I was doing okay. I just kept dancing. I felt a bump on my left arm, so I turned in that direction.

"Lola!" No answer. The floor sounded crowded but I wasn't making physical contact with anyone. I was bumped again from the back, so I whirled around.

"Lola?" I reached out and my hand landed on what felt like a big breast, a torpedo. I curiously lingered for a moment, trying to figure out if it was what I thought it was. I squeezed. The missile carrier squealed.

"Hey, buster! What seems to be your fuckin' problem? If you can't see what you're grabbing, take those dark glasses off! Do it again and I'll smack you!"

There was a break in the music, and from behind, I heard Lola's voice and then felt her hand grab mine.

"I'm sorry, George. An old friend asked me something. I took my eyes off you for a second, and you sort of drifted away. The next thing I knew that crazy woman was yelling! Okay, I'm back! Let's keep this party going!"

We danced practically all night. When the music slowed, we held each other and I was delighted to find that Lola was more shapely than I had imagined.

When we got back to the hotel Lola stopped the car, turned toward me and said softly, "Let me give you my home number. Call anytime." She handed me a small piece of paper along with a big hug and a quick kiss. "Well, brother, this is it," she said, grabbing and shaking my hand.

Back in my room I regretted that the evening ended without something more than a kiss. But Lola had been a wonderful antidote to my loneliness and the sadness that lingered after talking to some of the vets. I was single for the first time since I had been blinded. It was nice to know that I still had something to offer the ladies.

Chapter 26

Back in Chicago, my crowded apartment was beginning to feel like home even though I was seldom there. I had to be in the field two weeks each month. The first six months were exciting, but then the traveling got old.

While I was in the Windy City I had a reunion of sorts with Theresa, the child I may have fathered with Chris, the married woman who I'd dated back in Federalsburg when I was a youngster. Theresa had gotten pregnant as a teenager and now had a baby of her own. She needed a place to be and a job, so I invited her to come live with me and work for the BVA, which she did for several months.

It was a good arrangement for both of us. She had plenty of time for herself during the long stretches when I was away, and she was a great help to me when I was home. We formed a familial bond then, but I lost track of her in later years.

As for Chicago, it was a long and challenging winter. Often by the time I got to work my beard was transformed into a curly cube of ice. The fierce wind off Lake Michigan was hard to walk through and once nearly blew me off a train platform into the path of a bus.

Living in the city, for a blind person, presented other obstacles—literally. Homeless people cluttered sidewalks and parks. There were spots that had webs of treacherous railroad tracks crossing the streets and sidewalks. Those were places where I listened hard for pedestrians I could follow. I singled out a particular set of footsteps and followed as fast as I could, swinging my cane.

One day, on a deserted stretch of sidewalk, I heard footsteps approach rapidly from the rear. I stopped, turned and backed off the sidewalk so the traveler could pass. Instead, the shoes scraped slowly to a stop, squarely in front of me.

"Hey motherfucker, gimme your damn money!" A muffled black male voice.

I gulped for air. "Okay, okay!" I reached for my wallet. Something hard, small, and round poked my right side.

"Don't do nuthin' stupid," he growled. "Just give it up."

"Hey, STOP! HALT!" voices yelled in the distance. Approaching footsteps picked up speed, more than one pair.

"Shit!" the man spat. Then he farted, and sprinted away. I burst out laughing.

When I explained why I laughed, my rescuers had a hearty guffaw as well. One man in the party extended an arm and I latched on to it, laughing with them all the way to my train.

A few weeks later, with spring well on its way, I somehow got off track and unwittingly walked up a truck ramp and into a trailer before my laser cane went off, letting me know there was a ceiling. An older white woman saw me and got me back on track. She was from Evansville, Indiana, and when I said I was headed there soon and needed a driver, she gave me the phone number of a niece she thought might be interested. I phoned the woman, Joey, and made arrangements for her to meet me.

She picked me up from the airport and I learned that she was married and had two teenage daughters and a seven-year-old adopted biracial son. Joey's voice was hard, almost masculine, but she was caring and thoughtful and had a gentle demeanor.

The second day she drove me around, she started to become exceptionally friendly, even flirty. When we were done for the day she asked if I needed to do any shopping on my way back to the hotel. "We're downtown, in the business district."

"Thanks," I said. "It's been a long day and I wouldn't mind having a tall can of beer to take back with me."

"Well! I might just have one with you," Joey declared. "I haven't had a beer in a year." She parked and left, returning with a six-pack. She escorted me to my room, followed me in, and set the sack of beer on the dresser.

"Boy, it sure feels good to get out of that car!" Joey said. I could hear buttons unsnapping. Then her shoes hit the floor and she brushed past me, playfully patting me on the stomach.

"I got some beer, a peach cooler for me for later, and some chips." She popped two cans and handed me one.

I sat at the head of the king size bed and felt her sit at the foot. She took a couple of sips and then I heard her beer can thump on the table top.

"You kno-o-ow George, you said some things that turned me on today."

"You must be kidding."

"No, really! It wasn't exactly *what* you said, but how you said it."

Oh boy. Women!

"Ya see, me and my husband... Well, we haven't had sex in about three years. He had an affair and when I found out, I lost all my feelings for him.

"But you got my motor running today, honey." She slid closer to me. "Hey! Why don't you just stand up and check me out?" She grabbed my hand and put it on her shoulder. "I'm not too big, am I?"

She had shoulders as wide as a fullback's, with a Humpty-Dumpty torso. It wasn't the first time I got hit on by women because I was blind. I had come to understand that I was a man who seemed sympathetic and gentle, maybe in need of nurturing. I also understood that being blind meant I was oblivious to certain flaws that the rest of the male world could plainly see. But there was no mistaking what was going on here!

"Look at my behind and legs, George. They're not big at all." She was practically pleading, and grabbed my hands and rubbed them down her sides, top to bottom.

Joey was right. Her behind was just a crack in her back, and her legs were tooth picks. The poor girl must have been desperate.

She turned, wrapped her big arms around me and

pulled me hard against her sagging belly. I tried to be chivalrous and respond with a warm embrace, but my arms wouldn't reach.

"Joey, look. I'm flattered but I'm not in the mood. Besides," I lied, "I have a girl friend."

She turned me loose. Thank God! But then I felt her fingers trying to unbuckle my belt. I covered it with both hands. Then she tried to pull down my zipper. I covered the zipper with my right hand, while holding the buckle with my left. She pushed a shoulder into my chest and gently forced me backward onto the bed.

"You got me burnin', baby, so you got to do something about it," she demanded. "So, is it true? Once you go black you never go back?"

"Joey!" I shouted. "I'm REALLY not interested."

She finally stopped pulling and sat on top of me. At least she couldn't manipulate my zipper as long as she was sitting on it.

"I'm not through with YOU yet," Joey vowed, bouncing up and down. I twisted and unseated her onto the bed. She was on me in a flash, washing my face with juicy kisses, bumping and grinding.

I pushed her away and finally, her feelings hurt, her feet hit the floor and she was gone.

I couldn't say which was worse, being mugged or molested. I was relieved to be alone again and settled in for the night.

From a deep sleep, I awakened to a relentless knocking at the door. I found my watch and popped the cover—three o'clock in the morning! "Who is it?"

A muffled voice: "It's me, Joey." Jesus Christ!

"Joey, I'm in bed! It's too early to get up. Come back

in the morning."

"Please! Let me in. I just need to talk to you. Just for a minute. I promise." I hesitated. She might be smashed and then I'd have a real scene on my hands. She'd said she hadn't had a beer in a long time. Maybe she was a binge drinker and I had become part of one of her binges. Fuck it! I'll make sure she understands she's wasting my time and hers.

I took my sweet time getting fully dressed—my suit of armor against her assaults. When I let her in, she immediately apologized for her behavior earlier, and we ended up having a long chat about her failed marriage, her trouble raising a biracial son, her hopes for the future. She finally ran out of gas at six o'clock and went home.

She left me in a funky mood. She was a sad character in what had started to feel like a world full of sad and damaged characters. And listening to people like her, I had lost all confidence in marriage. Where does love go? Would I ever have it again?

My first year working for the Blinded Veterans Association had been long, but it was productive and stimulating. I criss-crossed six states on my own, visited countless veterans, and had helped most of them in one way or another. I had stayed in grand hotels and appeared on television and radio. I'd also gotten involved with the veterans' movement, serving on a committee to organize the Welcome Home Vietnam Veterans' Parade in Chicago, a major success. I had the honor of pushing the Grand Marshal's wheel chair, marching beside General William Westmoreland, the retired US Army Chief of Staff.

The irony was not lost on me that Westmoreland had been the commander when I was sent to Vietnam, the General who became infamous for predicting that we would win the "hearts and minds" of the Vietnamese people. Well, General, I thought, I guess we showed *them*! But I played the good officer and gentleman and kept my mouth shut.

The Grand Marshal was a paraplegic, a former Marine who was legally blind. In spite of his impairment, he had just days earlier managed to pull a drowning five-year-old from his neighbor's swimming pool. I couldn't help wondering if being blind allowed him to hear that she was drowning.

A few days after the parade, I got a phone call from my boss, National Field Service Director Roberto DeJesus. "I wanted to let you know that I'm moving on to a new job in the Veterans' Administration."

"Well, that's wonderful," I said. "Congratulations! I'm sure gonna miss working with you." Of course, I was also thinking, And now what for me? The answer was fast coming.

"George, you've done an absolutely fantastic job out there. In fact, I have some advice for you that I think you should seriously consider. If I were you, I'd get your application in for this job."

"Your job? *Your* job? Director of National Field Service? Are you kidding? I've only been working for a year."

"You heard me, George. No bull. It's up to you. I can't exactly say what I know, but let's just say I think you're more than qualified and I'm prepared to say so, if anybody asks."

I sat in my cramped little apartment in Chicago with my heart racing, knowing I had no choice. It was perfect. I'd be escaping Chicago's miserable winters and be close to home again. I sat down and composed a letter to Headquarters asking to be considered for the position. A week later I was summoned to Washington, D.C. for an interview. They hired me, practically on the spot. A month later I was living in a small apartment in Washington, the Blinded Veterans Association National Field Service Director.

I was intensely proud of what I'd accomplished and as soon as I was able, I took a bus back home to Federalsburg to visit my relatives. On the way from the depot, I asked Donald to drive by the cemetery in Bethlehem, so I could visit Grandma's grave and leave some flowers I'd bought.

I sat on the grass, leaning against the headstone and tracing her carved name with my fingers. Donald pulled a few weeds while I had a private conversation with Miss Susie.

THE END

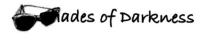

Epilogue

A few weeks after I was injured, I received a letter from one of my fellow sergeants in A Company that still brings tears to my eyes when I have it read to me. I had asked my wife, Blanche, to write a note to my unit asking what the hell happened to me on June 6, 1966, at a dusty crossroads in wartime Vietnam. It all happened so quickly, and then I was in a morphine-induced fog. I wanted to know what happened to the other men in my Band of Brothers, who were feet away from me when the bulldozer triggered those landmine explosions.

The letter was written on six sheets of lined tablet paper, addressed to my wife. It was written by a fellow sergeant, Bob Louis from Kansas. I had many white friends in the service, but Bob was one of my black brothers. We were both twenty-year-olds at the time.

Although I have given most of the people I've met fictitious names in the telling of my story, in this letter I have left in the actual names of the men mentioned, in honor of the sacrifices they made.

1966 June or July
Dear Mrs. Brummell,
I do not know if you remember me or not, but

we have met on one occasion [when our unit was stationed in Hawaii].

I hope to recall as much as possible and to inform George of the things that may not be clear to him.

As he may well remember, that day we were moving out to clear a road junction. His squad was to secure a bulldozer [which] moved without incident to the road junction at which time they dismounted and prepared to set up the platoon perimeter to secure the road junction. Standing in the road junction at this time were Sgt. Tompkins and Capt. Norberg, checking our position on the map.

As your squad started to move into the platoon perimeter, someone motioned the bulldozer to be brought forward. At this time you were either in front of or behind Pfc. Rivera. It is generally thought you were behind him.

The two of you started around the left side of the bulldozer. [The driver] let his blade down and moved forward. He only went about a foot. There were two sharp explosions about 5 seconds apart. Immediately after the second, there was the cry for a medic.

People in the immediate area started rushing about. Finally Sgt. Lanter came up to the NCOs and told us it had been mines. Capt. Norberg was dead. Pfc. Rivera had been standing about 1 foot from the mine. All that was found of him were his legs. Sgt. Tompkins was badly burned on his sides.

You yourself were just barely alive. Your clothes and flak jacket were ripped to shreds.

When I came back to attempt to find Rivera, I saw you were lying under the trees where they had *moved you. You were covered head to toe with bandages and gauze. I could see that you were still breathing. We all knew it would be touch and go until you got to the hospital. But we were pulling for you.*

Before they flew you out, they threw smoke for the choppers to come in and, as always, George had to complain. The smoke was blowing in his face. Right then I knew you had too much heart to let "Charlie" get a good soul brother down.

The next day we moved out again. Capt. McQuillan was our new CO. We went seven thousand meters and a machine gun hit us with one long burst. One man, Orland, SP/4, was killed, shot through the heart. No one else was even hit. He just didn't know what was happening and didn't get down fast enough. Right now we are still on Fort Smith. Tomorrow we end it.

I am leaving it up to Mrs. Brummell as to whether or not she tells you of this letter but I honestly hope that she does. I know this will give you a brighter picture of what happened. It was something unexpected. It shook us all up. But even though you were seriously injured, you were still extremely lucky and we were all glad to hear that you had pulled through.

Well this is all for now from us all. God bless you and take care. Drop us a line from time to time and let us know how you are doing.

As Always, Your Buddy and Comrade at Arms.
Sgt. Robert L. Louis
For the NCOs at the 2nd Bat. A/2/14, 25th Div.

Sgt. Louis's letter helped me redefine myself as I was learning to live in the dark. It contained a subtle, and intuitive, challenge: don't let Charlie get a soul brother down. It was a huge challenge: he and I both knew well how ordinary life got soul brothers down. I grew up in a town where blacks couldn't go inside the local ice cream parlor to get a cone. We had to stand outside at the window. Somehow, through good social skills and instincts, we all managed to co-exist peacefully in segregated Federalsburg, and I never had any problems of a racial nature.

Now that I was blind, I would need more than good social skills and instincts to survive and thrive. So I took the challenge and made a commitment to meet it.

During my forty years living in the dark, I have tried to make the most I could of being blind, just as I had planned to make the most of being whole when I joined the Army—I had wanted to move up the ladder and make the military my career. In a way, I accomplished my goal. I spent twenty years working with and helping veterans, with no regrets. I'd sooner carry a cane than a gun any day. I can't say I enjoy being blind, but I have enjoyed the challenge of it.

One of the veterans I was able to help was my own Uncle Noble. Through my deep involvement in veterans affairs, I learned that he'd received a less-than-honorable discharge from his World War II Navy service. Curious, I reviewed his records and determined that he had been unjustly denied an honorable discharge. I began a campaign to get his status upgraded. It took four years and a lot of persistence, but one day I received a phone call from Uncle Noble excitedly telling me he'd gotten his Honorable Discharge. It was one of my happiest moments on the job.

One of the most exciting experiences was meeting Stevie Wonder at a phone booth in Chicago's O'Hare Airport. We ended up chatting for a half hour, mostly about my new laser cane. He took my name and phone number when we parted. A few months later he was performing at a benefit concert in the Washington, D.C. area and asked that the Blinded Veterans Association receive some of the proceeds. As a result, BVA received a fifty-thousand-dollar recording studio for creating audio tapes for members.

In the late 1980s, I was instructing a class for veterans in Beckley, West Virginia, and mentioned to the state program director that my closest Army buddy, Traver, was from West Virginia. A couple of days later, he told me he had located Traver and that he lived and worked close by. We had a great reunion and have stayed in close touch ever since.

In 1989 I met Maria S. Peregrino, a native of the Philippines, at a party for members of the visually-impaired community. She attended with her blind female cousin. Maria and I hit it off and we were married in 1994.

I had only occasional contact with my mother over the years. When she died in 1990, I was curious to learn about her health history as it might relate to me and contacted a doctor who had treated her. I was interested to learn that she had been treated off and on for mental illness, which helped explain her bizarre behavior toward me and others.

I was privileged to be invited to return to Vietnam in 1998 with other injured vets to participate in a goodwill bicycle tour of twelve hundred miles, from Hanoi to Saigon, now known as Ho Chi Minh City. The ride was timed to commemorate the twenty-fifth anniversary of the Paris peace agreement of 1973 that set the stage for the withdrawal of American troops from Vietnam.

The Vietnam Challenge was set up by World TEAM Sports, a charity that sponsors events that bring together the disabled with able-bodied athletes. The participants included disabled vets from both sides of the war. Some men had lost limbs or were disfigured or, like me, had lost their sight.

I rode on the back seat of a tandem bicycle, rolling up and down the hills, through deserts and jungle, memories triggered by long-forgotten but distinct smells. It was an unforgettable experience, emotional for all. Some of the men refused to visit a monument at the site of the infamous My Lai massacre, where US soldiers killed hundreds of civilians in 1968.

A veteran nurse who went on the trip, after being teased by an ex-soldier because she hadn't seen battle, reminded him, "We put you back together when you were crying for your mothers, and at night we went into the villages to take care of the children you shot up that day."

In the end, it was a healing experience and the Vietnamese shot us this time with smiles, not bullets. A film crew traveled along and NBC broadcast the documentary they made, on Christmas Day, 1998.

I enjoyed the biking experience so much, I participated in a similar ride from the site of the World Trade Center to the Pentagon, to commemorate 9/11.

I've been honored by several Veterans Administration commendations and in 2001 received the Congressional Black Caucus Veterans Braintrust Award, recognizing exemplary national and community service on behalf of African American veterans.

I recently began to volunteer at the Washington, D.C. Combined Nursing and Rehabilitation Center two days a week. I help residents write their personal stories for the center's newsletter. With the completion of my own story, I hope to begin a new chapter of my life, reaching out to others with a message of hope.